The Democratic Regression

The Democratic Regression

The Political Causes of Authoritarian Populism

ARMIN SCHÄFER AND
MICHAEL ZÜRN

Translated by Stephen Curtis

polity

The original German edition of this book was published as *Die demokratische Regression. Die politischen Ursachen des autoritären Populismus* © Suhrkamp Verlag AG Berlin 2021. All rights reserved by and controlled through Suhrkamp Verlag Berlin.

This English edition © Polity Press, 2024

Polity Press
65 Bridge Street
Cambridge CB2 1UR, UK

Polity Press
111 River Street
Hoboken, NJ 07030, USA

All rights reserved. Except for the quotation of short passages for the purpose of criticism and review, no part of this publication may be reproduced, stored in a retrieval system or transmitted, in any form or by any means, electronic, mechanical, photocopying, recording or otherwise, without the prior permission of the publisher.

ISBN-13: 978-1-5095-5876-6 – hardback
ISBN-13: 978-1-5095-5877-3 – paperback

A catalogue record for this book is available from the British Library.

Library of Congress Control Number: 2023936628

Typeset in 11 on 14pt Warnock Pro
by Cheshire Typesetting Ltd, Cuddington, Cheshire
Printed and bound in Great Britain by CPI Group (UK) Ltd, Croydon

The publisher has used its best endeavours to ensure that the URLs for external websites referred to in this book are correct and active at the time of going to press. However, the publisher has no responsibility for the websites and can make no guarantee that a site will remain live or that the content is or will remain appropriate.

Every effort has been made to trace all copyright holders, but if any have been overlooked the publisher will be pleased to include any necessary credits in any subsequent reprint or edition.

For further information on Polity, visit our website:
politybooks.com

Contents

Acknowledgements	vii
1. Introduction	1
2. Measuring Democracy: From Optimism about Progress to Democratic Backsliding	16
3. The Ideology of Populism and the New Cleavage	44
4. The Crisis of Representation and the Alienated Democracy	69
5. Crises of Democracy	103
6. Opportunities and Dangers	133
7. Democratic Action in the Face of Regression	156
Notes	179
Bibliography	193
Index	220

Acknowledgements

At a conference in Potsdam on 10–12 November 2016, political scientists from various countries got together to discuss the condition of our democracies. Shortly before heading for the conference, on 8 November – the day of the US presidential election – some of our American colleagues gave interviews in which they forecast victory for Hillary Clinton, only to find out, upon arrival in Germany, that things turned out differently. There was much to discuss at this conference. It was also the first opportunity that we, the authors, had to present our reflections, still separate at that stage, on why contemporary explanations of the rise of populism were unsatisfactory and why we had to look at how democracy functioned. Coming from two different perspectives, we offered explanations that pointed to the selectivity of political decisions.

The conference in Potsdam marked the beginning of a series of workshops held under the aegis of the German Research Foundation's (DFG) project 'Concerns about Democracy in North America and Europe', which concluded at the Villa Vigoni, the German–Italian Centre for European Dialogue on Lake Como, shortly before the coronavirus outbreak in Lombardy. Working within the context of this project offered

viii Acknowledgements

us numerous opportunities to discuss facets of the material in the present book with various colleagues from different countries. We are grateful in particular to Claudia Landwehr and Thomas Saalfeld, who not only helped to create this context but also were always available for discussions. The two of us then held another workshop at the WZB Berlin Social Science Center in order to promote still further the idea of a joint text on what we call the *political* causes of authoritarian populism. We profited greatly from the comments and pointers we received at this meeting, especially from Swen Hutter, Cristóbal Rovira Kaltwasser, and Céline Teney. This book is also an outcome of those joint discussions.

We have each had important opportunities to discuss and improve the work that has gone into this book. As scholar in residence at the Max Planck Institute for the Study of Societies in Cologne during the winter semester 2019/20, Armin Schäfer had the chance to present the core ideas of the manuscript in a lecture series and to discuss them with those present. He is grateful to Jens Beckert and Lucio Baccaro for the invitation. Some of the ideas developed here came out during a joint research project with Lea Elsässer and Svenja Hense, in the course of which the three of them often talked about the meaning of representation and the nature of the shortcomings related to unequal responsiveness. Armin is grateful for the very stimulating exchange of views that resulted. He is also indebted to Miriam Hartlapp-Zugehör, Martin Höpner, Andreas Nölke, Simone Leiber, and Hubert Zimmermann, with whom he has repeatedly discussed many aspects of the manuscript. Although the participants did not always agree, the exchanges were always valuable in helping him to refine his own perspective.

Michael Zürn conducted his own research within the framework of the Cluster of Excellence 'Contestations of the Liberal Script', which is financed by the German Research Foundation (EXC 2055, Project ID: 3-0715469). Throughout many discussions with Tanja Börzel, Jürgen Gerhards, Johannes Gerschewski, Heiko Giebler, Christoph Möllers, and Stefan Gosepath he received important suggestions for which he is especially grateful. Subsequently these ideas found their way into the present book. As always, his work also benefited from the Global Governance unit of the WZB Berlin Social Science Center. He is immensely thankful to Alexandros Tokhi and Johannes Scherzinger for their data-collecting work. His discussions with Jelena Cupać, İrem Tuncer-Ebetürk, Rainer Forst, Edgar Grande, Peter Katzenstein, John Keane, Cédric Koch, Wolfgang Merkel, and Christian Rauh proved to be particularly significant. Michael would like to thank especially Karen Alter, with whom he undertook a thematically related project on backlash politics. He had much to learn from it.

Last but not least, we both would like to thank Katinka von Kovatsits, Lisa Scheuch, and Barçın Uluışık for supporting us in preparing and editing the English version of the manuscript; Stephen Curtis and Barçın Uluışık for their meticulous work on the translation; Manuela Tecusan for superb editing; and Elise Heslinga for her excellent efforts in coordinating the publication of the English version of the book.

Armin Schäfer and Michael Zürn, April 2023

1

Introduction

A line that runs in a peculiar hump-shaped curve between the X- and Y-axes has made a name for itself. What is called the elephant curve[1] first appeared in a World Bank report of 2012. It shows how incomes developed across the globe between 1998 and 2008. Income groups are marked off in 5 per cent increments along the horizontal axis, and they range from the very poorest on the far left to the super-rich on the far right. The income growth of each group is captured on the vertical axis. With a little imagination, the curve can be seen to resemble the outline of an elephant (see Figure 1).

The world's absolute poorest registered almost no growth in income over the period under consideration. Things went as miserably wrong for them in 2008 as they had in 1998; this is the elephant's tail dangling in the dirt. However, the curve then climbs steeply along the elephant's back, the groups at its head chalking up increases in real income of up to 80 per cent. It is not until about three quarters of the way along the X-axis that the curve drops – and sharply. The trunk reaches right down to the ground. Only the tip of the trunk, the part that represents the richest 1 per cent of humanity, points steeply upwards again. To put it plainly, the new middle layer in the

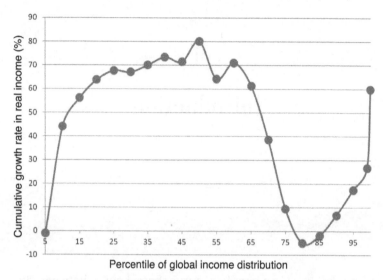

Figure 1 The elephant curve of global income growth.
Source: Milanović 2016, p. 31.

newly industrialized countries, above all in East Asia, together with the richest of the world's rich, profited massively from globalization. By contrast, the poorest of the poor in Africa and the old middle classes in more prosperous countries were left moaning about small growth and relative loss of prosperity. The upshot has been the 'new geography' of income inequality, in which differences between countries diminished, whereas within (western) countries they increased.[2]

That the income of the poorest of the poor remained stuck at under one dollar a day while that of the super-rich increased dramatically is a moral scandal. This is where global capitalism showed its ugly side of injustice. On the other hand, global capitalism's enormous ability to get things done was on display in Asia, especially in China, where hundreds of millions of people escaped from absolute poverty.

What interests us in this book, however, is not the implications of the elephant curve for distributive justice as much as its meaning for democracy. By 'democracy' we mean the principle

Introduction

of collective self-determination and its institutional realization as a form of government that is bound up with promises of political equality, legitimate reasons [*guten Gründen*], and power control. The elephant represents a problem for democracy because autocratic countries showed greater increases in prosperity than consolidated democracies – where, besides, the rich profited most. This is in marked contrast with the situation in democratic countries during the postwar decades, when prosperity soared even as income inequality declined.

The distribution of global economic growth points to two central challenges to the democratic form of government. On the one hand, it tells the story of the enormous success of an autocratic political system such as China's. From the time of the financial crisis, if not earlier, western liberal democracy has been faced with a political competitor that, in contrast with really existing socialism, is both different and successful. It is different because it does not explicitly link the emergence of economic market dynamics to the institutions of liberal democracy, and thereby calls into question the seemingly indissoluble connection between democracy and the market. It is successful because the authoritarian ruling elites in countries such as China and Singapore cannot simply be written off as self-seeking despots. Pursuit of the common good is a recognizable component of their policy, and they can claim considerable progress in combating poverty in particular. These states demonstrate that social progress is possible without those in power being subject to democratic oversight and without individual rights being guaranteed; in this way they undermine the notion, entertained especially after 1989, that there is no alternative to liberal democracy. If China is seen today in parts of the global South as an acceptable political alternative, then the question concerning the correct political order is back on the agenda.

What is more, the upward-pointing trunk on the elephant curve relentlessly draws attention to a further weakness of democracy: the growing inequality in the rich countries of the West. The material basis for supporting democracy is becoming weaker. The attractiveness of the political systems in Europe, North America, and Japan since the end of the Second World War was not sustained exclusively by the normative logic of freedom and self-determination – that was a delusion of columnists and thinkers who argued in purely normative terms; it also relied on the empirical observation that individual prosperity and the availability of important collective goods in the long run could best be achieved within the framework of a liberal democracy. For a long time, the lesson of history seemed to be clear: a materially rich life, innovative and comfortable products, an efficient political system – all these things were only to be had in western democracies. But this promise has lost credibility as a result of the income growth depicted in the elephant curve.

1.1 Double Alienation

Are these shifts in world society leading to a regression in democracy – that is, to a sustained movement away from the ideal of collective self-determination based on political equality and on a strong support base in the population? From our point of view, one can start talking about a *democratic regression* when two different changes become apparent at the same time. One is about the increasing distance between the democratic ideal of collective self-determination and an actual practice in which decision-making has been transferred to bodies that are not legitimized by elections and that are barely under citizens' control. The other involves an aversion to democracy from (parts of) the citizenry, as they no longer feel that they are adequately represented. Hence we propose to speak of democratic regression when we perceive a *double alienation*: the abstract alienation of practice from

Introduction 5

the democratic ideal and the concrete alienation of citizens from democratic institutions. In this connection, Rainer Forst (2020) speaks of a 'neglect of democracy'. The outcome of this dual disengagement is that democracy forfeits a portion of its charisma.

The reference point for our concern with democratic regression is to be found in Chapter 2: the great self-confidence that followed the collapse of the Soviet Union. Democracy seemed at last to have permanently rid itself of all its rivals and become the only game in town. Sooner or later, or so many diagnoses assumed at the time, its light would brighten even the darkest corners of the world. This optimism has not really survived the past decades – not unscathed at least. For one thing, there are authoritarian regimes that have steadily resisted becoming even a tiny bit more democratic; for another, the number of democracies has, again, declined during the past few years. If the rate of democratization simply slowed down, or if it came to a halt periodically, one might still assume that this was merely a blip in an unstoppable historical trend. But when democratic states turn into electoral autocracies,[3] in other words into autocracies with more or less free elections, and when the quality of democracy declines in its core countries, then hope of linear progress with a few little wiggles on the way can be kept alive only with a great deal of effort.

There is currently much talk of democratic backsliding,[4] above all because the quality of democratic government has gone down even in supposedly consolidated democracies. For a long time the decay of democracy was, from a Western European perspective, something that happened only in faraway countries; now the damage is being done closer to home. In the past ten years things have got worse for democracy, not just in Venezuela or Brazil but in the United States and Poland, too. It is true that in many of these countries there are hopes that a change of government would bring about a reversal of the trend; yet in countries where democracy has already been

6 The Democratic Regression

replaced by an electoral autocracy the prospect of the government's being voted out becomes more and more unlikely.

The current withdrawal of democracy appears to be more than a temporary blip. The optimistic story of democracy's spreading in waves separated merely by short-lived periods of partial regression hardly seems to square with actual developments. Instead, especially the period from 1945 to the end of the twentieth century has turned out to be, in retrospect, a phase of worldwide democratization. That half-century was characterized by positive basic conditions that no longer hold today in the same way. The advance of democracy was less the result of an inescapable logic of progress and much more the outcome of a specific historical constellation. The change in this constellation, a process that we trace in Chapter 2, now makes democratic regression possible. Societies are not gliding smoothly down a predetermined path towards the goal of liberal democracy; they develop through political conflicts and struggles over the extension of social and democratic rights. These conflicts may not only slow down the journey but also lead to a change in its destination.

1.2 The New Populism

The new populism stands at the centre of current debates about democracy. This is our main topic in the present book. In almost every country, populist parties have been founded and claim that they want to save democracy by giving 'the people' a voice again. Unlike the old parties of the extreme right, populists have nothing in their election manifestos and party programmes to say that democracy should be replaced by a different form of rule. On the contrary, they advocate an expansion of direct democracy and profess to represent people who are overlooked by the established political parties. Their claim to be the true voice of the people is presumptuous, but

Introduction

it strikes a chord with a not inconsiderable number of citizens. Our aim in this book is to explain why this is the case. To begin with, we need to grasp the ideas contained in authoritarian populism and delimit them with definitional precision. This we do in Chapter 3.

The predominant understanding of populism in political science today has been shaped by the works of Cas Mudde, who sees it as an ideology that divides society into two homogeneous and mutually antagonistic groups: the 'pure people' and the 'corrupt elite'.[5] According to this view, populism is a 'thin' ideology that can be combined with some other, more substantial ideology. We shall argue in Chapter 3 that neither of the elements of this established definition goes far enough. First, it produces too many 'false positives', the peaceful revolution in the last days of the German Democratic Republic being one example. That, too, was a case in which a movement opposed to an elite cartel rallied around the homogenizing formula 'We are the people'. Movements that want to prevail against authoritarian rulers must necessarily take a stand against the establishment and present themselves as relatively homogeneous. But that alone does not make them populist.

Second, populism is not an empty form that can be filled with any type of content, at will. Its ideological substance is not as thin as a mere confrontation between the establishment and the people represented as a homogeneous body might insinuate. We argue that contemporary populism is pre-eminently authoritarian and functions as an ideology in its own right. It is a political ideology built on an unmediatized form of representation of the majority that takes a nationalistic stance against 'liberal cosmopolitan elites'.

Contemporary populism is nationalist because it is exclusionary in two respects. On the one hand, it denies the legitimate interests of other countries by adhering rigidly to the topos 'our nation first'. On the other, from the very start it lays down who is allowed to belong to 'our nation', 'our people'.

The 'us against them' logic is not only directed at those who strive for other goals, it also always makes clear who does not belong. The anti-pluralism of authoritarian populism grows out of its vision of a homogeneous people with unanimous political aims. Anyone who claims to know and represent the will of the people cannot tolerate the idea that there may be other legitimate opinions. This is why the political opponents of authoritarian populists are always labelled 'traitors to the people' or 'corrupt power cliques'. The only possible reasons for wanting something different from what the populists themselves want are morally corrupt ones.

This specific understanding of politics also leads to the rejection of established procedures for shaping the will of the people. Unlike in a deliberative and participatory understanding of democracy, what is right is not something that has to be negotiated through democratic argument because, come what may, it is already established. The notion that political positions can be further developed and changed through participation in public discourse is foreign to authoritarian populism. This is why parliaments are derided as mere talking shops, which talk without deciding. And this is why claims that can be exempt from their reference to truth serve exclusively as weapons in a political dispute. Populists' own utterances are aimed more at casting contempt on politics in general than at shedding light on substantive positions on concrete and factual questions. Populists typically have no love for detail, they much prefer gross simplification. In the end, their deproceduralized understanding of democracy goes together with a very specific idea of what representation means. Here, too, the focal point is not the constant exchange between representatives and the represented, but the implementation of a (pre-established) will of the majority. In short, authoritarian populism builds on a specific understanding of politics that is not equally compatible with every type of content and that represents far more than just a 'thin ideology'.

1.3 The Causes of Populism

In Chapter 3 we develop the kernel of a *political* explanation of authoritarian populism, taking as our starting point the idea that neither socioeconomic nor sociocultural explanations suffice to account for its rise in and of themselves. Socioeconomic accounts start from the economic situation, in particular from a (feared) loss of social status. The losers of globalization, so the short version goes, are especially susceptible to the siren songs of populism. Yet it remains a mystery why this group turns to authoritarian populist parties and not, say, to parties of the left, as the very essence of their brand is the struggle against inequality and for social safeguards. Why should voters who feel economically disadvantaged and expect more state support vote for tax cutters par excellence, people like Silvio Berlusconi, Donald Trump, and Boris Johnson, who, besides, belong in the top 1 per cent of the income distribution? It is also noticeable that the Netherlands, Austria, and France – precisely the countries in which authoritarian populist parties enjoyed their first success – have been relatively less plagued with growing inequality. All in all, it remains unclear from a socioeconomic perspective why authoritarian populist forces have prevailed in countries that have profited exceptionally from globalization, at least at times – think of Turkey, or even India, for instance.

The sociocultural explanation for authoritarian populism that interprets it as a reaction to processes of cultural liberalization is equally inadequate when taken on its own. For one thing, it does not seem very helpful to restrict authoritarian populism to the cultural sphere. In disputes over the acceptance of refugees – to take one example – cultural aspects are not the only thing that matter; economic aspects such as the consequences for the labour market[6] matter just as much. Besides, the culturalist reading runs the risk of confusing cause and effect. In fact sociocultural conflicts often intensify only

10 The Democratic Regression

after an authoritarian populist party has chalked up some successes at the polls.[7] When all is said and done, it is unclear why authoritarian populism is particularly strong in countries with comparatively low levels of sociocultural liberalization, such as Russia and Turkey.

Both of these established explanations need to be completed, because they ignore the political sphere. They observe macrosocial changes – globalization and modernization – and see in populism an understandable but futile revolt against them.[8] The political reaction to these changes, however, is not a foregone conclusion. Our thesis is that only the *politically selective handling* of these social changes provokes a populistic defence reaction. A genuinely political explanation of populism sets out from liberal democracy's real deficits in the sphere of representation. Not all social groups are equally well represented, and the interests of the resource-rich receive more than their fair share of attention. Those who want to explain populism cannot close their eyes to the weaknesses of democracy.

Two factors in particular ensure that political decision-making is tilted in favour of the better-off. First, as political science pointed out back in the early days, the choir of democratic representatives sings 'with a strong upper-class accent'.[9] The responsiveness of parliaments in liberal democratic political systems has shown virtually no sign of improvement since then. Rather there is evidence that the accent has become even stronger in the course of globalization, and this is precisely what authoritarian populist parties have complained about at the top of their voices. At the heart of their criticism is the claim that representative democracy, the 'system parties', and the media pay no attention to ordinary folk – your average person in the street. This makes the perfect backdrop for a rhetoric that pits the ordinary people against a corrupt elite.

Second, over the past three decades decision-making powers have been transferred, on a large scale, from majoritarian institutions (MIs) such as parties and parliaments to non-majoritarian institutions (NMIs) such as central banks, constitutional courts, and international bodies. Decisions are increasingly made by institutions that are subject neither to the majority principle nor to the duty of accountability that binds representative bodies. The purpose of many NMIs is to impose the threefold liberalism of individual rights, international rules, and free markets. The more powerful these institutions become, the harder it is to implement an illiberal or protectionist policy, even if the majority of the population is in favour of it. So, to find the causes that underlie democratic regression, one should look particularly at changes in the political systems concerned (see Chapter 4).

As a result of these two developments, the impression of many people that politics no longer takes any account of them has grown – and there is a real basis for it. Not all groups enjoy the same opportunity of having their concerns heard and dealt with politically. This is the background that enabled the idea to spread that there is a homogeneous political class set apart from the rest of the population, a class that does its own thing and thereby serves the interests of a spoilt and tendentially corrupt cosmopolitan layer of society. Consequently, the target of the vast majority of authoritarian populist campaigns is not this or that particular economic or cultural policy, but the system that brings them into being.

This political explanation of the rise of authoritarian populist parties focuses on two developments in modern democracies: the professionalization or cartelization of party politics;[10] and the fact that NMIs are a main target of contemporary populism.[11] The cartelization of party politics has rendered the selective responsiveness of legislators more pronounced, and this, in turn, has revealed that the lower orders have little influence on the laws passed by parliament. As a result, trust in the social democratic and conservative people's parties, the 'cartel parties', has declined. A subsidiary transfer of trust to NMIs functioned only temporarily. Increasing criticism of NMIs

12 The Democratic Regression

testifies to their loss of the magic touch. This has brought the political system as a whole into focus, and the outcome has been the rise of authoritarian populist parties whose principal targets are the political system, the system parties, and the political class.

According to this reading, democratic regression is the consequence of the double alienation mentioned earlier: the abstract alienation of political processes from the democratic ideal and the concrete alienation of sections of the population from democratic institutions. This has prompted us to take up the rhetoric that authoritarian populist parties direct against the political system and to ask whether this rhetoric speaks to what motivates people to vote for those parties and whether the political systems in question show systematic changes that explain those parties' relative strength. We will show that dissatisfaction with the lack of openness of the political institutions results in high approval ratings for authoritarian populists – not because the voters who back them want to venture more democracy, but because they feel neglected by the existing system. This is how the lack of representativeness in the critical decision-making organs of democracy has contributed to alienation from democracy.

But why is it only in the past few years that these changes led to a rise in authoritarian populism and to a weakened democracy? Why have these structural changes been considered a problem and made an object of scandal? Why have they been prevented until now from mobilizing support for authoritarian populist parties? In our explanation, the role of trigger mechanism gets assigned to the major crises that have plagued democratically constituted societies throughout the past fifteen years, as we shall show in Chapter 5. These crises took structural changes in the functioning of democracies – changes that had already been under way for a long time – and turned them into a springboard for the rise of authoritarian populism. We are particularly interested in crises that largely played out

Introduction 13

within the consolidated democracies rather than affecting them only from the outside. These are the financial and euro crisis, the crisis surrounding the admission of refugees, and the Covid crisis. Each of these worked on democracy like a magnifying or burning glass:[12] they made changes to political processes more clearly visible, and they also threatened to start fires. In times of crisis, essential decisions are taken not by elected parliaments but by other political institutions. Thus the crises prove to be not only 'the hour of the executive' but also the hour of the experts – and that above all. That is when NMIs contribute substantially to policy orientation. But NMIs are not neutral. Their preferences tend to be cosmopolitan. In controversial cases, NMIs stand for individual rights, open markets, and international rules. Internationally agreed austerity policies thus take precedence over national referendums (e.g. Greece during the financial crisis), and the impositions of the open society cannot be countered simply by closing national borders (e.g. Germany in 2016 on refugees from Syria). Insofar as people come to realize not only that unpopular decisions get made but that they get made in committees that are largely insulated from people with other ideas, the political system itself comes under scrutiny. If, according to the logic of TINA ('there is no alternative'), the system allows for no alternatives, there ought to be a different system.

By concentrating rays of light, a burning glass threatens to set fire to anything that the light falls onto. A series of crises in quick succession accelerated the double alienation from democracy. They laid bare the decreasing representativeness of consolidated democracies and at the same time led to the strengthening of anti-democratic forces.

14 The Democratic Regression

1.4 Authoritarian Populism and the Future of Democracy

Authoritarian populism points to genuine weaknesses in democratic practice while using democratic institutions. The weaknesses of democracy thus drive many to cast their votes in favour of authoritarian populist parties. These parties claim that they will make the interests of ordinary people and silent majorities count again. Our analyses of the causes of the rise of these parties show that this appeal does indeed help to explain their successes. Thus, among other things, these parties give a voice to people who feel that they are not represented by the political elite. Could populism act 'as a productive force that may serve as the catalyst for a profound realignment of West European party systems' – a reorientation that better reflects the 'transformed conflict structures of West European societies'?[13] Can populism possibly even have a positive effect on democracy? We doubt it.

In Chapter 6 we investigate the effects that authoritarian populist parties have had on the development of the quality of democracy. The result is quite clear. If authoritarian populist parties, on their own, make up the government, they speed up democratic regression and even attack liberal democracy in its institutional foundations. It is particularly noteworthy that in countries such as the United States under President Trump, India, Poland, and Hungary the quality of democracy has come under fire in all its aspects. When in government, authoritarian populist parties do not strengthen the electoral components of democracy at the expense of the liberal ones, as talk of illiberal democracy would seem to imply. When they rule, authoritarian populist parties do democracy no good, no matter which aspect of democracy is at stake. Illiberal democracy – which is a contradiction in terms, anyway – is not their aim; electoral authoritarianism is.[14] Authoritarian populists may avoid destroying the façade of democracy, but they distort its normative core beyond recognition.

The rise of authoritarian populism is a sign of real problems in the functioning of liberal democracy. But it does not spell salvation for this form of government; it is a threat to it. The result is a democratic dilemma: while the growing complexity of decision-making procedures in globalized and pluralized contexts leads to a double alienation from democracy, the answer – in the shape of simplification through renationalization and homogenization – undermines its institutional foundations. So then, what is to be done? In the final chapter we argue that ultimately democracy can be defended only through more democracy.

2

Measuring Democracy
From Optimism about Progress to Democratic Backsliding

At least the future looked rosier in 1989 than it does today. Before the fall of the Berlin Wall, an essay appeared in the summer of the same year that gave expression to the optimistic zeitgeist. In 'The End of History?', Francis Fukuyama argued that the reforms introduced in the Soviet Union by Mikhail Gorbachev had brought an end not only to the Cold War but to history as such.[1] If up to that point history had been shaped by the struggle between different blueprints for society, it was now emerging that the idea of liberal democracy was undisputed and would remain so.

Fukuyama put forward his argument in the context of the philosophy of history. He followed the Hegelian conception according to which '[w]orld history is progress in the consciousness of freedom, a progress which we must recognize in its necessity'.[2] In this sense of a succession of dialectically evolving ideas, then, history came to an end with the Cold War. From then on, neither fascism, defeated in 1945, nor communism, only recently overcome, were able to challenge liberal democracy any more. Fukuyama was certain that the light of democracy loomed even in the earth's darkest corners: sooner or later other countries would turn to this ideal. The endpoint of Hegel's historical eschatology had been reached.

Fukuyama's essay was primarily read as a prognosis of an institutional triumph of democracy. Although his theoretical argument did not necessarily depend on empirical evidence, in the book version of his thesis – a version that dispenses with the question mark in the title – Fukuyama fell back on data intended to substantiate the triumph of democracy.[3] In the meantime, democracy had gained a foothold in non-western regions. As far as Fukuyama was concerned, this was a testament to the universal validity of liberal democracy, even though regions such as the Near East and the Middle East were still a long way from experiencing sustainable democratization.[4] Progress was not to be halted.[5]

In tune with the optimistic zeitgeist, people also read Samuel P. Huntington's highly regarded book *The Third Wave: Democratization in the Late Twentieth Century* as evidence of democracy's unstoppable onward march. The first wave, according to Huntington, rolled in in the 1820s, with the introduction of general suffrage in the United States. After the end of the First World War there were twenty democracies. The countermovement began with Mussolini's seizure of power in Italy in 1922. By 1942 the number of democracies had shrunk to twelve.

Allied victory in the Second World War led to a second wave, which by Huntington's system of counting amounted to thirty-six democracies in 1962. But then the emergence of military dictatorships in Greece and parts of Latin America and the expansion of the Soviet sphere of influence brought another period of withdrawal, until 1975. The third wave of democratization began – again, according to Huntington – with the end of the dictatorship in Portugal in 1974.

Back in the 1990s, Huntington had already recognized the first signs that the third wave had run its course and he had forebodings of a new, reverse wave. But, in spite of all setbacks,

18 The Democratic Regression

the number of democracies still increased in the long run, because only some of the countries fell behind the status they had achieved. The image of waves modified the concept of linear progress, yet by the same move reinforced the basic idea of a secular trend towards democratization. Does such a trend really exist? The answer depends to a significant degree on one's underlying understanding of the nature of democracy.

2.1 What Is Democracy and, if There Is Such a Thing, How Many Are There?

According to David Held,[6] democracy is based on a principle of self-determination. Consequently people should be free and equal in determining their own living conditions and the framing of their communal existence, so long as their freedom is not used to negate the rights of others.[7] From this perspective, individual and collective self-determination depend on each other. Democracy is a process of public will formation and decision-making in which all those affected have the same opportunity to participate freely and with equal rights. At the same time, democracy must produce normatively justifiable decisions. In particular, it must not affect negatively its own foundations. A double anchoring like this rules out both purely procedural conceptions of democracy, which concentrate solely on decision-making processes, and strictly liberal interpretations, which consider individual rights to have priority over the democratic process. This perspective takes individuals as being endowed with autonomy and the democratic process as being reciprocally constitutive; hence it ties in both with the idea that rights and democracy have the same origin[8] and with the neo-republican notion of democracy as the absence of 'domination'.[9] The democratic process is characterized by two principles: the principle of affectedness, whereby all persons affected by a decision should have the right to have a say in its making; and the principle of deliberation, which demands that all decisions be publicly discussed and justified through argument. We follow this sophisticated conception of democracy.

Against this yardstick, how many countries can be classified as democracies? To calculate empirically the number of existent democracies is an undertaking with a long tradition; and it is still a growth industry in political science. Many of the current indexes go back to the work of Robert Dahl, who built a series of bridges between the theory of democracy and empirical research. In one early attempt, Dahl called a system of government democratic if it remained permanently responsive to its citizens and treated them equally in the process.[10] In order to capture how far these aims are achieved, Dahl[11] identified eight conditions, which cover degree of public contestation on the one hand and inclusiveness on the other.[12] In Dahl's view, countries can manifest both a high degree of participation without genuine competition and a marked degree of political competition with limited opportunities for participation. Under the apartheid regime in South Africa, for example, there certainly was competition for power, but the opportunities for black South Africans to participate were extremely limited. On the contrary, in countries under state socialism the electoral law was comprehensive and the voter turnout high, but there was no competition for the responsibility to form a government in which opposition parties could win elections. Only countries with an inclusive electoral law and with genuine competition between parties attain the status of a 'polyarchy', as far as Dahl is concerned.[13] This concept comes close to a sophisticated understanding of democracy, but still leaves out much of the deliberative component. The extent to which really existing regimes correspond to such a lean conception of democracy can be determined without great difficulty.

The Finnish political scientist Tatu Vanhanen has been working for decades to simplify still further the two dimensions identified by Dahl and to translate them into a concept for measuring democracy. According to Vanhanen, competition can be operationalized by subtracting the proportion of votes gained by the strongest party from the value of 100. The degree of participation is measured by the percentage of the population that took part in the election. To set boundaries, Vanhanen laid down a series of thresholds, freely defined. The degree of competition must be no lower than thirty – in other words, no party should obtain more than 70 per cent of the vote. The degree of participation should amount to at least 10 per cent.[14] As a result, this straightforward operationalization of democracy looks only at elections and ignores the legal and social requirements for free and fair elections. It follows that a great many countries are categorized as democratic. Other frequently used indexes of democracy broaden their understanding of the concept somewhat. For example, the Polity IV Index of the Center for Systemic Peace takes elements of the separation of powers into account, and the Democracy Index of Freedom House also covers individual rights to freedom. What these measuring devices have in common, however, is that they work with relatively simple concepts of democracy.

More recent attempts to measure democracy go beyond these lean approaches. Dahl's 1989 conception of the democratic process developed still further and now covers aspects related to deliberative will formation,[15] political equality,[16] and the population's ability to join in determining the political agenda.[17] These more recent efforts also start out from different variants of democracy that, from the normative point of view, may all be of equal value.[18]

A good example of the more complex attempts to measure democracy can be found in the Democracy Barometer, originally developed by the Berlin Social Science Center (WZB) and the Centre for Democracy in Aarau. It identifies three fundamental principles: freedom, control of power, and equality. Each principle is assigned three requirements, and its implementation is assessed with the help of a total of

Measuring Democracy 21

100 indicators.[19] The authors realize that there are different ways of attaining a democracy of high quality. The Varieties of Democracy (V-Dem) project, which aimed from the outset to assess different variants of democracy, goes even further.[20] Apart from distinguishing between 'electoral' and 'liberal' democracy, it pays heed to 'deliberative', 'egalitarian', and 'participative' variants – such that the electoral variant is the base form, to which different components are added:

(1) *electoral democracy*: free and fair elections, universal suffrage, freedom of opinion and association;
(2) *liberal democracy*: electoral democracy plus constitutional–legal oversight of political decisions, separation of powers;
(3) *deliberative democracy*: electoral democracy plus public justification of political decisions related to the public good; acceptance of counterarguments and extensive consultation of various groups in the course of the decision-making process;
(4) *egalitarian democracy*: electoral democracy plus comprehensive freedoms, equal access to power (decision-making bodies), and something that resembles an equal distribution of resources;
(5) *participative democracy*: electoral democracy plus extensive involvement of civil society actors in decision-making processes; the possibility of referendums; and a consequent reversal of subsidiarity (decision-making to be as decentralized as possible).

Each of these variants can point to a long line of ancestors in political theory, and one can find good reasons to emphasize one component or another.[21] Which elements of democracy are given particular prominence and are included in the measuring process has an immediate effect on which countries count as democratic, how many they are, and what shape the spread of democracy takes over the course of history. In what follows we start by looking at a series of current democratic indexes and supplement them with the Liberal Democracy Index from the V-Dem project, which encompasses both the electoral and the liberal components of democracy.[22] When the number of democracies is mentioned in public discourse, the figures are taken for the most part from less sophisticated indexes, such as Polity IV or Freedom House. In a second step, we shall add in the various conceptions of democracy in the V-Dem dataset.

As can be seen in Figure 2, all the indexes shown indicate a clear proliferation of democracies since 1900. In addition, all the curves are roughly similar in outline. At first glance these data support the position of the optimists of democratic progress. Make a few allowances, and the waves of democratization and

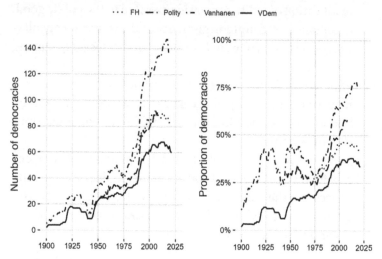

Figure 2 Absolute number and proportion of democracies worldwide.

Source: Data from https://github.com/xmarquez/democracyData.
Note: FH = Freedom House, Polity = Polity IV, Vanhanen = Vanhanen Index, V-Dem = Varieties of Democracy, Liberal Democracy Index. The graphs represent the absolute and the relative number of democracies according to various conceptions of democracy.

Measuring Democracy 23

undemocratization identified by Huntington become visible as well. On the basis of these data, the interpretation of history as a secular trend (punctuated by a few backslidings) towards the expansion of democracy as part of modernizing and civilizing society cannot be dismissed out of hand.

At the same time, the measurements clearly diverge. The Vanhanen Index, which has an exceptionally simple construction, rates 137 countries worldwide as democracies.[23] According to Freedom House and the Polity IV Index, there are just above eighty democracies, and the V-Dem's Liberal Democracy Index counts sixty. As the right-hand graph in Figure 2 indicates, the percentage of countries classified as democratic can range from 33 to 76, depending on the procedure adopted. This is a remarkable difference.

The measures also diverge when it comes to the most recent developments. The Vanhanen Index shows a downward trend only at the very end of the time series. The other indices show at least a flattening of the curve over the past two decades and a decline after 2010. If the measurement includes not only elections but also the rule of law and the protection of individual rights, the picture is less rosy. This already suggests that recent changes are not primarily about restricting or eliminating the right to vote, but about circumventing the legal and social preconditions for free, secret, equal, and fair elections.

None of the indexes used so far corresponds to a sophisticated participatory or deliberative understanding of democracy. This is why we take a second look at developments, in Figure 3. Here we use the different notions of democracy of the V-Dem project. The basic concept of electoral democracy focuses on elections and nothing else, just like the Vanhanen Index. In 2021, ninety countries – just over a half of the countries with available data – met these minimum conditions. Yet if we look at the liberal, egalitarian, deliberative, or participatory variants, the figures are much lower (see the left-hand graph in Figure 3). At no point does the proportion of democratic

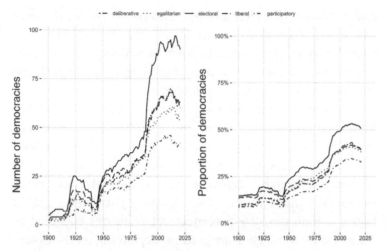

Figure 3 Number and proportion of democracies worldwide, according to various notions of democracy.
Source: Data from V-Dem, Version 10.

countries come close to 50 per cent, if we take anything but a minimalist approach (see the right-hand graph in Figure 3). If we were to combine the participatory and deliberative elements of democracy – which the V-Dem data do not do – this share would fall even further.

If we change the perspective by dividing the V-Dem indexes into two periods of development, the picture changes again. It becomes apparent that the relative proportion of democratic states was no higher in 1945 than in 1900. The spread of democracy, then, is a time-limited phenomenon, which basically got going only after the end of the Second World War. We can see a steep rise after 1945 that accelerated in the 1990s, but then it flattened and even went into reverse in recent years.

An overall view of empirical trends gives rise to four observations that are important in the context of our study:

(1) No matter how we measure democracy, over time a rise is discernible in both the absolute number of democratic

Measuring Democracy

regimes and their relative proportion. At present significantly more countries are democratic than was the case in 1920 or 1970.

(2) Depending on the concept of democracy, both the absolute number and the relative share of democratic states differ markedly. According to the purely electoral variant of the data from the V-Dem dataset, there were ninety democratic countries in the world in 2021; but if we take into account liberal requirements, there were only sixty of them. If we focus on the deliberative elements of democracy, the number is sixty-three; if we focus on the egalitarian elements, the number drops to fifty-three; and if we ask how many countries meet the requirements of a participatory democracy, the answer is forty-two. Only on the basis of a very narrow understanding of democracy, limited to holding elections, is it possible to regard more than half of the world's countries as democratically governed.

(3) The lion's share of the increase took place only after 1945. If we take the end of the Second World War as a reference point, any movement in the figures up until then was roughly on a level with the nineteenth century. However, the period between 1945 and 2010 witnessed a truly breathtaking expansion, in which the number of (liberal) democracies rose from 11 to nearly 70.

(4) But at the same time, as Figure 3 clearly shows, this expansion began to slack off, then in recent years the number of democracies has actually fallen. We are currently living through a reverse wave – hence a renewed democratic decline, which is now already more clearly marked than the crack between 1960 and 1974 in the line that displays the absolute number of democracies – the crack that Huntington identified as the second reverse wave.

A second look at the measurement of democracy casts further doubt on the optimistic view of progress peddled by

Fukuyama, Pinker, and Co. The spread of democracy may owe not so much to a long-term secular trend of political modernization as to specific historical conditions that obtained in the post-war period but now are no longer the same. In this case it would be more likely that, as this contingent historical constellation comes to an end, democracies decrease in number. The democratic form of government could then lose its status as a role model and sink back numerically to a noticeably lower level. We would then face not a temporary blip but a democratic backsliding, entirely unforeseen on the progress model. At any rate, it seems advisable to abandon any explanations based on progress and, instead, to tell a historically embedded story of the rise of democracy. Then the warning voices that urge us to be wary of a 'backsliding', a 'de-consolidation', or a 'recession' of democracy would make more sense.[24]

2.2 Democracy and the Postwar Order

We should do justice to Samuel Huntington. With his concept of waves of democratization, he placed less of an emphasis on teleological optimism about progress than did the other theorists of democratic growth mentioned here. He considered the third wave of democratization to be a consequence of five specific causes. First, he anticipated growing problems of legitimation for authoritarian regimes in a world in which the democratic principle enjoyed a high degree of recognition. This first cause rested on political modernization theory[25] and, to that extent, pointed to long-term and seemingly irreversible trends. However, Huntington also referred to historically contingent factors such as the lengthy phase of economic boom – his second cause – and the change in the political doctrine of the Catholic Church, which declared its support for democracy only in the 1960s: Huntington saw this as the third cause. Lastly, he identified changes in the foreign policy of the United

States, the Soviet Union, and the European Union, as well as the general snowball effect, respectively as the fourth and the fifth cause.

Of course, these causes seem to have been thrown together rather at random and without any theory. A systematic stocktaking of democracy's success would need to start out from the historical turning point that all its measurements so unequivocally indicate: the end of the Second World War. From there everything went steeply upward – more steeply and for much longer than ever before. Figures 2 and 3 show this unmistakably.

When political developments happen more or less at the same time in similar format in many countries, places, and regions, it makes sense first of all to abandon the comparative perspective and take a look at the international context. When one compares democratic states among themselves and asks about the factors that condition development in individual countries, one acts as if development occurred in one country independently of what was going on in the others.[26] But in the real world societies watch, learn from, and imitate one another. At the same time, they are all embedded in the same common global context – in the world order or global system. After 1945, this global context was democracy-friendly. The post-war world order made the world safer for democracy.[27] Yet in the meantime this context, propitious as it was for the spread of democracy, has changed in a number of decisive respects.

During the final years of the conflict the Allies were already beginning to plan for the post-war world. The meeting of experts from the United States, the Soviet Union, China, and the United Kingdom that took place between August and October 1944 at Dumbarton Oaks is the best known in a series of such gatherings. The outcome of the deliberations carried out in that picturesque mansion in Washington, DC was a plan for the United Nations, already quite thorough, that included a

28   The Democratic Regression

strategy for winning the support of the rest of the world, despite the privileged position allotted to the great powers in the UN Security Council. At roughly the same time, at a conference in Bretton Woods, a little town in New Hampshire, plans for a liberal economic order with open borders were drawn up in order to avoid a repetition of the economic chaos that gripped virtually the whole world in the aftermath of Black Thursday, in 1929. The United States gave up its isolationist position,[28] striving instead for an institutionalized world order under its own leadership. Advocates of this policy in the United States saw it as a means of both advancing the interests of the world's most productive national economy by far and exporting the political ideas that stood behind American exceptionalism.[29] Further steps in this process were the UN Charter of 1945, the Marshall Plan of 1948, and the North Atlantic Treaty of 1949.

While Great Britain accepted the role of junior partner in this endeavour, Stalin and the Soviet Union had their own ideas, as did communist China. The conquest of Eastern Europe and its integration into a Soviet empire brought about a *de facto* split between the East and the West. As a result, the international order existed at two separate levels: the regional level of the two blocks, each led by a superpower and character- ized internally by a high degree of cooperation; and the global level, dominated by East–West relations and by the conflicts between the two superpowers.

Within the western world, the plan to coordinate trade and currency policy in order to lower customs tariffs and avoid devaluation contests prompted Anglo-American collaboration in setting up the General Agreement on Tariffs and Trade (GATT), the International Monetary Fund (IMF), and the World Bank (WB). Harry Dexter White in the United States and John Maynard Keynes in the United Kingdom are regarded as the architects of this system. The international trade regime came into existence on the basis of GATT in 1947. It called on states to do away with quotas for trade in industrial goods and to reduce tariffs. But above all it introduced the 'most favoured nation' principle, whereby any advantage or privilege granted by one contracting party to the products of another had to be granted to the products of all other contracting parties as well.

The IMF had already been founded in 1944. It was intended to support a liberal international economy through a system of free convertibility of currencies, which were anchored in fixed exchange rates with the US dollar. In addition, the World Bank was set up to boost development projects and processes in economically disadvantaged parts of the world. Although these international institutions functioned on principles of executive multilateralism with little or no social participation, they served a clearly recognizable social purpose: the global enabling of the democratic welfare state, which required a specific international context.[30]

The social goal that these institutions relied on is aptly captured in the concept of embedded liberalism. Embedded liberalism was an arrangement that involved free trade and open borders but that would nevertheless make it possible for national political systems to mitigate the shocks and inequalities unleashed by the global market.[31] The international institutions created on the basis of the principle of embedded liberalism enabled relatively unlimited trade to take place between all industrial states, and at the same time allowed for considerable differences in the political and social development of national regimes of production and welfare states.[32] They also facilitated the development of democratic welfare states.

Within advanced capitalist economies, a historic compromise was reached between capital and labour. Trade unions accepted open markets, together with the economic uncertainties that the latter entailed; export-oriented business associations accepted the construction of welfare states in order to cushion the effects of these uncertainties. This historic compromise came in a variety of versions. It began in the

30   The Democratic Regression

United States in the 1930s, with Franklin D. Roosevelt's New Deal. The Scandinavian states followed immediately after the Second World War,[33] while the conservative welfare states in other European countries came on the scene from the second half of the 1950s on.[34] As a result, some of the emerging welfare states – Sweden, for example – ended up controlling more than 50 per cent of the gross domestic product (GDP). Other countries, for instance Switzerland, with an average of 30 percent, kept state involvement at a much lower level. Such multiplicity highlights the decisive characteristics and achievements of this embedding: it made it possible to cushion the social risks of competition in a liberal world market (welfare embedding), and it also enabled free decision-making as to whether and how (i.e. through which parts of the national welfare system) the cushioning was to take effect.

The achievements of this arrangement reached far beyond the economic sphere. Democracy, international institutions, and interdependence strengthened one another, leading to a stable peace between the democratic welfare states.[35] Against the background of the perceived threat from the Soviet Union, it was possible for the first time to establish a transatlantic, and even a partially transpacific, security community in what is called the OECD world. The historic compromise served both the foreign policy interest in international stability and in a united West and the interest of export industries and trade unions respectively in open markets and in the extension of the welfare state. This constellation brought about the age of social democracy.[36] From today's perspective, the 1970s and early 1980s represent the high-water mark of the democratic constitutional and interventionist state.[37] Democracy indicators show a very steep increase in the number of democracies, during this period in particular.

In some respects, post-war institutions were too successful. Embedded liberalism set in motion a continuous dynamic of liberalization and accelerated technological progress, and the interplay between these two gave globalization a boost.[38] From the mid-1980s on, the increase in the number of cross-border transactions meant that national policy could no longer achieve its desired aims in all areas – say, because environmental externalities made themselves felt, or because social measures reduced the competitiveness of businesses. The rapid increase in direct investment, and in particular the extreme sensitivity of financial markets, severely limited the scope for decision-making related to national market interventions and social safeguarding programmes. These developments chimed with the growing importance of transnational financial capital, the relative decline of national export industries, and the rise of a transnational class.[39]

Above and beyond this, the deepening of the liberal order brought with it a continual strengthening of international regimes that demanded that states open their borders to enable the free exchange of goods, capital, labour, and services. But on the other hand few regulations were developed to change or correct market results at the international level.[40] According to Scharpf (1999), 'negative integration' outweighed 'positive integration'. So the paradox of post-war liberalism lay in the fact that it attacked some of its institutional cushioning mechanisms. It undermined the bases of its own success and produced losers in industrial countries, where the welfare state and social support for weaker individuals were well established. At the same time, globally active enterprises were investing more and more in all parts of the world, exploiting lower labour costs in poorer countries. The results of all this are reflected in the elephant curve discussed in the opening pages of this book.

The dissolution of the socialist camp can be seen as a further step in this path-dependent story. With the relaxation of tensions between the East and the West, especially after the Helsinki Declaration of 1975, the concept of individual rights penetrated the area under Soviet rule, strengthening the

32 The Democratic Regression

opposition there. Gorbachev's *perestroika* was a reaction partly to opposition groups that demanded more freedom and partly to globalization and the pressure it exerted on the stagnating Soviet economy. The failure of *perestroika* brought down the Soviet Union.

The end of the Cold War created new possibilities for strengthening international cooperation. The most dramatic change took place within Europe. To embed German reunification in European integration, the Kohl government gave way to pressure from France and accepted a currency union. Apart from this consolidation of the European Union, the other most noteworthy development was its expansion. Immediately after the fall of the Berlin Wall, there was a rush towards the European Union. For most Eastern European states, membership was tantamount to a guarantee of economic prosperity and independence from Russia. In reaction to this demand, the European Union developed the Copenhagen criteria, which stipulate that a state must accept human rights, be a democracy, guarantee a free market, and be prepared to adopt the communal body of rights and duties known as the *acquis communautaire* before it can become a member. In this way, the European Union exerted enormous pressure in favour of liberal democratic reforms in these countries. EU extension can, in this sense, be regarded as the most successful instance of external intervention in the domestic affairs of other states in recent history.[41] In little more than a decade, a large number of the former socialist states of Eastern Europe were integrated into the European Union, and in many cases into NATO – notwithstanding critical voices in the West and in Russia.[42]

On 1 May 2004, eight Central and Eastern European countries – Czechia, Estonia, Hungary, Latvia, Lithuania, Poland, Slovakia, and Slovenia – together with two Mediterranean ones – Malta and Cyprus – joined the European Union. In terms of numbers of people and number of countries, this was the largest single extension. Romania and Bulgaria, which had not been regarded as accession-ready in 2004, joined on 1 January 2007. Croatia followed in 2013. The European Union's expansion eastward served the integration of Eastern Europe into an open global system, even though this step possibly undermined political reform in Russia, where western expansion was seen as a threat and strengthened authoritarian defensive reactions.

At a global level, a series of large-scale conferences in the 1990s,[43] generally with the participation of non-state actors, led to a wave of international agreements that were no longer restricted to the opening of markets but also took in positive international regulations and interventions. Three of these agreements are of particular importance. First, the Uruguay Round of multilateral trade negotiations in 1992 led to the founding of the World Trade Organization (WTO) in 1995. Not only did this new agreement have considerable effects on trade (it was aimed at non-tariff restrictions such as subsidies, property rights, and product regulations);[44] the WTO went further and immediately made provision for a dispute resolution procedure that removed the veto right from states. Only in the event of a unanimous vote by member states can resolutions of the Dispute Settlement Body (DSB) or of the Appellate Body be rejected. National powers are thereby delegated to international bodies.[45] Currently 160 states are members of the WTO.

Second, the Kyoto Protocol of 1997 laid down binding commitments on industrial countries to reduce emissions of greenhouse gases under the United Nations Framework Convention on Climate Change (UNFCCC). Although it soon became clear that the commitments were insufficient to combat climate change effectively, many saw the agreement as a first step on the way to a strong global regime that would counter global warming.

Third, the United Nations Security Council began to play a much more active role in world politics. It defined humanitarian disasters and civil wars as threats to international peace and

34   The Democratic Regression

intervened in a number of relevant cases by military means.[46] Somalia, Haiti, Bosnia, and Afghanistan are well-known examples. The Security Council thus established a regime of peace enforcement; the international community was from now on supposed to be in a position to create internal peace from the outside.[47] In the case of Kosovo, the western states attempted to obtain further authorization from the Council to enforce peace in a civil war. As Russia's traditional ally Serbia was the target of the proposed intervention, it soon became clear that a draft resolution would not be passed in the Security Council. In the end, NATO intervened without a UN mandate. This was interpreted by some as an anticipation of a Responsibility to Protect (R2P) norm. The founding of the International Criminal Court (ICC) followed the same pattern. The Rome Statute that established the court was approved in July 1998; to date, the United States and a number of other states have not adopted the Statute.[48]

In consequence, the 1990s witnessed a systemic shift in the global order. Whereas an international multilateralism had taken shape after the Second World War, the end of the Cold War ushered in a postnational liberalism that intervened in national affairs to a far greater extent and mixed embedded liberalism with neoliberal institutions. One part of this development was another salient increase in the number of democracies (see Figure 2).

At the same time, the change to postnational liberalism has led to disputes that have come to light more and more since the end of the nineties.[49] Many postnational liberal institutions have been criticized for working for the benefit of western companies and elites, for being of a neoliberal character with considerable effects on distribution, for applying double standards, and for institutionalizing unequal power relations. The intensification of Islamic fundamentalism, Russia's revisionism, China's rise, anti-globalization movements, and the spread of right-wing populism and nationalism in Europe and the United States turned out to be new (or renewed) challenges. The understanding of individual rights as universal has been criticized on the grounds that it is underpinned by interventionist institutions and contributes to the spread of an 'unhealthy' multiplicity of lifestyles (multiculturalism, LGBTQ+). Borders are re-emphasized, the free movement of capital, goods, services, and people is increasingly being called into question. All this goes together with a growing rejection of political authority beyond the boundaries of the national state. Doubt has been cast on the legitimacy of multilateral institutions as protectors and promoters of economic freedom, security, human rights, democracy, and the rule of law – and not only by autocratic regimes but also by nationalist forces of the right as well as by left-wing movements, all of which are oriented against the neoliberal policies of western states.

Consequently, the global order is losing recognition and legitimacy because international institutions are seen as tools of the liberal globalists and of the executives in a small number of powerful states. Postnational liberalism urges states to respect human rights, the rule of law, and democratic principles, setting universal liberal ideas above national sovereignty. Above and beyond that, the distributional effects of international institutions are becoming more visible. Generally speaking, the liberal international order benefits people via mobile resources that operate in accordance with a liberal cosmopolitan worldview. These features of postnational liberalism have not only led to a noticeable increase in the politicization of institutions[50] but also fired up the defensive reactions of authoritarian populists inside and outside liberal societies.

Embedded liberalism made life easier for democracies. The blossoming of consolidated democracies and the third wave of democratization depended on this liberal international order. The order underwent changes nonetheless – it was deepened and radicalized; it encroached more than before on the politics of states. The triumphal progress of democracy came to an end

36 The Democratic Regression

because economic progress can obviously proceed without it, and sections of the population resisted liberal cosmopolitanism. Quite possibly, the change in international framing conditions has put an end to a period in which democracies have been able to flourish as never before.

2.3 Is There a Reverse Wave?

As we just saw here, after a long rise the number of democracies has finally fallen again. But is this finding enough for us to talk of democratic backsliding? To be able to answer this question, we need to know not only whether some democratic countries have become autocracies but also whether the quality of democracy has deteriorated in many countries at the same time. This we shall investigate by making use of data from the V-Dem project once again. We begin by identifying the countries in which the quality of democracy has gone down by at least ten percentage points over a five-year period.[51] Of course, not every deterioration in the quality of democracy leads directly to dictatorship. Even so, changes that exceed a certain level would justify talk of 'autocratization';[52] and, if we are dealing with a sufficiently broad development, that would point to democratic backsliding. Figure 4 plots the number of countries that have experienced an accumulated fall in the Liberal Democracy Index of at least five (light grey) or ten (dark grey) percentage points over the previous five years. Particularly since the 2010s, there has been a clear increase in the number of countries in which the quality of democratic processes has declined. Unlike in the 1960s and early 2000s, worsening results in some countries have not been offset by progress in others and are thus reflected in the net values for deterioration and improvement.

In almost two thirds of the sixty-two countries that qualified as democratic in 2000 according to the standards of

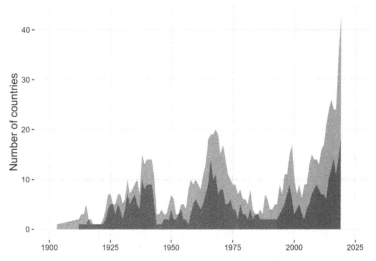

Figure 4 Waves of democratic regression since 1900.
Source: Data from V-Dem, Version 10.

Note: The numbers represent the countries in which the Liberal Democracy Index showed a fall of five (light grey) or ten (dark grey) percentage points for a period of five years before each reference year.

the Liberal Democracy Index, the figures have gone down since that year. The same applies to one third of the non-democratic countries. Of course, the figures looked at so far do not cover the full extent of the democratic backsliding yet. For, when all we do is count the number of democracies, we leave aside the question of whether these countries have large or small populations. That way, if India is demoted from being a democracy to being an autocracy, the result is on a par with, say, Lesotho's going the same way; yet 1.3 billion people live in India and only 2.2 million in Lesotho. A feature of the current phase of democratic backsliding is that we witness it especially in heavily populated countries. Overall, one third of the world's population has experienced a retrenchment of democracy, and only 8 per cent live in countries where the quality of democracy has improved.[53] The picture therefore doesn't get any better if we look at developments in the world's nine largest countries.

Altogether 4.3 billion people live in China, India, the United States, Indonesia, Pakistan, Brazil, Nigeria, Bangladesh, and Russia. They make up more than half of the world's population. In this group, only Pakistan and Nigeria show qualitative improvement in their democracies, although here, too, all we find is low-level changes – and for a number of years the curve has been pointing downwards again in Pakistan. No progress has been recorded in Indonesia, which lies, generally speaking, around the middle of the scale. The lowest values are recorded for China, which has become not a jot more democratic in the past twenty years. Bangladesh and Russia are more undemocratic today than they were in 2000. Three countries that counted as liberal democracies at the beginning of the period we are examining, namely Brazil, India, and the United States, display a sharp or moderate decline in the quality of their democracies. In India, which was long considered a model of success in spite of its poverty, inequality, and ethno-religious conflicts, the deterioration of liberal democracy has clearly accelerated since the Hindu nationalist Bharatiya Janata Party (BJP) under Narendra Modi took office. In India, democracy never fared as poorly as it does today ever since independence in 1947, except during the state of emergency between 1975 and 1977. Brazil, too, has retrogressed noticeably: this started under the first presidency of Lula da Silva, plagued as it was by corruption and scandal, and intensified after his replacement in office by Jair Bolsonaro. So far, democratic backsliding in the United States has been comparatively less catchy, even though during his period in office President Donald Trump showed little understanding of the separation of powers, the independence of the judiciary, or press freedom,[54] let alone the contempt for democratic processes that he demonstrated by refusing to accept his defeat in the 2020 election, if not before. The storming of Capitol Hill on 6 January 2021 and the subsequent reaction of many Republicans document the erosion of the losers' consent.

Democratic backsliding is most pronounced in, but not limited to, the most populous countries. Table 1 shows that the quality of liberal democracy has deteriorated seriously since 2010 – by ten percentage points or more (see the dark grey areas in Figure 4) – in twenty-five countries across the globe.[55] The index has fallen by more than twenty percentage points in twelve countries, the sharpest declines being registered in Poland and Hungary. Although the quality of Turkish democracy improved between the late 1990s and 2005, there has been a dramatic reversal after that year, and Turkey is now considered an autocratic country. Hungary, too, is now well below the threshold for countries to be allowed in the group of liberal democracies. Research has shown that, while the goal of EU membership has a positive effect on democratic reform, the European Union has so far lacked effective instruments to sanction states if the quality of their democracy deteriorated after accession. This is particularly true when several such countries prevent a concerted action.

The data in Table 1 also show that the withdrawal from democracy proceeds little by little. Nowadays democracies die differently and more slowly. In earlier periods they were removed at a stroke, through military putsches, coups d'état, or great power interventions. Today elections continue to take place, but the governments that are elected use their (parliamentary) majorities to manipulate the rules of the democratic game.[56] Erosion takes the place of eradication, wilting away that of sudden extinction.

Very slim indexes of democracy that concentrate only on elections do not capture the full extent of these changes, because elections are not completely abolished and voting rights are not always restricted. What gets restricted is those very freedoms that enable free and fair elections, the separation of powers, and the control of the executive in the first place.[57] Citizens can

Table 1 Change in the Liberal Democracy Index

	LDI 2000	LDI 2010	LDI 2021	Change 2010–2021	Democracy in 2000?
Poland	0.805	0.824	0.413	−0.411	yes
Hungary	0.761	0.678	0.362	−0.316	yes
Serbia	0.273	0.533	0.242	−0.291	no
Brazil	0.740	0.786	0.512	−0.274	yes
Turkey	0.438	0.389	0.115	−0.274	no
Benin	0.511	0.541	0.280	−0.261	yes
Mali	0.384	0.422	0.183	−0.239	no
India	0.595	0.574	0.357	−0.217	yes
Mauritius	0.657	0.678	0.464	−0.214	yes
El Salvador	0.320	0.426	0.215	−0.211	no
Afghanistan	0.028	0.227	0.021	−0.206	no
Slovenia	0.759	0.802	0.599	−0.203	yes
Thailand	0.398	0.338	0.169	−0.169	no
Nicaragua	0.397	0.216	0.055	−0.161	no
Greece	0.793	0.812	0.668	−0.144	yes
Comoros	0.108	0.266	0.126	−0.140	no
Zambia	0.389	0.430	0.296	−0.134	no
Botswana	0.602	0.617	0.486	−0.131	yes
Philippines	0.446	0.408	0.281	−0.127	no
USA	0.808	0.856	0.735	−0.121	yes
Hong Kong	0.315	0.315	0.199	−0.116	no
Ghana	0.557	0.678	0.568	−0.110	yes
Czech Republic	0.808	0.819	0.709	−0.110	yes
Indonesia	0.518	0.537	0.428	−0.109	yes
Yemen	0.126	0.137	0.033	−0.104	no

still vote in electoral autocracies, but are not free to organize themselves as an opposition, cannot seek information on political matters without depending on the government, and cannot defend themselves (successfully) against legal restrictions by taking legal action. A distinguishing feature of new autocratic rulers is that they change the rules of the liberal democracy game to benefit themselves – so that, although elections take place, the chances of their being voted out are extremely slim.

With the aid of V-Dem data, it is possible to determine which components of democracy are particularly under fire.

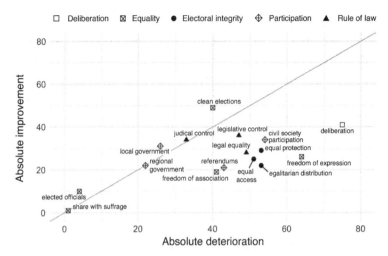

Figure 5 Changes in partial aspects of democracy.
Source: Data from V-Dem, Version 10.
Note: These are countries in which a subindicator of democracy has registered either an improvement (vertical axis) or a deterioration (horizontal axis) of at least 0.05 points on a scale of 0 to 1 since 2010. If the indicator is below the diagonal line, more countries showed a deterioration than an improvement; if above, more countries showed an improvement.

Figure 5 indicates where improvements and deteriorations have been observed since 2010. If the number of countries in which a particular element or indicator has deteriorated is greater than the number of countries in which it has improved, that number appears below the diagonal. Comparing positive and negative trends allows for a series of conclusions to be drawn.

First, between 2010 and 2021 more aspects of democracy deteriorated than improved. The value indicated for 'freedom of opinion', for example, fell in sixty-four countries and rose only in twenty-six. Second, the conditions that are necessary for free and fair elections often worsened. In many countries, freedom of opinion and freedom of association were restricted, as were the participation of civil society actors and equality

42 The Democratic Regression

before the law. Discrimination against particular social groups also increased. Third, although ballot rigging, too, became more frequent in forty countries, an even greater number of countries registered an improvement. Finally, there were hardly any changes in the right to vote and in the allocation of functions through election.

2.4 After Optimism

Thirty years ago, many commentators were looking ahead to the future with optimism. Liberal democracy had established itself against its challengers, and even the most unyielding autocrats feared for their power. It was only a matter of time, thought Fukuyama – and he was not the only one – before North Korea, Saudi Arabia, and South Africa developed into liberal democracies. History would not become uneventful as a result, but would no longer be a contest between rival social models; one design would have finally proved its superiority. The expectation was that there would be no more global cleavages or system conflicts.

But talk of the end of history rapidly became history. It was soon very clear that democracy was not going to continue sprawling out. There is no evidence of a secular trend in favour of democracy; it was rather the specific historical conditions after the Second World War that promoted its spread. Now that these conditions have dropped out, autocratization seems to be making headway. The current trend towards less democracy is a source of concern because it has taken hold in countries that are (or were) considered to be consolidated democracies. It is not just the usual suspects – countries plagued by relative poverty and social inequality, marked by a variety of religious or ethno-linguistic lines of conflict[58] – but richer and less unequal states, long regarded as embodiments of democratic stability, that are nowadays showing a tendency to erode. The fact that large and powerful states have been chiefly affected by this trend is especially conspicuous and worrying. And, as we shall argue in the next chapter, it is also the sign of a new cleavage that opens up.

What is new about the current reverse wave in democratization is not just the countries that are involved but the way in which the dismantling of democracy is implemented. Whereas in the old days tanks rolled through the streets, now democratic regression is implemented by stealth, at the edges of perceptibility to begin with. In the end, of course, it is quite clear that a country is no longer democratically ruled because its media are not free, the opposition is hamstrung, the separation of powers has been undermined, and its courts have been brought into line. But when exactly the first step was taken along this road is often a mystery to contemporaries.[59] It is therefore difficult to ascertain exactly when the struggle for the survival of democracy begins, because the new autocrats claim to want to 'dare more democracy' and are able to point the finger at real problems in existing regimes. If democracy functioned perfectly, it would offer its opponents fewer points of attack.

3

The Ideology of Populism and the New Cleavage

For some years now, democracy has been in retreat. This development can be observed not only in countries that have recently adopted a democratic form of government but also in a number of venerable democracies that have proven to be resilient to the temptations of autocracy. We have witnessed how established parties have been pushed aside by the likes of Marine Le Pen, Geert Wilders, or Giorgia Meloni and how parties with rich traditions have bowed to ostentatious personalities such as Donald Trump or Boris Johnson. Against this background, a whole series of books have been preoccupied with the current state of democracy, casting a worried eye not only over Latin American and Central and Eastern European countries but also over France, Great Britain, the Netherlands, Sweden, Germany, and the United Sates.[1] One way or another, all these countries have shown that they are vulnerable to right-wing populism, although they are among the richest states in the world and have been classified as liberal democracies for decades.

It is predominantly with this internal development in established democracies that we shall concern ourselves in the remaining chapters of this book. By that we do not mean to

The Ideology of Populism and the New Cleavage   45

say that the rise of technocratic autocracies such as China and Singapore presents less of a challenge to democracy. Quite the contrary: in terms of world politics, China's economic success is of central importance. However, the measurement of democracy in the previous chapter points to the fact that, as far as the presently observable decline in democracy is concerned, the increasing strength of autocracies is less decisive than the internal weakening of existing democracies. As a result, it is the second development that will matter most in the chapters that follow.

Anyone who talks about the rise of populism needs to engage with the inner weaknesses of established democracies. For, although many of the populist demagogues have managed to destroy their own magic auras in short order, populism as such has been able to establish itself as a lasting phenomenon. But why do messages from populist parties and movements hit home? Only when we find convincing answers to this question will we be able to think sensibly about strategies for the defence of democracy. Current answers seem to overlook the fact that, if it is true that the strength of populism leads to the weakening of democracies, the reverse statement is also true, and this has to do with real weaknesses in how liberal democracy currently functions. The social, ideological, and spatial distance between representatives and the represented has in fact increased. The composition of parliaments, advisory bodies, and local authorities diverges considerably – and more than before – from that of the population at large. Unelected bodies that are only indirectly legitimated and remain below the threshold of public attention often take decisions with major political consequences, without consulting those affected by these decisions. And it is precisely in times of crisis that the population's participation on a large scale is put on hold, while the advice of experts is increasingly sought. There may be good reasons for all these trends, but they are not without consequences for the way in which politics is perceived. The fact that the most

46   The Democratic Regression

important decision-making organs of democracy lack representativeness is a central cause of the rise of populism.

Democratic regression is the consequence of a double form of alienation. On the one hand, over recent decades, in the course of the historical developments sketched in Chapter 2, the consolidated democracies have put a greater distance between themselves and the democratic process in its ideal form. On the other hand, broad sections of the population are aware of a gulf between ambition and reality. The part of the population that really is negatively affected by developments – or feels that it is – loses faith in democratic institutions, which come to be perceived as distant and operating in conformity with a logic of their own. Authoritarian populism is a result of this development.

Before venturing a political explanation for the rise of authoritarian populism, which we shall do in the next chapter, we would like to shed light on the intellectual content of the new style of populism and to situate it within the context of a new social cleavage. The chapter ends with a discussion of the explanations – currently predominant, but from our point of view inadequate – of the rise of authoritarian populist parties.

3.1   Populism: A Controversial Concept

Populism is not a new phenomenon but, for a number of years now, it has been gaining a new significance. Among those reckoned to be early precursors in the United States are actors as diverse as the People's Party, which was active at the end of the nineteenth century as a political movement that represented the farming community, Huey Long, governor of Louisiana from 1928 and later US senator, and George Wallace, who fought in the 1960s to maintain segregation. The Narodniks, who saw the germ cells of Russian socialism in village community and peasant life, are often cited as early populists too. From the 1930s

The Ideology of Populism and the New Cleavage   47

onwards, movements emerged in Latin America that promised to assert the will of the people against established elites and imperialist powers. Among the representatives of this form of populism were Juan Perón in Argentina and Getúlio Vargas in Brazil. In the 1980s, Alberto Fujimori in Peru, Carlos Menem in Argentina, and Fernando Collor in Brazil continued this tradition: they retained the same anti-establishment stance but had totally different economic programmes, mostly neoliberal. Finally, Hugo Chávez in Venezuela and Evo Morales in Bolivia represented a decidedly left-wing populism, which Nicolás Maduro, Chávez's successor, claims today as his own.

From the second half of the 1980s, European parties dispensing an anti-establishment rhetoric began to grow in importance. Jörg Haider in Austria, Jean-Marie Le Pen in France, and, later, Pim Fortuyn in the Netherlands were the leading lights in this development. The term 'populism' was often applied to the parties they led. Then, in the past two decades, right-wing populist parties have established themselves in numerous European countries, and in many cases gained comparatively high shares of the vote.

For a long time, a *strategic* understanding of populism predominated, especially against the backdrop of the Latin American experience. Consequently populism tends to be seen as 'a political strategy, through which a personalistic leader seeks or exercises government power based on direct, unmediated, uninstitutionalized support from large numbers of mostly unorganized followers'.[2] Only with the rise of populist parties in Western Europe did an *ideational* understanding of populism gain importance, whereby populism is an ideology or a worldview, and not an opportunistic strategy to obtain power.[3]

But what are the ideas and concepts at the basis of populism? Most basically, populism rests on the conviction that ordinary people ought to determine their own destiny and should be empowered to do so. This corresponds to an original idea of

48   The Democratic Regression

Edward Shils (1954), who used the term 'populism' to capture various anti-elitist trends in US history. Thus understood, populism counter-balances representation and elite formation; it pairs them up as a counter-concept [*Gegenkonzept*]. This grassroots democratic conviction, as it were, can be made out to be the lowest common denominator in all movements that are normally described as populistic. Among them are the early US grassroots movements, the grassroots elements of the Greens in the 1980s, the anti-elitist tirades against corrupt elites in Washington and Brussels, and anti-imperialistic aims and objectives that include the repudiation of foreign powers and international institutions. This core is important, if one is to understand the intellectual roots of contemporary populism. But it is too unspecific and too vast to capture all its particularities.

The predominant understanding of populism in political science today has been strongly influenced by the work of Cas Mudde, who defines populism as 'a thin-centered ideology that considers society to be ultimately separated into two homogeneous and antagonistic groups, "the pure people" and "the corrupt elite", and argues that politics should be an expression of the *volonté générale* [general will] of the people'.[4] Thus understood, populism has two components: anti-elitism and the idea that the people are a homogeneous entity with a single, unified will. Populism is not a fully developed ideology, like socialism or liberalism. Fully fledged ideologies are comprehensive; 'thin' ideologies, on the other hand, have limited programmes.[5] On account of its ideological thinness, so the argument goes, populism docks onto more substantial ideologies, so that, from this perspective, it can turn out to be left-wing just as well as right-wing populism, or even some religious or ecological variety of populism.

3.2 Why Populism Is More Than a Thin Ideology

We follow Mudde and Kaltwasser (2017) in that we regard populism not simply as a political style or as a strategy for gaining power but as a set of substantive political positions and ideas. But, unlike these authors, we see more in contemporary populism than just a thin ideology.

Authoritarian populism possesses a specific understanding of politics and democracy that can be described with the help of four distinctive features:

(1) Political communities end at national borders. For populists, political responsibility is coterminous with the boundaries of the national territory. They deny that people on the other side of the border could be members of the political community. Simply paying heed to the interests of people who do not live in their country is something they reject. Political decisions must be taken exclusively in the interest of their own population. Cross-border responsibilities and solidarity count as a betrayal of ordinary people. Correspondingly, democracy beyond the national state is regarded as impossible as a matter of principle. This set of convictions makes contemporary populism *nationalistic.*

(2) The nationalism at play here is anti-pluralist and presupposes a homogeneous popular will. For not everyone is part of the people; a sharp dividing line is drawn between the true people and those who do not belong. In the United States, the heartland counts for more than the inner cities; in France, *la France profonde* [the French heartland] outweighs the multiethnic cities; in Germany, the slogan 'We are the people' [*Wir sind das Volk*], when chanted by supporters of Pegida or Alternative for Germany, does not extend to people with a history of migration, or even to the other residents of Kreuzberg, Berlin. Authoritarian populism works with an *image of the people as homogeneous.*

50 The Democratic Regression

(3) Political attitudes and interests are a given. What aims represent the will of the people, or how those aims are to be achieved – these are not matters to be shaped or changed through dialogue and confrontation with others. There can be no legitimate dispute over aims or the best ways of attaining them, because what is right is fixed from the outset. Hence there is no need for complicated procedures in order to arrive at correct political decisions. Contemporary populism is *decisionistic*.

(4) The will of the majority must be implemented. Representation does not consist in a continuous exchange between the represented and those who represent them, such that the latter would retain the power to take decisions autonomously but would be under an obligation to explain themselves and give reasons for their decisions.[6] What matters instead is to implement the (given) will of the majority without distortion. The best means of achieving this end are quick referendums, since they can give adequate expression to the popular will. In this context, individual and minority rights are merely a distraction. This is *the component* of authoritarian populism that is *fixated on the majority*.

Authoritarian tendencies are inscribed into these four features of contemporary populism. If dissenting opinions are inadmissible, the work of the opposition must be impeded or entirely suppressed. If courts prevent the true will of the people from being put into effect, measures are needed to remove these blockades and to prohibit them in the future. The authoritarian tendency shows up in attacks on the separation of powers, on newspapers or television channels regarded as hostile, or in open displays of contempt for parliamentary procedure. Where populist parties are in power, they often make it their aim to alter the regulations that govern democracy and the rule of law in such a way that effective opposition

The Ideology of Populism and the New Cleavage   51

and independent oversight become impossible, so that these parties can secure their power indefinitely. The attempts by the PiS [Law and Justice] party in Poland and by the Republican Party in the United States to fill the Polish and the American supreme courts with faithful followers, the change to electoral law in Hungary, and Donald Trump's attacks on the liberal press are examples of authoritarian tendencies in populist parties and actors.

Contemporary populist movements do indeed push for 'people's empowerment', but what they offer the people is a strangely deproceduralized form of empowerment. The popular will is to be realized through the delegation of power to one or several leaders.[7] This is the unmistakable message of an election poster for Heinz-Christian Strache, erstwhile head and lead candidate of the Austrian Freedom Party (FPÖ): 'HE wants what WE want.'[8] Contemporary populism not only demands the empowerment of the popular will or *volonté générale* but contains a precise understanding of what that will is: something pre-political and deproceduralized, which is embodied in the leadership of the populist party.

The ideological background to contemporary populism goes beyond a simple confrontation between the establishment and the people, imagined as a homogeneous entity. It also contains an authoritarian conception of how politics has to give effect to the popular will, which only exists in the singular.[9]

The distinction between supposedly thin and more substantial ideologies is problematic in another respect as well. No ideology can speak to every imaginable problem or question. An ideology is an answer to the urgent questions of the time and develops in interaction with other, rival ideologies. It has the 'capacity to fuse ideas and sentiments to create new public justifications for the exercise of power'.[10] So you need no weighty tomes of philosophical discourses before you can start talking about a thick ideology. An ideology can count as content-rich (hence thick) if it develops a narrative that brings together the

52   The Democratic Regression

various issues that are contentious at one particular time. This does not prevent some ideologies from evolving over time and adapting to new social challenges and objections, so that they become more comprehensive and detached from their original conditions. This is what happened with liberalism: it started in the eighteenth century, by way of opposition to absolute monarchy, but subsequently developed into a far broader conception of bourgeois society.[11] Unlike other ideologies of that time, it developed into a liberal script in the sense of a dominant constellation of ideas and institutional regulations for governing the organization of society, one that covered moral principles, cultural norms, ethical values, instrumental grounds, and cultural routines and customs.[12]

Contemporary populism is, admittedly, neither a dominant nor a historically developed script, but it is a fully fledged political ideology characterized by more than a simple confrontation between 'corrupt elites' and 'pure people'. Its ideas on the content, determination, and implementation of the popular will are what makes it specific. Otherwise it would be too vague to give enough definition to political parties and social movements. Nadia Urbinati uses very similar arguments to criticize the conception of populism as a thin ideology. Such a perspective can explain neither

> what makes populism a ruling power, nor how it transforms democratic institutions. Certainly, the thin-centered moral orientation is an important step, because it provides a minimal criterion for ordering the empirical analysis of various populist experiences. But it seems too broad and unpolitical to capture the form of representation that qualifies populism in its relation to democracy.[13]

Contemporary populism is pre-eminently an *authoritarian* populism that functions as an ideology on its own. It can be defined through a specific combination of procedural and

The Ideology of Populism and the New Cleavage   53

textual ideas. Authoritarian populism designates an ideology that takes up nationalistic positions against liberal elites and claims that political decisions should correspond most authentically to the unmediatized will of the majority.[14]

This understanding stresses the 'negativist approach' of authoritarian populists.[15] The positions they adopt are primarily directed *against* this or that, and much less shaped by their own aims. Authoritarian populism is anti-pluralistic insofar as its starting point is the homogeneous will of the people. It is anti-liberal insofar as it calls into question individual and especially minority rights. It is anti-procedural insofar as the will of the people ought to make itself felt directly and not be softened up by deliberations and multifarious checks and balances. Finally, authoritarian populism is anti-internationalist insofar as unrestricted emphasis on national sovereignty as a prerequisite for the effectiveness of the people's will implies an outright rejection of any political authority outside national borders and sets itself against the institutional complexity of multilevel political systems. On this agenda, closing the borders replaces interdependence and national sovereignty replaces international responsibility.

Authoritarian populism is an example of a self-standing ideology that brings together various themes in a more or less coherent political programme, from which specific aims can also be derived. It does not depend on another, more substantial ideology to which it can be attached. Even so, left- and right-wing variants can be discerned. The left-wing variant instrumentalizes the critique of imperial dominance for justifying power, seeks to protect the national economy, and offers comprehensive social benefits. What is fair is beyond dispute as far as the people is concerned, but its implementation is impeded by corrupt elites. The right-wing variant, on the other hand, focuses on the exclusion of people who, from its point of view, are not members of the national community. It advocates tax reductions and privatizations. In practice, however, the

54 The Democratic Regression

difference seems to blur over time. Some of the populist parties labelled right-wing, such as the Rassemblement National in France led by Marine Le Pen, have adopted a protectionist and state-interventionist agenda. At the same time, Jean-Luc Mélenchon's La France Insoumise, which is regarded as a left-wing populist party, has taken up similar positions on questions of migration. In fact the uprising led by the Gilets Jaunes (Yellow Vests) showed how well these French movements can work together – unsurprisingly perhaps, since they represent different varieties of authoritarian populism.

But not all the new parties of the left belong in this category. Many are pluralistic and open to international cooperation. For instance, we do not regard either the Coalition of the Radical Left in Greece – Syriza – or the Spanish party Podemos as populist.[16] They were formed against the background of extreme austerity policies, but the concrete decisions and positions they took, for example in the Greek case, turned out to be largely liberal, pluralist, and internationalist.

Is contemporary populism dominated by authoritarian populist parties? In political science research, there are various ways of identifying populist parties. Party and election manifestos can be assessed, political communications can be analysed, or experts can be consulted. We followed the third of these methods and made use of the PopuList dataset.[17] In order to classify parties in thirty-one European countries, a research team consulted eighty specialists who were asked to assess case by case whether, by populist standards, parties were to be assigned to the radical left or to the radical right and whether, beyond this, they were Eurosceptic. The data covered the period from 1989 to 2020 and all the parties that have won at least one seat in a national parliament or at least 2 per cent of the vote since that year. By this method, 102 parties out of a total of 211 were classified as populist or right-wing populist. This classification rested on a broader understanding of populism than the one we have sketched here, but nevertheless

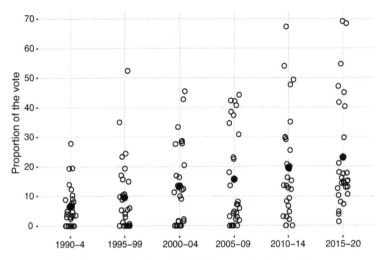

Figure 6 The rise of populist parties in Europe.
Source: Data from PopuList dataset (see Rooduijn et al. 2020) and ParlGov databank (see Döring and Manow 2019).
Note: The chart shows the proportion of the vote obtained by populist parties in thirty-one European countries. Countries in which there were no (qualifying) populist parties during the periods marked off on the horizontal axis received the value 0. Filled circles represent the average value for the relevant five-year period.

one that allowed us to trace the trend of the past three decades. Figure 6 shows the proportions of the vote obtained by populist and right-wing populist parties during the period 1990–2020.

Two trends are noteworthy. The number of populist parties – in other words, the number of empty circles in Figure 6 – clearly rises. In the 1990s there were still quite a few countries without populist parties of any significance; but after 2005 this situation changed almost everywhere. Right-wing populist parties have established themselves even in countries like Germany (AfD)[18] and Spain (Vox), which were previously considered by and large immune to this phenomenon. Furthermore, longer-established parties obtain over time larger voting shares (see the position of points on the Y-axis). The voting shares of the

56 The Democratic Regression

relevant parties have risen rapidly in Finland, Sweden, the Netherlands, and especially in Poland and Hungary, where they now dominate the party system. This increase was not evenly distributed or entirely without setbacks, but overall (right-wing) populist parties have managed to establish and consolidate themselves in almost every country in Europe.

3.3   The New Cleavage

Authoritarian populism is an ideology with a specific understanding of politics, community, and democracy. Ideologies bundle up solutions to the urgent problems of the time and give them internal cohesion. But they reach their full development only when they interact with opposing ideologies. When such ideologies shape societies, when they consolidate their system and rely on a socio-structural network, political science starts to speak about social cleavages. Since the 1980s, a political dispute has developed that pits liberal globalists against authoritarian populists in both national and international contexts. The two groups represent opposite attitudes to a social cleavage that has been identified and commented on in a variety of studies.[19]

Cleavage theory views the history of modern Europe as a succession of four basic social conflicts.[20] Each of the four cleavages was caused by a revolutionary social change. The nation-state revolution brought about the cleavage between church and state and, later on, between the centre and the periphery. The Industrial Revolution gave us the opposition between labour and capital and between town and country. As far as the twentieth century was concerned, the decisive cleavage was the one between labour and capital, which pitted the parties of the left against their bourgeois counterparts. True, the parties operated under different names in different countries and in each camp there were different subgroups, but in

The Ideology of Populism and the New Cleavage   57

principle most party systems were ranged along the left–right axis. For a long time this phenomenon could be observed in Great Britain, where, thanks to the first-past-the-post electoral system, parties faced each other by way of a Labour and a Conservative or Tory Party: together, these two constituted the poles of the labour–capital divide. Even in countries with proportional representation, the old centre-left and centre-right parties clearly dominated. In Austria, for example, the social democrats (SPÖ) and the conservatives (ÖVP) obtained 89 to 93 per cent of the vote in national parliamentary elections between 1956 and 1983. In the 2010s, the situation changed at remarkable speed. In the National Assembly elections of 2019, the SPÖ and the ÖVP still won between them 58.7 per cent of the vote; but, in the first round of the presidential election of 2016, the candidates for the two old-style people's parties were able to muster only 23 per cent of the vote. Similarly, in the run-off for the 2017 presidential election in France, Emmanuel Macron of La République en Marche, a new party, was facing Marine Le Pen of the Front National, since the Parti Socialiste won only 6.4 per cent of the vote in the first round. Changes have not been quite so dramatic in every country. Even so, the shift away from the old centre-left and centre-right parties and towards new challengers happened almost everywhere.

Since the 1980s, a cleavage has formed that runs orthogonally to the left–right axis. The social revolution that triggered it is globalization, which not only produced economic inequality but triggered fundamental disputes as to how the demos should be defined in the 'postnational constellation',[21] how permeable borders should be, and whether political decisions should be taken at the national or the international level. The poles of this new conflict are captured by various different concepts: green–alternative–libertarian (GAL) versus traditional–authoritarian–nationalist (TAN),[22] integration versus demarcation,[23] universalistic versus particularistic,[24] cosmopolitan versus communitarian.[25]

58   The Democratic Regression

One can speak of social cleavage only when breaches within society are sustained by both a socio-structural and an ideological network and when they crystallize in a corresponding form of political organization.[26] The Industrial Revolution, for instance, rendered the opposition between labour and capital more acute. This opposition had its intellectual foundations in the ideologies of socialism (with its social democratic variant) and liberalism (with its conservative manifestation) and organized itself in trade unions and industry associations, in the familiar mould of left- and right-wing parties.

(a) In a ground-breaking 1989 study titled *Commerce and Coalitions*, Ronald Rogowski worked out the intra-societal distributional effects of open borders, and hence the *socio-structural element* in the new cleavage. According to him, those who benefit structurally from the opening of the borders in western societies are the people whose capital is held in forms that are plentiful at home but in short supply on the world market: financial capital, physical capital, and knowledge (educated human capital). Before the globalizing shift of the 1980s and 1990s, the opposite was true of simple manual activities; they were plentiful on the world market but in short supply in western societies. This group lost out when borders were opened because such activities were transferred elsewhere, or competition increased as a result of migration. The new distribution is also reflected in the elephant curve of the global income growth discussed in Chapter 1.[27] The winners were the highly educated (or trained) graduates from the world's best universities and the owners of financial capital – a new global middle class.[28] The winners of globalization show an above-average level of education, as well as a high degree of cultural and human capital. They are both spatially and professionally mobile. On the other side of the divide stand the losers of globalization in the rich industrial countries. Their level of education or training is below the average, they have limited cultural and social capital, and they are much less present outside national borders.[29]

The Ideology of Populism and the New Cleavage   59

(b) Cosmopolitanism and communitarianism are a pair of concepts that invite the description of *intellectual bases* of the new cleavage. The concept of cosmopolitanism suggests first of all a world of philosophical values and ideas that, until two decades ago, was known to very few people outside academia, although it has left the academic sphere for a long time. The moral and political convictions that make up philosophical cosmopolitanism can be brought under three core elements: individualism, universalism, and generalizability. These elements are the starting point of the cosmopolitan belief that all the people on the globe deserve the same respect, regardless of nationality, religion, and the like.[30] Even theorists who take no radically universalist position and emphasize the relevance of social contexts often argue that in this day and age the decisive social context is the global one. According to them, globalization has opened up national societies and placed them in a global context. In a situation where everyone shares the same global fate,[31] cosmopolitanism is an adequate normative solution.

In the opposite corner, the philosophy of communitarianism prioritizes the constitutive role of community and identity in the development of social attitudes and ways of thinking. In this reasoning, distributive justice and democracy depend on social contexts that are, for the most part, territorially defined. They require an active community, a strongly participative democracy, and a pluralistic republicanism.[32] Communitarians understand freedom, self-government, civic virtues, and a participation-oriented institutional infrastructure as being fused with the political community. They take freedom to be the result of political communication and participation.[33] At the same time, in philosophical communitarianism the concept of community is little specified – the community could be local, regional, or national.

Our use of this pair of concepts has little to do with the 1980s' philosophical debate about principles of justice. Our

60   The Democratic Regression

aim is to reconstruct the ideational foundations of the two opposite poles of the new social cleavage. Understood in this way, cosmopolitanism and communitarianism sum up political attitudes that are bound up with each other when it comes to this cleavage.[34]

There are three reasons why this pair of concepts appears to be better suited to describing the new cleavage than the alternatives mentioned. First, unlike GAL and TAN for example, or demarcation and integration, cosmopolitanism and communitarianism refer not only to the content of positions but also to the ideational foundations at their core. Second, the ideational components of the cleavage need to be captured by concepts that put the two sides on an equal footing. Other confrontations, such as those between materialists and postmaterialists or between GAL and TAN, create an asymmetry insofar as they tend to regard one side as atavistic, as a brake on the process of secular modernization. Even if the two positions are not considered to be of equal moral value, none of the teleology from the philosophy of history should be allowed to creep into the analysis of cleavages. Third, the juxtaposition of cosmopolitanism and communitarianism, like that of integration and demarcation, ultimately captures the fact that the cleavage at stake here has something to do with fighting for borders. The new cleavage differs fundamentally from previous ones in this respect, as was worked out by Stein Rokkan.[35] The question is no longer how national societies are shaped. It is about the borders of the nation-state themselves – about their permeability, their normative dignity, and their meaning to the political process.

Of course, the creation of a two-dimensional political space as a result of the emergence of a new cleavage makes it necessary to distinguish between different variants of communitarianism and cosmopolitanism. Anyone who, at least for the foreseeable future, perceives national demarcation as a prerequisite for democracy and as a form of redistribution that

The Ideology of Populism and the New Cleavage   61

fights inequality, is on the side of left-wing communitarianism. This may carry authoritarian connotations, but not necessarily. By contrast, right-wing communitarianism is almost always authoritarian. With their eyes on the formative phase of the new cleavage, Herbert Kitschelt and Anthony McGann premised that there is a 'winning formula' for the new right – a formula that combines nationalism and neoliberalism.[36] But right-wing populism has proved to be more flexible on this front. Many authoritarian populists nowadays advocate a strong welfare state, so long as its benefits improve the lot of the true people. By the same token, cosmopolitanism cannot be restricted to its 'dirty variant', radical neoliberalism. There is now also a left-wing variant, represented by human rights individualism and movements in defence of the environment, for instance. Those who support open borders, strong international institutions, and defensible human rights will often demand a markedly intensified regulation of the global financial markets, a strong climate regime, and often even redistributive mechanisms and solidarity beyond the nation-state.

(c) Finally, in order for the structural and intellectual contrasts described here to turn into a permanent cleavage, one needs powerful and effective actors, who can mobilize their supporters and represent their interests in society and politics. In everyday political debate, liberal globalists and authoritarian populists take up opposite positions. There are three points that come at the top of the list. One is about controlling the national borders for people, goods, and capital. Whereas advocates of liberal globalism tend to support open borders, authoritarian populists stress, from either nationalistic or sociopolitical motives, that borders ought to be protected. The second cluster of issues is linked to this point. Liberal globalists regard the transfer of competences to European and international institutions as functionally necessary and normatively desirable. Authoritarian populists, on the other hand, fear that it will undermine the sovereignty of

62   The Democratic Regression

the people and damage democracy. The third cluster concerns the relationship between individual rights and majority will. While the authoritarian populist coalition puts majority will ahead of individual rights, liberal globalism does mainly the opposite.

To the informal coalition of liberal globalists belong most of the established parties and many notabilities from government, the civil service, and the law, as well as important media and international organizations. Against them stand the authoritarian populist parties, plus movements such as Pegida and the Identitarians, who are classed as belonging to the extreme right. The Danish People's Party, the Freedom Party of Austria, the Rassemblement National in France, the PiS Party in Poland and Geert Wilders's Party for Freedom in the Netherlands are prominent, but by no means the only, examples of parties of this type. They are clearly illiberal, above all with respect to immigration policy and Islam, and at the same time they reject any kind of extension of supranational competences.[37]

In Western Europe, the tension between cosmopolitanism and communitarianism has also left its mark on the profiles, membership, and constituencies of the old-style catch-all parties [*Volksparteien*], as Otto Kirchheimer described them – which, historically, defined themselves through their positions on the left–right continuum. This kind of camp forming within parties has to be understood as a specific expression of the new cleavage. Admittedly, even today centrist catch-all parties exercise a moderating function in the matter of the old cleavage between labour and capital, which has a lot to do with the fact that a popular party cannot afford to lose the support of a large social stratum or a relevant cultural environment. But when smaller parties are in a better position to make their mark along the new line of conflict and to mobilize voters, the vote shares of the centrist parties will erode. While the silent revolution[38] and its post-material, liberal values encouraged

The Ideology of Populism and the New Cleavage   63

the rise of the New Left, including the Greens, it was in the course of the silent counter-revolution[39] that the authoritarian populist parties came to light.

As a result, all three aspects that have to be present before we can speak of a new cleavage are now in place. The structural opposition between globalization's winners and losers is underpinned by the ideological confrontation between cosmopolitan and communitarian positions. Organizationally, a liberal–globalist coalition faces up to an authoritarian populist one.

3.4   Inadequate Explanations

Cleavages come into being as a result of social revolutions. Thus the new one is an outcome of the globalization that began in the 1980s and accelerated during the 1990s. Globalization means that social spaces where transactions are thickly clustered no longer stop at the borders of states. Karl W. Deutsch described the situation with admirable operational clarity. The borders of national societies are in a process of dissolution when no clear density reduction is to be seen in the frequency of social transactions.[40] In the 1960s, over 98 per cent of all telephone calls were domestic, and investments and goods deliveries were made primarily within states. Things have changed drastically since then.

With the aid of the KOF Globalization Index, it is possible to show the extent to which transnational interactions have increased in density (Figure 7). The index covers numerous indicators, which range from tourism through business to the spread of international non-governmental organizations. In addition to being an aggregated globalization index, it distinguishes various subareas such as politics and various activities such as social and economic ones. Furthermore, it registers both the legally (*de iure*) codified transnational and

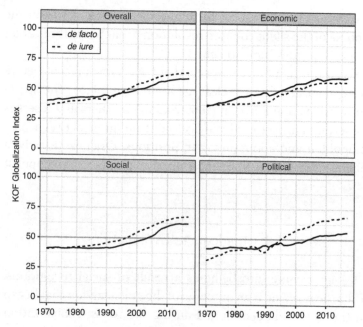

Figure 7 Globalization since the 1970s.
Source: Gygli et al. 2019.
Note: The KOF Globalization Index measures the economic, social, and political dimensions of globalization.

international regulation and the actual (*de facto*) number of transborder interactions.

As a sum of all indicators, between 1979 and 2017 the *de facto* index rose from 40 to 59, while the *de iure* figure rose from 36 to 64 (on a scale of 0 to 100). These figures reveal a clear growth in the number of cross-border interactions in cultural and economic areas as well as an increase in international agreements. The lines showing economic and social globalization follow very similar trajectories. Only *de facto* globalization in the political area lags behind somewhat.[41]

The globalization push described here represents the social revolution that brought the new cleavage into being. But the question of which mechanisms can translate globalization

The Ideology of Populism and the New Cleavage 65

into a new cleavage and thus propel the rise of authoritarian populism remains. Two answers dominate both the public and the scholarly discussion. One stresses the cultural effects of globalization, the other its economic dynamics. Among the explanations on offer, the socioeconomic one is the most prominent. It follows on from the distributional effects of globalization demonstrated by Rogowski (1989) and Milanović (2016). By this account, it is mostly the economic losers of globalization who have joined the authoritarian populists, and mostly its economic winners who have joined the liberal globalists. At the centre of all this stands the growing economic insecurity, which has increased in the most established democratic systems during the past three decades. Numerous studies have shown that the probability of the election of an authoritarian populist party rises when income and job security are below average.[42] Neither Brexit nor the election of Donald Trump as US president would have succeeded if they had not received substantial support from declining regions with old industries.[43] Furthermore, the economic explanation points to an increasing friction between dynamic metropolises and disconnected rural regions.[44] So Hillary Clinton received more than 80 per cent of the vote in each of the ten largest US cities, while Donald Trump achieved even better results in some rural states. This is the sign of an enormous polarization. Even in the heyday of the left–right opposition, mainstream parties of either stripe generally fell quite a bit behind such figures.

The economic explanation certainly recommends a series of follow-up questions. For one thing, people of low status and people with strong fears of status loss have always shown above-average support for authoritarian populist parties;[45] and the fact that there are so many more of them now than there were twenty years ago can hardly be attributed to a general deterioration of the economic situation in Western Europe and North America. For another, it remains a mystery, as we

66 The Democratic Regression

have mentioned before, why the losers of globalization turn to authoritarian-populist parties and not to left-wing parties, whose brand essence is the struggle against inequality and for social safeguards. Why should voters who feel economically disadvantaged and expect more state support vote for Silvio Berlusconi, Donald Trump, and Boris Johnson, who belong in the economic elite and support political programmes that aim to bring tax relief to the richest of the rich? Ernest Gellner has called this, ironically, the theory of the wrong address: 'The wake-up message was meant for *classes*, but, through a terrible mistake of the messenger's, it was sent to nations instead.'[46]

Similarly, the socioeconomic approach does not explain how the pool of populist voters in almost all OECD countries remains relatively constant, at slightly over 20 per cent. This applies to Scandinavian countries, where inequalities are still limited, as much as to Anglo-Saxon societies, which are much more unequal. One could argue at this point that the decisive element is not the absolute degree of inequality, but its increase during the past few decades. Even then, questions remain. In only three Western European countries has inequality either not increased or increased very little during the past twenty years.[47] These are the Netherlands, Austria, and France – precisely the countries in which authoritarian populist parties enjoyed their first successes. Moreover, from a socioeconomic perspective, it remains unclear why, in countries that have profited exceptionally from globalization, authoritarian political forces should have broken through and be in government. Turkey, India, and Poland are particularly striking examples.

Apart from economic explanations, cultural changes are frequently cited to account for the rise of populism. In this case, the cleavage between capital and labour is often considered to be an economic dimension of political space, while the new cleavage is perceived mostly as a cultural dimension.[48] By this account, thanks to social (and cultural) globalization, cultural liberalism and universalism have become so dominant that they eliminate all the dissenting positions as politically incorrect. This has elicited a cultural defensive operation from the more traditionally minded sections of the population. According to this explanation, the anywheres and the frequent travellers are lined up on one side, the somewheres and the homebound on the other. The distinction between bourgeois and working-class culture has been replaced, in this view, by the gap between the supposedly 'chic' and the supposedly 'square'. As a result, the opposition between borderless globalism and nation-oriented populism is reflected with exceptional clarity in the contrastive attitudes of the elite and of the broader population, especially on matters of migration.[49]

The sociocultural explanation, of course, leaves central questions open as well. First, it does not seem either helpful or in line with the theory of cleavages to restrict the conflict between cosmopolitanism and communitarianism to the cultural sphere. Cleavages encompass all dimensions. Even the conflict between capital and labour has a cultural component – which is apparent, among other things, in the different lifestyles of working-class circles and of the bourgeoisie. Likewise, the cultural practices of liberal globalists are bound up with certain socioeconomic conditions[50] – people don't get to be frequent travellers without having adequate finances. Second, the culturalist reading runs the risk of confusing cause and effect. Sociocultural contrasts frequently start to become intense when an authoritarian populist party has achieved some electoral successes.[51] Christoph Nguyen (2019) shows, for example, that anger and fear do not correlate too strongly with decisions to vote for right-wing populist parties, but the values for anger and fear rise once these parties have been elected. From a cultural perspective it is something of a mystery why authoritarian populist parties fight with great vehemence and unanimity against European and international institutions, when these institutions can hardly be said to count as spearheads of the LGBTQ+ movement and of post-material thinking; oftentimes, all they stand for is market liberalization on materialistic grounds. Finally, it remains noticeably unclear why authoritarian populism is uncommonly strong in countries that do not distinguish themselves through their liberal culture. Russia and Turkey spring to mind.

Both explanations show deficiencies and ignore the political sphere. Even their empirical powers of prediction seem relatively limited.[52] By contrast, a genuinely political explanation of populism would point to deficits in the functioning of democracy. It would concentrate on the reduced representativeness of the political system when the preferences of the decidedly communitarian social strata are at stake. Among these strata, the impression of not being heard in politics is becoming entrenched. The perception of a political class that serves its own interest and those of the cosmopolitan elite is spreading against this background. Authoritarian populist parties claim to speak on behalf of those who have been left out. Hence they criticize the political system and the mainstream parties absolutely and as a matter of principle – and their charges stick because in reality the politics of the past few decades has been a supporter and an ally of liberal globalists.

4

The Crisis of Representation and the Alienated Democracy

The main thing that anyone who listens to representatives of authoritarian populist parties will hear is complaints about the political system. In Germany, for instance, the Alternative für Deutschland (AfD) wants to overcome the 'filthy horrible' red–green system. It talks about the 'system parties' or, in Jörg Meuthen's watered-down version, the 'old parties'. The 'political class' is held responsible for Germany's aberrations and wrong turns.[1] The 'lying press' refers not to individual media but to the media landscape as a whole. In the AfD manifesto, the renewal of democracy (with a heavy emphasis on referendums) and pruning the European Union are pretty much top of the agenda. In other words, the first in line to be criticized are the ruling institutions, not the policies – and this in the name of democracy.[2]

But if the aim is to identify ideas for specific policies and measures that are part of the AfD's brand essence, one needs to take a closer look at its basic political manifesto.[3] One will find there just a handful of claims that mark the party as an outsider. Of course, the claim to strengthen the country's external borders is uttered very loudly, but there is nothing special about it in the current political landscape. In the sociocultural sphere, conspicuously, gender research should be terminated; and this point comes straight after a section that upholds academic freedom. Commitment to the traditional family is only rarely expressed with the same degree of openness, and the same can be said of the demand for a dominant (German) culture instead of multiculturalism. Socioeconomically, almost nothing falls outside the familiar framework: the minimum wage is to be retained, bureaucracy reduced, the social market economy strengthened, and all the rest of it.

Besides, complaints about the unjust and degenerate political system predominate in the AfD. They are followed by complaints about migration and the sociocultural state of the country. Criticism of the socioeconomic conditions seems, by contrast, to be relatively light. Much the same goes for authoritarian populist parties in other consolidated democracies. If one looks more closely at the ones with governmental responsibilities, a similar picture emerges: it is mostly a picture of the whole, without details – and political institutions and procedures are almost invariably in the foreground.

In the consolidated democracies, this criticism of the way in which democracy functions resonates with a great many people. In 2019, the Pew Research Center published the results of a survey according to which attitudes in Great Britain, France, and Germany show a very similar profile.[4] Here is a question whose answers stand out on account of their negativity: 'Do you believe that the elected officials in your country are interested in what people like you are thinking?' Only 33 per cent of respondents replied in the affirmative in Germany, 28 per cent in Great Britain, and just 23 per cent in France. So a clear majority is dissatisfied with the political class.

But if the questions are more specific and relate to concrete problems, the population tends to side with the old mainstream parties rather than with the authoritarian populist ones. In all three countries the gender equality goal, for example, received extremely high approval ratings: 90 per cent in Germany and

France, 92 per cent in Great Britain. Moreover, a positive assessment of living standards prevailed in all three. In West Germany 64 per cent of respondents had a positive view and in East Germany 59 per cent – more than in Great Britain (57 per cent) and France (53 per cent). All these figures are much better than in 1991, when the same question was asked and authoritarian populist parties were not yet on the scene (the improving runs from 12 percentage points in West Germany to a whopping 44 percentage points in East Germany). There was only one area in which a large minority of respondents took the side of the authoritarian populist parties: migration. But even here, according to the Pew Research Center, the majority were still satisfied with the existing policies. In sum, people are less dissatisfied today with equal rights policies and with their own standard of living. Traditional ideas about gender roles had little resonance and, just before the Covid crisis, people were overwhelmingly positive about their economic circumstances. A large majority was dissatisfied with the political class – and a significant minority with migration policies.

These observations need to be taken seriously if we are to explain the rise of authoritarian populism. Hence the existing economic and cultural explanations must be supplemented by a political one. And that explanation is not about dissatisfaction with specific policies but about the political system as a whole and about lack of trust in decision makers. It is about the feeling that one is inadequately represented in democracy, and about the alienation from democracy that comes with it. In our view, such an explanation has the additional advantage that it integrates economic and cultural distortions and can thus yield a more complex interpretation.

There are always two sides to explaining social phenomena. On the one hand, a good explanation takes account of the insider perspective of the actors, in any situation. What motives underlie the election of an authoritarian populist party? If the dissatisfaction of those who vote for authoritarian populist parties is focused more on the political system and less on socioeconomic inequalities and concrete sociocultural policies, this is an important indicator from an internal perspective. But it is not enough for us. We also have to identify any generalizable causal factors that have brought about the social development we are interested in. So then: causes are prior events or developments that regularly produce the observed result. Causes stand for generally valid social patterns, which can be expressed through statements of probability and their framing conditions. For this reason, we pinpoint the rhetoric that authoritarian populist parties direct at the political system; then we ask whether the latter contains any obvious systematic changes that have influenced the rise of such parties (see sections 4.1 and 4.2) and whether the dissatisfactions generated by those changes are reflected in what motivates people to vote for these parties (see section 4.3).

Two distinct developments account for the growing dissatisfaction with established democracies. First, legislative parliaments are selectively responsive: they pay special attention to the upper social layers and classes. This unequal responsiveness is one of the generalizable causes that produce dissatisfaction with the 'system'. Second, parliaments and parties – the classic institutions for majority decisions – have lost some of their importance over time. Today decisions are often taken by bodies such as central banks or international institutions. The growing significance of non-majoritarian institutions (NMIs) of this type is a second reason for discontent with the functioning of democratic systems. Hence we agree with David Runciman: 'Democracy is not working well – if it were, there would be no populist backlash.'[5]

The Crisis of Representation and the Alienated Democracy 73

4.1 The Inadequate Responsivity of Parliaments

In 1960, shortly before the election of John F. Kennedy to be the thirty-fifth president of the United States, Elmer Eric Schattschneider published *The Semisovereign People,* a political science classic. It was a harsh critique of the theory of pluralism. Schattschneider noted a bias in the system towards business and the upper classes. The notion that the interests deputized for in Congress could be representative of the American population as a whole was nothing but a myth. The upshot of this attitude was the famous statement that '[t]he flaw in the pluralist heaven is that the heavenly chorus sings with a strong upper-class accent'.[6] The unequal responsiveness of parliaments in liberal democratic systems has scarcely diminished in the meantime.[7] There is even a lot to suggest that, in the course of globalization, the accent has grown more pronounced over the past two decades. This is precisely what the authoritarian populist parties are complaining about, and they do it at the top of their voices. The core of their criticism is that representative democracy, the 'system parties', and the media pay no attention to the ordinary person – the people in the street. It is against this background that the antagonism between ordinary people and a distant elite takes place. The rhetoric comes from an authoritarian mindset, but it is based on a reality: there is indeed a gap between the representatives and the represented.

4.1.1 Who governs?

When democracy first arose in antiquity, it was a direct democracy. The thought that decision-making may be transferred over the long term to professional politicians would not have occurred to the Athenians. Every citizen – and in those days theirs was, admittedly, a very exclusive circle of wealthy men – had the right to take part in the popular assembly, and

74 The Democratic Regression

offices were allocated by lot for short spans of time and, as a rule, only once. The principles of Athenian democracy were intended to ensure that the people ruled themselves. There was no 'political class' in the system. However, this form of democracy, which constituted a revolutionary recasting of traditional rule, could not be simply transferred to nation-states when the rule of the people had to be established, from the late eighteenth century onwards. In a second democratic transformation, the direct democracy of small city-states became representative democracy in large territorial states. Self-rule by citizens was no longer practicable in the modern version of democracy, so representatives had to take decisions in their stead. Although the representative variety is the one that we take for granted today, it would not have been regarded as democratic in antiquity.[8]

If we do not govern ourselves but select a small group to take decisions on our behalf, there is always a risk that the elected representatives will decide differently from the majority. For this reason, political representation always remains a fragile construct, a potential breaking point on the borderline between representatives and the people they represent. In spite of the promise that democracy would guarantee equality among citizens, there remains an elitist element in representation.[9] The threat of being voted out of office is a mechanism intended to prevent the difference between the represented and their representatives from being systematically translated into decisions that go against the interests of the former.[10] The representatives have to be free, but also under an obligation to the citizens. They need to justify their own actions, and their re-election depends on how convincing those justifications are.[11]

Parliaments have never been a mirror image of the population. In most countries, men have always been overrepresented, the representatives have been older than the population average, and people with a migration history have been strongly underreprensented. These representational deficits have been somewhat mitigated in recent decades. In another area, however, the imbalance has become more pronounced: Mark Bovens and Anchrit Wille (2017) have investigated how the composition of parliaments in Western Europe has changed in point of educational outcomes. Even though the proportion of people with higher education has always been higher in parliaments than among the general population, nowadays academic achievers are particularly strongly represented, which is why Bovens and Wille called their book *Diploma Democracy*.[12] At issue here is not only the difference between those people and the general population but also the increasing homogenization of their career paths. The three-step progression school–university–politics is much more common now than it was in the past. The danger of parliaments becoming insufficiently responsive to underrepresented population groups intensifies when everything that almost all their representatives know about building sites (if they know anything at all) comes from vacation jobs or topping-out ceremonies and when these representatives never go into bakeries other than as customers.

4.1.2   For whom is government meant to be?

Unequal representation carries over into parliamentary work. The representatives' legal responsibilities towards their constituents do not work the way Hanna Pitkin hoped it would. Wouter Schakel and Armen Hakhverdian (2018) show, for example, that the political positions taken by members of parliament in the Netherlands tend to correspond to those of the voters whose characteristics they share: higher education and higher incomes.[13] Congressmen and -women in the United States differ in their political preferences on the basis of their social origins: a representative from a working-class family and a representative with a privileged family background fight for different causes.[14] Similar findings are available for Latin

America,[15] and in debates in the British House of Commons 'career politicians' position themselves differently from working people.[16] The numerical underrepresentation of certain groups leads to the underrepresentation of certain political views. A good many representatives outside populist parties incline towards liberal globalist views.[17]

Do the decisions that parliaments eventually reach also favour better-off groups? The starting point of this line of research is in the United States. Martin Gilens (2005) altered at a stroke the standard research into responsiveness when he examined almost 2,000 answers to survey questions in order to ascertain which members of the population had supported which policies and what political decisions had subsequently been taken. Gilens's innovation consisted in assessing surveys over more than three decades and dividing the respondents into various income groups. This research design allowed him to capture differences regarding whose preferences were implemented. His results showed there was a clear tilt in favour of the rich. Now, it is not the case that the political concerns of poorer groups are never implemented; but whether they are depends on whether these groups have the same aspirations as the rich. In many instances, 'coincidental representation' takes place,[18] as all income groups are in favour of similar policies; but when there are notable differences between the rich and the poor, politics normally sides with the rich.

There is a specific mechanism that can explain this imbalance in responsiveness. Since election campaigns in the United States are very expensive and become even more so over time, while no public reimbursement of campaign costs is in place, all candidates rely on private funding. The campaign can be financed through an abundance of small contributions, but more often a small number of big spenders carry the lion's share of sponsorship. The need to raise money is a strong incentive not to offend current and potential donors.[19] This is one reason why political decisions look more to the preferences of the rich. He who pays the piper (or the heavenly choir) calls the tune.

If the financing of election campaigns were the deciding factor in unequal responsiveness, the models in Europe would have to look different. In most European countries, election campaigns are financed according to a clearly different model, because the state bears a part of the costs. In order to test whether political decision-making in Germany is less distorted than in the United States, for example, one can compare the voters' political preferences with the decisions taken by the Bundestag.[20] For the period 1980–2013, survey data are available on more than 700 topics, which all involved a concrete change of policy. The respondents stated in each case whether they were for or against the proposal, and on this basis it was possible to determine how high the proportion of those who supported a reform was within various educational, income, and professional groups.[21] Next, we examined whether the proposed policy change was implemented by the German Bundestag during the next four years.

Although Germany presents none of the United States' dependence on private campaign funding, the results are similar. The Bundestag, too, is more likely to implement policy changes if they are advocated predominantly by professional groups of higher social status (civil servants, the self-employed) and by higher-income groups or groups with higher educational qualifications.[22] As can be seen in Figure 8, there is no more than a coincidental connection between the preferences of workers, skilled workers, and lower-grade employees on the one hand and the implementation of reforms on the other. For other professional groups, by contrast, the connection is positive and statistically significant. As far as the probability of implementing policy proposals goes, it makes little difference whether very few or very many (skilled) workers favour a change, for example. But the situation looks very different for civil servants, the self-employed, and entrepreneurs: the

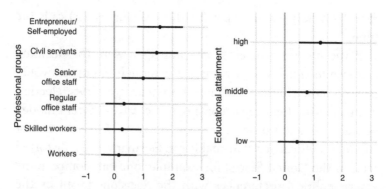

Figure 8 The responsiveness of the German Bundestag.
Source: Data from ResPOG dataset.
Note: These are the Logit coefficients of separate regression models in which the probability of implementation is estimated as a dependent variable and the degrees of agreement in six professional and three educational groupings are estimated as independent variables. If the horizontal black line does not cut the value 0, then a statistically significant connection exists. The higher the degree of agreement with a reform, for instance among entrepreneurs and self-employed, the greater the probability that it will be implemented by the Bundestag.

greater the number of supporters, the more likely it is that a change of policy will take place. Concretely, this means that there is a 43 per cent probability that a change will take place if 10 per cent of the self-employed or senior businesspeople are for it, but the probability rises to 73 per cent when support for the measure reaches 90 per cent. By contrast, the likelihood of implementation increases only by five percentage points when 90 per cent rather 10 per cent of skilled workers are in favour of it. The results are no different if we look at groups classified by educational attainment plus the associated differences in income; here too, the connection between political preferences and political decisions seems to be much stronger in the case of groups with more resources.

As in the United States, in Germany, too, professional groups of lower social status and citizens of lower educational levels or

The Crisis of Representation and the Alienated Democracy 79

with lower incomes sometimes get the policies they wish for. But this depends decisively on how much their views coincide with those of better-off groups. If the desires of workers differ from those of entrepreneurs, or the desires of the less educated differ from those of the highly educated, or the desires of the poor differ from those of the rich, politics will mainly go along with the latter in each of these cases. Similar studies are now available for the Netherlands, Sweden, and Norway, and they confirm that the patterns outlined here operate even in these egalitarian countries.[23]

The influence of people with smaller incomes, lower educational levels, and lower-grade professions on parliamentary decisions is limited in Europe as well. There, too, the parliamentary choir sings with an accent. The accent may be rather less pronounced than in the United States, where campaign financing is a source of inequality; but it can still be clearly heard. There is also a good deal of evidence to suggest that it is stronger today than it was in the 1960s and 1970s, when Schattschneider called attention to it for the first time, in relation to the United States. The selective responsiveness of political decision-making goes together with a double dose of liberalism. People with higher educational qualifications and incomes often have liberal preferences not only culturally: they also cherish free markets more strongly. If their interests are given more weight, this fact shifts politics further towards the liberal cosmopolitan end of the spectrum.[24]

4.2 The Disempowerment of Parliaments

Parliaments deal selectively with society's requests. Their responsiveness to the interests of the lower classes is only superficial. Nevertheless, parties and parliaments remain the central institutions that can give people with fewer qualifications any influence over decisions. Parliaments based on an

80 The Democratic Regression

equal suffrage represent a historical achievement of the working class. The introduction of a universal and equal right to vote for representation in parliament was the prerequisite for the welfare state. Only when this right was guaranteed could laws be enacted with the support of the majority of the population, which enabled the building of institutionalized national solidarity and the redistribution that goes with it. Majority decisions were required to set up a progressive tax system. On its own, the selfless and public-spirited willingness of the better-off would hardly have been enough. Thus, in liberal democracies, parliaments and the parties are the institutions that give the majority principle its validity and make it theoretically possible for the interests of the majority to prevail against the interests of the privileged. This inherent threat alone prompts the better-off also to adopt, now and again, political positions that are in line with the interests of the lower classes. Thus most of the decisions of parliaments are in unison with the interests of the better-off *and* with those of the disadvantaged.

In consequence, a discreet but dramatic change in the institutional landscape gains importance – namely the transfer of the decision-making power from majoritarian institutions such as parties and parliaments to non-majoritarian ones such as central banks, constitutional courts, and international bodies. This shift is the result of a dynamic that set in exactly at the time when Schattschneider was writing about the accent of the parliamentary 'heavenly choir'. At the end of this chain are the initial upswing of the new authoritarian populist parties and the call for an anti-pluralist notion of majority rule.[25] The full extent of the process could be observed in the consolidated democracies of Western Europe and North America, but an accelerated version was also on display in Central Eastern Europe, Turkey, and Latin America.[26]

We need to add the relative disempowerment of parliaments to their inadequate responsiveness. As shown in

The Crisis of Representation and the Alienated Democracy 81

section 4.1, majoritarian institutions are less responsive than they once used to be. What is more, they have lost to NMIs their decision-making competence on many issues, as will be shown in what follows. This twofold institutional dynamic, which combines the unequal responsiveness of parliaments with their disempowerment, has led to their alienation from democracy and has facilitated the rise of authoritarian populist parties. It strengthens the authoritarian narrative, in which a strong leader figure knows best how to translate into action the will of the people (if necessary, on a plebiscitary basis).

4.2.1 Majoritarian and non-majoritarian institutions in democracy

According to the World Values Survey (WVS) of 2006, more than 85 per cent of the world's population wanted to live in a democratic political system.[27] The figure is still similarly high today. A closer look reveals, however, that around that time the population had little faith in parliaments and parties, especially in most OECD countries, and preferred institutions that did not depend on majorities and elections.

In eight out of the sixteen countries surveyed (see Table 2),[28] the respondents showed more faith in the justice system, the European Union, and the United Nations than in parties, parliaments, and governments; in the table, these countries are marked with three stars (***). In three other countries, marked with two stars (**), parties and parliaments recorded the lowest figures among institutions, although there at least governments did somewhat better. In four more cases, marked with one star (*), trust in the listed NMIs was on average higher than trust in the MIs. Only Finland and Turkey departed somewhat from this general pattern of low trust in majoritarian institutions (MI), although both countries showed very low values for trust in political parties. Almost all the people in these countries want to live in a democracy,

82 The Democratic Regression

Table 2 Trust in various democratic institutions

Country	Courts	Government	Parties	Parliament	EU	UN
Australia***	53.8	40.1	14.3	35.4		45.5
Chile	30.0	48.2	19.1	26.2		45.4
Germany***	56.4	23.9	13.0	22.0	30.6	37.8
Finland	81.8	64.5	29.1	56.2	36.8	63.7
Italy***	51.6	26.4	16.5	33.1	67.2	59.0
Japan***	82.0	31.0	18.3	23.2		64.1
Canada***	65.6	38.4	23.1	36.5		61.4
Mexico**	37.7	44.7	23.9	25.5		53.0
Netherlands*	43.4	26.7	22.5	28.4	28.3	35.5
Norway*	86.0	54.1	28.6	62.3	44.3	85.2
Poland***	32.9	18.2	07.1	12.5	46.2	49.5
Sweden*	74.2	42.3	33.4	54.9	36.6	78.2
Switzerland*	76.8	69.3	27.6	57.4	43.5	52.8
Spain***	55.6	44.9	28.5	50.8	61.3	59.8
Turkey	75.0	62.7	33.0	60.0	30.2	30.4
USA**	58.2	38.6	15.4	20.3		33.4

Source: World Value Survey 2006; cf. Inglehart et al. 2014.
***: all NMIs > all MIs.
**: parties and parliaments have the worst values.
*: ø NMIs > ø MIs.

but most of them dislike majoritarian institutions. This is a democratic paradox.[29]

The democratic paradox has its roots in the relationship between majoritarian and non-majoritarian bodies. In theory, parties and parliaments play a central role in democratic political systems.[30] Parliaments enact laws through majority decisions taken by elected representatives. The latter are chosen in free elections based on the competition between parties. Parties and parliaments embody the idea of popular rule. Any decision can, at least in principle, be reversed as soon as a new majority is formed. As everyone has the opportunity to make their voice heard, decisions made by majoritarian institutions should reflect the views of the majority. On the whole, despite unequal responsiveness, majoritarian institutions give everyone the possibility of using their individual vote

The Crisis of Representation and the Alienated Democracy 83

to influence the composition of parliaments and thereby their decisions – at least indirectly.

Constitutional courts and central banks are the best-known non-majoritarian institutions. The main task of NMIs consists in controlling and *restricting* public power in such a way that it does not infringe individual or minority rights or endanger the democratic process itself.[31] In addition, NMIs are required to implement the norms set by the legislature.[32] International institutions are NMIs inasmuch as they protect democracy and human rights, helping to put agreed policy goals into practice. NMIs are often appointed by majoritarian institutions to make the 'right' decisions. In this sense, NMIs exercise epistemic and moral authority. Their decisions build on the assumption that these bodies know better what the correct decision is. At the same time, NMIs generally do not possess the resources for enforcing their decisions. No constitutional court can force the executive to follow a judge's ruling. NMIs are also not directly accountable to the electorate. They can thus be defined as governmental entities that (a) possess and exercise specialized public authority, which is separate from that of other institutions, (b) are neither directly elected by the people nor managed by elected officials, and instead (c) refer to the epistemic quality in justifying the decision.[33]

According to the theory of constitutionalism, parliaments are the legislators. Together with the executive, they form of the basis of government by the people. The role of NMIs, on the other hand, is to limit the rule of the people.[34] Arguably NMIs have increased so much in recent decades, in both quantity and quality, that they now fulfil a role that not only restricts authority but also establishes it. NMIs take fundamental decisions in many important areas. One need only look at the part played by the European Central Bank during the euro crisis. But when an institution that is not directly accountable to the people takes far-reaching decisions, it is easy to get the impression that decision-making is being withdrawn from

84   The Democratic Regression

large sections of the population, whose interests are not being heard.

This power shift in favour of NMIs is the result of a political sequence with four stages.

4.2.2   Increase in the power of non-majoritarian institutions

The starting point was the historic compromise at the end of the Second World War that was described in Chapter 2. Thanks to this arrangement, the opening up of world markets was cushioned by the development of the welfare state, which enabled democracies to stabilize. At the same time people's parties [*Volksparteien*] emerged, for which Otto Kirchheimer coined the term 'catch-all parties'. A catch-all party is a political party that aims to appeal to broad sections of the electorate and to people with different political views. These parties tend towards the centre. Only there can elections be won in a two-party or three-party system.[35] Through the dominance of parties of this kind, liberal democracies were able to consolidate themselves in Western Europe and North America. At the same time, the rise of catch-all parties had the effect of blurring the distinctions between left and right, slowly but surely. Research into party manifestos shows that 'programmatic differences on the classic socioeconomic issues (such as: the role of the state, market regulation, nationalization, social welfare, fiscal policies) have virtually disappeared during the last decades'.[36] Social democratic parties moved to the center and became more moderate. Subsequently, all catch-all parties found themselves confronted with problems of internal discipline because, time and again, their core supporters were critical of the official party line. This necessitated centralization, and the strengthening of party leadership, and a professionalization of political careers. At the same time, centre-right and centre-left parties formed very close ties with the interest groups that represented capital and labour.

This phenomenon was labelled 'corporatism'.[37] Corporatism reinforced the trend towards a negotiating democracy among party leaders and heads of associations.[38]

In the early 1960s, the outstanding political scientist Robert Dahl anticipated that the rise of centrist catch-all parties would cause problems. In his view, this phenomenon led to a

> politics of compromise, adjustment, negotiation, bargaining; a politics carried on among professional and quasi-professional leaders who constitute only a small part of the total citizen body; a politics that reflects a commitment to the virtues of pragmatism, moderation and incremental change; a politics that is un-ideological and even anti-ideological ... [Many citizens see this form of politics as] too remote and bureaucratized, too addicted to bargaining and compromise, too much an instrument of political elites and technicians.[39]

As a result of this development, the responsiveness of parliaments to the lower social classes sank (as shown in section 4.1), and trust in parties and parliaments started to dwindle along with it. The process began relatively soon after the rise of catch-all parties. Early surveys from three consolidated democracies – the United States, Sweden, and France – ascertained the degree of trust in parties with a similar prompt ('Do politicians care about their concerns?'). The proportion of positive responses began to decline in the United States from the late 1950s. A similar development took place in Sweden and France during the early 1960s.[40] From the mid-1970s on, the proportion of negative answers crossed the 50 per cent threshold in all three countries. The question of trust in parliament has been asked directly and systematically in WVS surveys since the 1980s. Data are available for sixteen OECD countries that were deemed to be democracies in 2001 (see Figure 9). A clear and permanent diminution of trust in majoritarian institutions is evident. Only very recently has the trend been reversed.

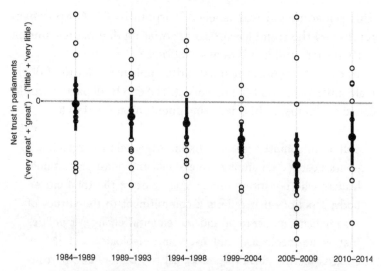

Figure 9 Trust in parliaments.
Source: Data from WVS, various waves (see Inglehart et al. 2014).
Note: To obtain the values presented here, the proportion of people with little or no trust in parliaments was subtracted from the proportion of people with (very) high trust in parliaments. Zero value indicates equal size; negative values indicate that mistrust predominated. Every empty circle stands for a country; the filled circles give the average values for the 16 countries.

Although there are a number of outliers (especially in the 1999–2004 wave), the values for all countries are significantly lower in the last two waves than in earlier ones. Poland is a particularly interesting case: the country underwent a democratic transformation only in the 1990s. Figures for trust in parliament sank from 55 per cent in the second wave and over 30 per cent in the third to 11 per cent in the fifth and sixth waves. It looks as though this new democracy took only twenty years to retrace a path that the established democracies had completed in four decades.

This finding supports the thesis that there has been a growing alienation between parties' members and voters on the one hand and parties' parliamentary representatives and leaders on

The Crisis of Representation and the Alienated Democracy 87

the other.[41] The diminishing faith in majoritarian institutions has led, in a second step, to an increase in the significance of NMIs. More and more, NMIs have not only scrutinized and implemented decisions but also acquired a central role in shaping policy and establishing norms.

Three mechanisms above all have led to the strengthening of NMIs when trust in MIs has diminished. First, the transfer of decision-making powers to institutions that enjoy a high degree of trust serves to legitimate them. The quest for legitimacy led to the strengthening of NMIs (see Table 2). Second, parties and coalitions sought to outsource compromise decisions that did not appeal broadly to party members and traditional voters. This second mechanism is often referred to as blame-shifting. We are accustomed to find this sort of thing in the transfer of competences to the European Union. Governments shuffle off the responsibility for unattractive policies and point the finger at 'Brussels', even if they agreed to a given policy in the EU Council.[42] The third and last mechanism is about building trust: NMIs send international investors a signal that the rule of law and economic rationality will protect them in the long run. Hence the move to NMIs was speeded up by the push for globalization and the neoliberal policies that went with it. Competition between investors heightened the value of institutionally guaranteed commitments.[43]

Did NMIs actually increase during the 1980s and 1990s, as these causal mechanisms would seem to suggest? Yes, they did, and very conspicuously. First, many of the world's legislatures, especially in the 1990s, decided to allocate more powers to constitutional courts. Ran Hirschl sums up this development at the very beginning of his study *Towards Juristocracy*: 'Around the globe, in more than 80 countries . . . constitutional reform has transferred an unprecedented amount of power from representative institutions to judiciaries.'[44] Second, according to Rappaport and colleagues, between 1990 and 2008 no fewer than eighty-four countries increased the autonomy of central banks, while not a single one weakened the constitutional position of a central bank.[45] Furthermore, Jordana and colleagues show that regulatory authorities that can take decisions independently of the majorities in their respective parliaments have been set up in larger numbers since the 1990s.[46] But the NMIs we are talking about are not merely internal to democracies; they also include international bodies that have withdrawn decision-making powers from national MIs such as parliaments and parties. Their authority has increased dramatically since the 1990s, too.[47]

We get a more detailed overview when the development of NMIs at the national and international levels is summarized in an index. Jordana et al. (2018) make available comparative data regarding the number of sectors in which at least one regulatory body plays a significant role. They chose sixteen sectors in order to cover a broad range of political areas in which NMIs are relevant. These include, for example, competition, the environment, financial services, food safety, gas, health, and insurance – but not the judicial system. The dataset comprises 799 regulatory authorities that were active on 31 December 2010. The International Authority Database (IAD) has measured international authority on the basis of an analysis of thirty-four international organizations and more than 1,000 international treaties. In this instance authority is determined on the basis of the institutions' autonomy, their binding power, and the range of their functions.[48]

The datasets for regulatory bodies and international authority can be combined in an NMI index. To do this, for the sixteen countries under our review, we have standardized the national-level scores between zero and one, for both national and international NMIs. The resulting index, shown in Figure 10, offers an exceptionally clear picture. The significance of NMIs doubled between the late 1970s and the early 2000s. If one starts with the assumption that the total amount of political authority over this period remained somehow constant, the

The Crisis of Representation and the Alienated Democracy 89

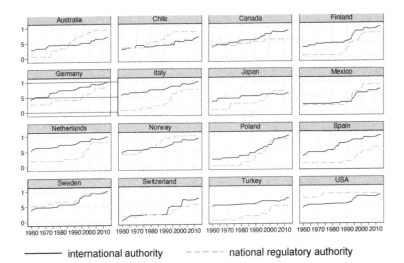

Figure 10 Index of the autonomy and powers of NMIs in 16 countries between 1960 and 2015.
Source: Data from the International Authority Database (see Zürn et al. 2021).

power of majoritarian institutions was drastically reduced in less than twenty-five years.

If we consider national and international NMIs separately, a number of further insights ensue. First, the rise of NMIs is apparent in all sixteen countries; there is not a single exception. Second, the relative significance of NMIs outside the nation-state depends on membership of the European Union and on the eurozone. In the Americas, Australia, and Japan, national regulatory bodies are more relevant than international organizations. The exception in this group is Canada – a country generally reputed for being an especially staunch supporter of multilateralism. The rise of NMIs was unusually rapid during the period 1980–2000, and especially in the 1990s.

From a general point of view, the transfer of decision-making powers to NMIs can be seen as part of the Madisonian turn in

90   The Democratic Regression

modern democracies – a term coined by Torbjörn Bergman and Kaare Strøm in a ground-breaking 2011 study of the political systems of Scandinavia. According to them, decisions taken in politics are more and more subject to the logic of checks and balances. Jan-Werner Müller is less moderate in his tone: taking his cue from John Maynard Keynes, he speaks of an 'euthanasia of politics'.[49]

4.2.3 The euthanasia of politics and cosmopolitan selectivity

Non-majoritarian institutions bring expertise and technical knowledge into politics. They are less subject to the political passions of the moment. They like to be considered comparatively neutral to the left–right axis in politics. But they are certainly not politically neutral when it comes to the new cleavage. The institutional purpose of NMIs already points in the cosmopolitan direction. Constitutional courts emphasize and defend individual rights, often against majority political decisions. Central banks control inflation, tend towards a supply-side economics, and try to stabilize international capital markets. Regional and international institutions insist on national policy compliance with international guidelines. Mostly they advocate that further powers and tasks be transferred to them. At the same time, important decision makers in NMIs are not accountable to the electorate; they are accountable only to other parts of the political system. Constitutional courts endeavour, even consciously, to minimize the dependence of their judges on political decision makers and on the public. For this reason, judges are often appointed for life or for a fixed period, without any possibility of reappointment.

Although all NMIs legitimize their decisions on the grounds that they are correct and necessary, these decisions are not politically neutral. They contribute to cosmopolitan policies'

The Crisis of Representation and the Alienated Democracy 91

being legally sanctioned and institutionally locked in. The consequence of NMIs' takeover of authority is a depoliticization of questions that until then had been political. They were taken out of the realm of collective decisions and transferred to the sphere of what is supposed to be, objectively, the right thing.[50] But the right thing has a recognizable accent – only this time a cosmopolitan one.

This cosmopolitan hue is evident in the use of data that show the positions of various actors on subjects that bring cosmopolitans and communitarians into confrontation with each other.[51] With the help of what is called 'claims analysis', we can place the focus on actors and on the positions they take vis-à-vis various topics.[52] To investigate attitudes to globalization, we used a dataset of 11,810 claims made in public forums in Germany, Poland, Mexico, Turkey, and the United States, in the European Parliament, and in the UN General Assembly.[53] We used two variables in our analysis: the actor's position on the question of opening the borders for goods, people, and capital; and the actor's position on the transfer of powers to international organizations. Aggregating the results on these two issues can produce four values: 'integrate', 'keep integrated', 'demarcate', and 'keep demarcated'. Second, actors were distinguished according to their functions within various political systems – the executive (e.g. the Secretary General of the United Nations, members of national governments, of the EU Council of Ministers), the legislative (e.g. members of the European Parliament, of national parliaments, of city councils), the judiciary (e.g. members of the European Court of Human Rights, of the German Federal Constitutional Court) – or as experts and actors who operate at the international level.

The results are clear and the differences are statistically significant (see Figure 11). Members of the legislature – legislatures being archetypal MIs – score 2.1, which is close to the middle position (2.5). In contrast, the demands of the

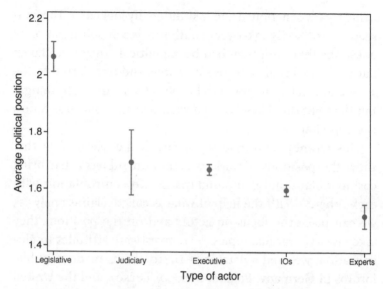

Figure 11 The cosmopolitan tendency of members of NMIs.
Source: Data from the International Authority Database
(see Zürn et al. 2021).
Note: Political positions range from 1 (cosmopolitan pole) to
4 (communitarian pole); 95% confidence interval.

representatives of all NMIs are much closer to the cosmopolitan pole (1 being the most cosmopolitan). Experts are the most cosmopolitan, with an average score of 1.5, and are followed by representatives of international organizations, the executive, and the judiciary, all of whom score between 1.6 and 1.7.

The more visible this cosmopolitan bias, the greater the gap between the positions of the elite and those of the population. Thus, in the countries studied, there are significant differences of opinion between elites and citizens on issues such as supranational integration, climate change, free trade, and immigration.[54] This gap underlies the growing distrust between large sections of the population and the political class and deepens the divide between authoritarian populists and liberal globalists.

The Crisis of Representation and the Alienated Democracy 93

In the final analysis, the advantages of the transfer of authority to NMIs come with new, long-term problems. As more authority is delegated to NMIs and the blame-shifting goes on for a longer period, the NMIs become more politicized.[55] Ultimately, the attempt to remove certain kinds of decisions from the realm of the political triggers the politicization of the institutions responsible for these decisions. In the end the NMIs also lose trust and support. The people's disillusionment with parties and politicians is then compounded by disillusionment with the NMIs. The latter are increasingly seen as instruments of the cosmopolitan elite and as enemies of 'ordinary people'. From there, it is only a small step to supporting an authoritarian populist party that rejects international cooperation.

Democratic alienation and the rise of authoritarian populism is therefore the result of a historical sequence set off by the rise of centrist catch-all parties. This process has instituted a dynamic that started with the decline of trust in MIs and led to the growth of authoritarian populism through the rise of NMIs with cosmopolitan tendencies. This narrative is summarized in Figure 12.

4.3   Alienation from Political Institutions

We have described two trends that have shifted political decisions in favour of liberal globalists. First, parliaments have become unequally responsive to the concerns of different social groups: people with higher incomes, with higher educational attainments, and in more highly qualified professions have been systematically receiving more attention than groups at the other end of the spectrum. This form of inequality fosters economically liberal positions (e.g. support for free markets). Second, parliamentary powers have been transferred to NMIs. Yet the decisions of NMIs are not politically neutral

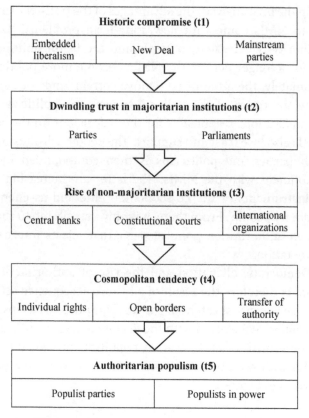

Figure 12 The historic compromise and the rise of authoritarian populism.
Source: Created by the authors.

either; rather they reveal an affinity with cosmopolitanism (internationalization and cultural pluralism) within the two-dimensional political space.

These two developments form the base of our political explanation for the rise of authoritarian populist parties, a phenomenon that brings together two general trends in modern democracies: the professionalization and cartelization of party politics;[56] and the fact that NMIs are a main target of contemporary populism.[57] The cartelization of party politics has

The Crisis of Representation and the Alienated Democracy 95

aggravated the selective responsivity of the legislature. The rise of NMIs has brought in a further degree of bias: it systematically favours the positions of liberal globalists. Trust in NMIs is diminishing, and this shifts the focus onto the political system as a whole.

The unequal responsiveness of parliaments and the shift of decision-making onto non-majoritarian bodies that are only indirectly legitimized represent, in our terminology, an alienation of political decision-making processes from the democratic ideal. If we turn the coin, this alienation of processes pairs up, on the obverse, with an alienation of groups whose members no longer feel that they are politically represented in a democracy. The rise of authoritarian populist parties can be viewed as a consequence of this double alienation.

To define authoritarian populist parties, we shall use the Chapel Hill Expert Survey (CHES), a database that contains information on 277 parties in thirty-two European countries. The classification of parties via CHES rests on a survey taken in the countries under investigation. With the aid of a questionnaire, 421 experts were invited to classify all the parties along various criteria – how far to the left or right they stand and whether they would judge European integration positively or negatively. We follow Pippa Norris and Ronald Inglehart[58] by using seven questions to position parties on a liberal-versus-authoritarian axis and two questions to gauge how populist they are.[59] The scores for both aspects are summed and rescaled to values between 0 and 100, higher values indicating more populist or authoritarian parties.

This procedure can be illustrated by taking a look at the German political system. In Figure 13, we order German parties along the two axes using the CHES database. It immediately catches the eye that the AfD's position was assessed by experts as both the most authoritarian and the most populist one. At the same time, when we consider relative positions on the liberal–authoritarian axis, there are clear differences between

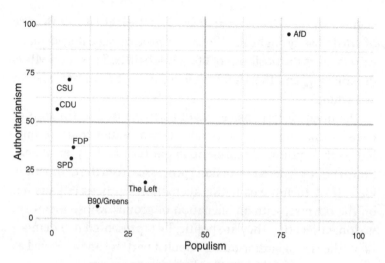

Figure 13 The German party system.
Source: Data from Chapel Hill Survey 2019 (see Bakker et al. 2019).

the Greens and the Left Party on the one hand, the CDU and the CSU on the other. The Greens espouse especially liberal positions, while the CSU inclines to more authoritarian values. Conversely, the experts attribute a slightly higher degree of populism to the Greens than to the CSU, which could be because the Greens are credited with an attitude that is more critical of the elite, no matter how established they may have become. At any rate, if we set the threshold in the middle of the scale in each case, it becomes clear that the AfD is the only party that features in the upper right quadrant. This procedure identifies authoritarian populist parties and immediately distinguishes them from other parties.

On the basis of this operational definition of authoritarian populist parties, we now consider the sixteen countries for which the WVS trust data are available. The successes chalked up by authoritarian populist parties can be seen clearly in Figure 14 (see also Figure 6). They began in the 1990s, accelerated during the 2000s, and turned out to be especially significant from 2009. These parties emphasize the logic of

The Crisis of Representation and the Alienated Democracy 97

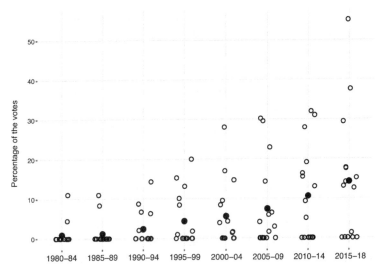

Figure 14 The rise of authoritarian populist parties in sixteen countries since the 1980s.
Source: Data from WVS, various waves (see Inglehart et al. 2014).

decision-making by majority and have turned their fire on NMIs. So it should come as no surprise that, with the rise of these parties, relative trust in parliaments has been growing again (see Figure 9 above).

Finally, we ask whether the rise of authoritarian populist parties can also be traced to the motivations of citizens and whether the alienation from democratic institutions of segments of the population whose voice remains unheard makes the election of an authoritarian populist party indeed more likely.

We want to base our understanding on empirical evidence. To do this, we combine two sets of data. We shall be using the European Social Survey (ESS) for one of them. The ESS is a scientific survey carried out in more than thirty European countries every two years. The latest edition that we were able to consult appeared in 2018 and offers a number of questions designed to ascertain how open to people's concerns a political

98 The Democratic Regression

system is. Two items form part of our investigation: (1) *How much would you say that the political system in [country] allows people like you to have an influence on politics?* and (2) *How much would you say the political system in [country] allows people like you to have a say in what the government does?* In addition, the ESS contains demographic information that we use to classify respondents in accordance with a system devised by Daniel Oesch (2006). We distinguish sixteen professional groups that exhibit four different levels of qualification, from semi-skilled through skilled to semi-academic and academic. Using these different sources of information, it is possible to deduce not only whether there is a connection between the perceived responsiveness of political decision-making systems and voting behaviour but also which groups feel less taken into consideration and are more inclined towards authoritarian populist parties. For this purpose we also use data from the Chapel Hill Expert Survey, which we illustrated previously in dealing with the case of Germany. Data covering twenty-two countries can be found in both the ESS and the CHES, which we now combine.[60] Of the parties named in the ESS, we list as authoritarian populist those with scores of over fifty on both axes.

Figure 15 shows the correlation between the perceived responsiveness of political systems and the voting behaviour of sixteen social classes. Two observations are particularly important. First, there is a close connection between the perceived responsiveness of political decision-making systems and voting behaviour: the more strongly people feel that they have no say in or no influence on political decision-making, the more likely they are to vote for authoritarian populist parties. Correspondingly, the feeling that they are being heard makes them less likely to vote that way. Second, perceptions vary considerably among social classes. Highly qualified respondents are more likely than respondents with fewer qualifications to think that people like themselves enjoy opportunities to

The Crisis of Representation and the Alienated Democracy 99

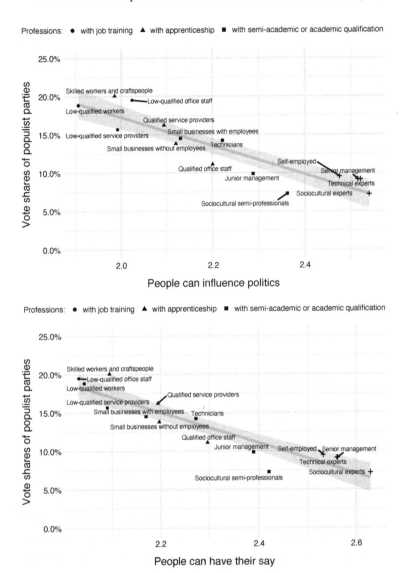

Figure 15 The openness of the political system and professional groupings' voting for authoritarian populist parties.

Source: Data from European Social Survey 2018 and Chapel Hill Survey 2019 (see Bakker et al. 2019).

Note: This figure shows weighted average values for twenty-two countries.

100　　The Democratic Regression

have their say and to influence politics – an entirely accurate impression, as both our studies of responsiveness and the offloading of decision-making competence onto international institutions indicate. Only a little over 5 per cent of sociocultural experts (university teachers, publicists, etc.) admit to having voted for an authoritarian populist party, as against the 20 per cent of skilled workers and craftsmen who do. This pattern fits in with the sociocultural dimension of the cleavage produced by globalization. People whose economic situation has been severely endangered through job relocation or as a result of growing competition from low-wage areas and whose outlook on life is rather local tend to be found at the upper left margin of the figures.

4.4　The Representation Crisis Gives Birth to Populism

Our explanation for the rise of authoritarian populist parties builds on the current weaknesses that affect liberal democracy. These include a good measure of political inequality[61] and the partial disempowerment of parliaments by NMIs,[62] a phenomenon that has accentuated the imbalance between the political influence of different groups of citizens and thus turned it into a new cleavage. The dominance of liberal globalists is one of the drivers behind the rise of authoritarian populist parties. Authoritarian populists criticize not so much individual political measures and laws as the way democracy is being turned on its head; it is for this reason alone that they can claim to stand up for more democracy. This criticism resonates with sections of the population because it is grounded in reality; citizens can see that democracy has become disconnected from its own guiding principles. But acknowledging this has no tendency to mean expecting authoritarian populist parties to be able to change the situation they are criticizing. On the contrary, they themselves are one of the drivers of democratic backsliding. This paradoxical effect is something we know from history. So, for example, although fascism can be understood, among other things, as a defence reaction against the accelerated modernization that characterized the first half of the twentieth century, national socialism furthered the modernization of German society.[63]

Our political explanation integrates the economic and the sociocultural ones insofar as the political measures and laws that it addresses are inscribed in the political opposition in various ways, depending on the political configuration and circumstances. At first glance, our political explanation bears some resemblance to another explanation, which regards the current crisis of democracy as a reaction to the rise of technocracy.[64] But our explanation differs from that one in two respects. First, authoritarian populists are primarily targeting not technocrats but the political class and NMIs. The latter have a liberal globalist hue and emphasize the rights of individuals and minorities with different lifestyles and preferences. Technocrats, on the other hand, seek solutions. Differences and disputes often have no place there. It can also be shown, empirically, that citizens are more inclined to support a technocratic regime if they have weaker democratic attitudes and are mistrustful of the political class. By contrast, respect for NMIs goes hand in hand with democratic attitudes and trust. Technocracy is, by this account, the less harmful sibling of authoritarian populism.[65] In consequence, technocrats and authoritarian populists are frequently seen as two linked challenges to representative democracies, whereas deliberative representation and NMIs count as necessary parts of liberal democracy that are quite frequently attacked by authoritarian populists – and sometimes by technocrats as well. Second, the cartelization of parties and the rise of NMIs constitute two separate processes and cannot be lumped together under the label of technocracy.

102 The Democratic Regression

A further explanation, which at first glance is not unlike the political one, treats authoritarian populism as a consequence of neoliberalism. By this account, liberal markets were protected and fenced off from politics[66] in order to allow the exploitative interests of businesses and shareholders to develop unimpeded. Once again, our political explanation does indeed show a number of overlaps with this view, but there are also significant differences. First, we do not share the assumption that there was a 'golden age' of democracy when politics was equally receptive to the concerns of all classes in society.[67] Besides, in terms of fuelling discontent, the imbalance between traditional economic classes seems to play much less of a role than cultural and educational differences and the difference between communitarianism and cosmopolitanism. But, above all, there have been far fewer attacks on specific policy measures and laws than on their institutional establishment through NMIs and selective representation. Our political explanation focuses not on individual decisions but on the politics that has enabled unpopular decisions and locked them in.

5

Crises of Democracy

The first two decades of the new millennium have seen an unexpected intensification of crises and crisis-like phenomena. It all started with the attack on the Twin Towers in New York, whereupon American politics immediately went into crisis mode. In 2008, the bankruptcy of the investment bank Lehman Brothers led to a global financial crisis. The stock market crash in the first few days after bankruptcy was as severe as the one that followed Black Thursday in 1929. Hard on its heels came the eurozone crisis [i.e. the European sovereign debt crisis], which revealed structural problems with the common currency. In 2014 Russia annexed the Crimean Peninsula. For the first time since 1945, territorial borders within Europe were unilaterally redrawn – the very epitome of an international crisis. The number of people fleeing to Europe from the Near and Middle East and North Africa increased dramatically in 2015 and, in the perception of broad sections of the population, led to a social crisis that precipitated a strengthening of xenophobic and racist political groupings. The frequency of further attacks by Islamist terrorist networks in 2015 and 2016 could well be interpreted as a security crisis; and 2020 will go down in the history books as the year of the Covid crisis. Its

104 The Democratic Regression

medium- and long-term effects are still unforeseeable. Finally, in February 2022 Russia invaded the Ukraine and began an atrocious war.

As a result of these crises, the liberal democracies are under pressure to act. The terror attacks we mentioned were indeed external attacks on democracy or on the liberal world order created in 1990. In reaction to them, almost all democracies set in motion processes that are often referred to as 'securitization'.[1] Securitization involves redefining a problem as a security problem, and thus removing it from the regular political process. Then, in order to solve it, it seems legitimate to resort to extraordinary means such as declaring a state of emergency, imposing martial law, or mobilizing the armed forces. The executive takes charge of the crisis and makes use of the situation to achieve aims that otherwise would not have been enforceable. After 9/11, this process was pushed to the extreme under the US administration of President George W. Bush. Vice President Dick Cheney in particular showed himself to be a master of securitization. Indeed securitization undermines the democratic process and strengthens the executive. But, even so, it often turns out to be only a temporary process.[2]

Of special relevance to us are the crises that were triggered within democratic societies, such as the financial crisis and the euro crisis, or that had to be dealt with within democracies, such as the ones known as the refugee crisis and the Covid crisis. These very crises shine a light on the changes that had taken place in political processes across democracies, and thus have burning glass and magnifying glass effects.[3]

5.1   Crisis as a Permanent State

The term 'crisis' comes from ancient Greek (κρίσις 'separation, decision, judgement' < κρίνειν 'to separate, distinguish'). In Greek medicine it often referred to situations in which the disease 'decided' between life and death. A crisis was considered to be an unsustainable in-between state; it led to either recovery or death (or at least permanent physical damage).[4] *A crisis threatens the organism as a whole with permanent damage or collapse*, even if the causes are specific to a particular organ. In the context of our study, we speak of a crisis when problems that belong to subsystems of society such as the economy spread and come to challenge society as a whole, so that they cannot be left unsolved for long. A small, passing blip in an economy's growth is no more of a crisis than a slightly elevated blood pressure. The deterioration of trust in politics or an insufficiently responsive parliament are deficits in political subsystems; they become crises only when they attack constitutive elements of democratic society and demand the imminent provision of suitable antidotes.

In the final analysis, political crises are *social constructs*. Admittedly, it seems almost impossible to proclaim something successfully as a crisis unless there is a kernel of reality to it; but public recognition of a state as critical is necessary before we can really speak of a crisis. We talk of crisis when it is intersubjectively acknowledged that the continued existence of the organism, society, or political regime is at stake and that immediate action is necessary as a result. So it is possible to have existential problems that are not perceived as crises, even though occasional alerts have been put out. Conversely, problem situations that in reality are only moderately serious can be magnified out of proportion and advertised as crises.

A situation described as a crisis requires *swift action*. In a modern society, the appropriate decisions are expected to come *from politics*. Accordingly, social crises require political solutions even if politics was not responsible for causing the crisis – or at least not directly. To that extent, a crisis leads to the politicization of anything that causes and reinforces it. Social contacts and hygiene regulations became a political issue only during the Covid-19 pandemic. At the same time,

106   The Democratic Regression

however, a crisis has the potential to narrow and depoliticize the space normally reserved for political decision-making and for public debate on the right decision.[5] The need for *immediate* reaction tends to lead to the suspension of processes of political mediation. A crisis tolerates no democratic deliberation; parliaments and opposition parties play a subordinate role. In a crisis, politics comes to the fore, yet is trimmed down to doing what is necessary. For this reason, crises can seem highly political and strangely depoliticized at the same time.

The matter of blame also comes to the fore. Does the crisis have an exogenous cause, and is there no one or nothing to blame for it? Did it burst in on a functioning community like a meteorite or a virus from some distant country, or was it the result of endogenous aberrations? These questions, too, are decided via social interpretations. In particular, if blame is laid at the door of endogenous developments and the political system's first reaction is seen as inadequate, the crisis may turn out to initiate radical change.

This connects with a further aspect of crises. As the German poet Friedrich Hölderlin once said, where there is danger, the rescue grows as well: crises conjure saving remedies. Appropriately enough, the Marxist concept of crisis has a positive connotation. From this point of view, crises accelerate progress; they serve as a means of reaching a new stage in development. Up until the 1970s this view of social crisis was predominant.[6] Right now, by contrast, negative connotations predominate. The theory of historical institutionalism does indeed point to the dual nature of crises, because they embody critical junctures that can break up path dependencies and institutional entrenchment. Crises, then, also present an opportunity structure for extensive changes. Although political actors perceive crises as situations of stress with severely limited room for manoeuvre, the force of structural constraints often weakens. In crises there is often a yawning gap between the 'objective' loosening of structural constraints and the 'subjective' perception of urgency by decision makers. Quite often, opportunity structures of this kind are in fact the starting point of structural changes.[7]

Summing up, what we mean by 'crisis' is the broad public perception of challenges that threaten society as a whole, necessitate swift political countermeasures, and, when endogenous, indicate a need for social changes.[8]

In addition to these defining characteristics, the crises of the past twenty years share a series of further commonalities. First, they do not stop at the borders of nation-states; this is why Arjen Boin (2009) has used the term 'transboundary crisis'.[9] Crises in the globalized world are transboundary in a double sense: their effect extends far beyond the subsystem in which they originated – and to this extent are systemic in nature. But their effect extends beyond their territory of origin, too – and to this extent they have a point of reference in the global society. Today crises are responsible for combining the geographical with the functional spread of problems. The insolvency of a number of American buyers of real estate eventually brought the Greek state to the brink of collapse; the despotic claim to power of the Assad family in Syria led to social splits in Sweden; the frustration of radicalized people in Islamic societies caused other people almost everywhere to become victims of senseless outbreaks of violence; and careless practices in animal markets or laboratories in Wuhan put almost the entire world on a staggered lockdown.

Second, most crises of the twenty-first century so far were not caused by democratic political systems and did not bring about an acute crisis of democracy. According to Wolfgang Merkel, an acute crisis requires at least one of two conditions to be true. Such a crisis is reached either 'if deficits increase in frequency and crowd out existentially necessary democratic procedures while hollowing out their basic normative content – freedom, equality, control of sovereignty', or 'if citizens recognize that this has happened and withdraw their belief in the

108   The Democratic Regression

legitimacy not only of the government but of the democratic system itself'.[10] In this sense, the periods 1965–7 in Greece and 1930–3 in Germany, for example, represent, each, an acute crisis of democracy. If we apply this model, however, the cases we are looking at in this chapter represent something different.

These crises were not directly caused by democracy either; on the contrary, the consolidated democracies proved to be comparatively good at managing them. The international coordination of spending and rescue policies ensured that the economic crash that followed the financial crisis was short-lived and had no lasting effects. Even the eurozone proved redeemable, and in many countries economic recovery was soon under way. Thus the crisis took an entirely different course from the one after 1929. The integration of refugees into Western European societies certainly did not merit ten out of ten, but it was still a creditable performance. It also managed to reduce the number of asylum applications. The moral content of the measures involved is up for debate, no doubt, but nobody resorted to very brutal methods of obtaining border security by force, although the number of people who drowned in the Mediterranean was alarmingly high. Even the reaction to the terrorist attacks in 2016 and 2017 can hardly be interpreted as a failure. Democratic societies reacted to this increase in insecurity[11] without surrendering their identity; they hardly restricted civil liberties at all, and in spite of that the number of attacks declined, especially in Germany, where they were well below the level of right-wing extremist attacks during the mid-1990s – at least on purely numerical grounds.[12] There was nothing to suggest that consolidated democracies would not cope too well with the Covid crisis on the whole. In short, the tight sequence we witnessed – a sequence of major crises of more or less global proportions – cannot be read as the direct manifestation of a crisis of democracy. But even if these events were not endogenous crises of democracy, their frequency put democracy under stress.

Crises of Democracy

Nowadays people are quick to call 'crisis' any state of affairs like this. Given the general expansion of this concept and its inflationary use,[13] developments with genuine potential to engender crises get labelled 'crises' too. A few influential analyses of the crisis of late capitalism played their part in this development.[14] Wolfgang Merkel[15] speaks of latent crises that come about in the 'fading levels of democracy',[16] post-democratic conditions,[17] or purely institutional facades.[18] The diagnoses often talk about a crisis of democracy, but in fact they point to a slow deterioration, structurally caused, and to a lack of effort or capacity to adapt. The fear that lurks behind all this puts you in mind of the controversial story of the boiling frog: the frog stays in the cooking pot while the temperature of the water steadily rises, until it's much too hot and the frog dies.

How do the acute crises mentioned so far contribute to a latent crisis, that is, to a creeping deterioration of democracy? In answering this question, the metaphor of the magnifying glass comes into play. A magnifying glass makes objects appear larger, and thus it enables one to see things that one would otherwise not see. Understood like this, acute crises have rendered visible various changes in the political processes of democracies. Key decisions were no longer taken by elected parliaments but by other political institutions. The crises put the spotlight not only on the executive but also on non-majoritarian institutions and experts: Mario Draghi and Anthony Fauci are two names that symbolize this development.

But, as a physical object, a magnifying glass is also a burning glass: it uses a convex lens to make the sun's rays converge as they strike it, and thus it enhances the energy density of the light to the point where it can set light to combustible materials. Some of these crises have in fact led to debates about the value of liberal democracy. In light of such crises, the question is often whether autocratic systems are capable of responding better. What is more, the rise of authoritarian

110 The Democratic Regression

populist parties has accelerated as a result of the crises. In this view, the fact that they have come thick and fast has exacerbated people's alienation from democracy and has exposed the declining representativeness of consolidated democracies while strengthening the anti-democratic forces. We focus here on three crises in order to analyse these effects.

5.2 The Lehman Brothers and the Lack of Alternatives

On 15 September 2008 bankers left a high-rise in New York laden with cardboard boxes. Distraught stock market traders stared at their screens. That was the day when a bank went bust in the financial capital of the world. Its name is second to none in evoking the start of a crisis that caused people to lose their jobs and savers to lose their savings all around the world. The bank's name was Lehman Brothers. The trigger of the crisis was the low-interest policy of the American Federal Reserve under Alan Greenspan. The low interest rates sparked a building boom. From 2002 to 2007, more and more people bought houses and apartments on credit, even when they could not really afford them. The banks did not worry. In order to acquire more customers, they often shut both eyes and reduced their security requirements. Thanks to the bundling and reallocation of various types of credit, the risk of failure seemed very slight, and this made it possible to grant new credit in vast quantities.[19] All went well until the real estate bubble burst and at the same time many clients became unable to continue servicing their mortgages. The houses (and consequently the securities) suffered a massive loss in value. Suddenly there were huge holes in banks' balance sheets.

The end of Lehman Brothers was not the start of the crisis, however. Back in February 2007, Alan Greenspan had warned of a recession and the dangers to the banks. Anxiety spread

Crises of Democracy

111

slowly, especially since the appropriate countermeasures seemed to be having little effect. In August 2007, the banks stopped reciprocally guaranteeing one another's credit operations, because they were afraid of bad subprime mortgages. Nevertheless, the American Federal Reserve continued to believe that low interest rates would be enough to restore liquidity and confidence. On 21 November the secretary of the Treasury, Henry Paulson, convinced three banks, Citigroup, JPMorgan Chase, and the Bank of America to set up a super-fund of $75 billion. The fund would provide liquidity to banks and hedge funds to buy up bad assets. Although the Federal Reserve lowered the interest rates further and the US government set up various reflationary programmes, the crash could not be prevented. The bankruptcy of Lehman Brothers finally triggered the financial crisis and the risk of a banking collapse that threatened to bring down entire economies.

The banking and financial crisis points to a double absence of borders. A crisis with origins in the banking system developed until it affected the whole society through an abrupt fall in economic output; its effect was as drastic as the one that followed Black Friday in 1929. Moreover, all the large banks were so tightly interconnected that the crisis turned out to be fully global.

In spite of a number of attempts by G20 states to coordinate their reactions to the crisis, national emergency measures were predominant before 2010. The German federal government in particular resisted becoming involved in extensive coordinated spending programmes. As national measures such as the scrappage premium and short-time work allowance cushioned the increase in unemployment and economic recovery followed swiftly after, the German federal government showed only limited interest in international cooperation. Still, the banking crisis was just the first phase of a long-lasting financial crisis, which struck with full force especially Southern European countries.

The Democratic Regression

Because of their interconnectedness, the banks were unable to escape the negative consequences of the US housing bubble burst. Of the twenty-nine banks in the United States that were deemed relevant to the system or 'too big to fail', seventeen had their headquarters in Europe.[20] Many of these banks consequently found themselves in a perilous situation: their customers threatened to panic. European governments had to spend billions to rescue national banks and stabilize the financial system. These financial rescue measures, together with the deep financial slump and the unemployment that exploded in many countries, generated a dramatic increase in public debt. The banking crisis turned into an economic crisis, and then into a sovereign debt crisis.

The negative consequences of all this were especially drastic in the southern states of the European Union and in Ireland, that is, in the GIIPS group (Greece, Ireland, Italy, Portugal, and Spain). Yet these countries started from different positions. In 2007, national debt in Ireland and Spain was well under 60 per cent of GDP – a lower ratio than Germany's or France's at that point. In Portugal it was 71 per cent. Only Greece and Italy, with 103 and 107 per cent respectively, were highly indebted even before the crisis. But between 2008 and 2013 debt increased in all the GIIPS countries, reaching 95 per cent in Spain and as much as 177 per cent in Greece. In Ireland, which never fitted very well into this group on account of its completely different economic structure, the debt burden fell again below the 60 per cent mark. In all other countries the rescue packages increased debt and unemployment considerably in the beginning, and no sooner had the first signs of recovery become visible than the Covid crisis kicked in, as we shall see later.

Although, at least in Spain and Portugal, increases in public debt were a result and not a cause of the financial crisis, there was nevertheless a demand that the countries in crisis carry out extensive savings programmes and make harsh cuts in their social systems. As for the euro, monetary policy was standardized without the creation of any additional balancing mechanisms or measures to mitigate economic imbalances. In the absence of compensatory mechanisms, however, differences in productivity and in economic structure quickly turned into crises, as comparative capitalism research had pointed out early on.[21] Since currency devaluations were not an option and labour mobility was insufficient to reduce these differences, the only choice available during crisis that could restore competitiveness was between institutionalizing transfer mechanisms and internal devaluation. A narrative was adopted according to which profligate spending policies had caused the economic problems and for this reason those policies had now to be countered by strict austerity.[22] Spending had to be reduced, which put wages and social benefits under pressure. As a result, the possibility for newly elected governments to adopt alternative economic strategies vanished. If anything, the economic and financial crisis in the European Union did not make parliaments into institutions of the hour. The most important decisions were taken intergovernmentally, and non-majoritarian institutions such as the EU Commission and the European Central Bank had their status enhanced. It is thus no coincidence that the populist revolt was directed at the excessive power of unelected institutions and has for the most part a Eurosceptic orientation.

Greece can serve as an example. In 2010, as a result of the various mechanisms described here, the country was on the brink of insolvency. The worst could be avoided only thanks to financial help from the European Union. But the aid measures had strict conditions attached to them, such that successive Greek governments were presented with wide-ranging and very detailed guidelines that were to affect not only their budgetary policy but their economic and social policies as well. The implementation of these policies was supervised by the Troika (as it is commonly known): the European Commission,

114   The Democratic Regression

the International Monetary Fund, and the European Central Bank – all non-majoritarian institutions. The first bailout established not only a fiscal consolidation plan but also a cut in the minimum wage and pensions, a reduction in the size of the public sector, an increase in VAT (value-added tax), and the deregulation of the labour and product markets. These reforms were intended to increase the competitiveness of the Greek economy in the medium term. In the short term they made a bad economic situation worse.

Already at the beginning of the financial crisis, the ruling party Nea Dimokratia (New Democracy) was voted out of office and replaced by a social democratic government. George Andreas Papandreou, who had been elected prime minister in 2009, negotiated the rescue package with the European Union and had to impose the unpopular austerity policy at a time when unemployment was rising higher and higher. In 2011 Papandreou resigned, to make way for a technocratic government of national unity. Between 2011 and 2012, only interim governments were in office, as it was difficult for any party to win a majority in parliament. A three-party coalition led by Nea Dimokratia took over the government business from 2012 to 2015, but after the dissolution of parliament in 2015 this alliance, too, had squandered all its credibility in the eyes of the electorate. In reaction to the continuing economic crisis and loss of confidence in the established parties, at the next parliamentary election the responsibility for governing the country was handed over to the left-wing opposition party Syriza, which had been an unimportant splinter group before 2012.

While previous governments had bowed to the Troika's decrees, Alexis Tsipras, the new prime minister, announced that a referendum would be held on the third bailout and the consolidation measures it demanded. On 5 July 2015, more than 60 per cent of the electorate voted against the suggestions of the Troika – which now, at the request of the Greek government, was referred to as 'the Institutions'. However, since the European Union refused to give in to Greece's demands, the Syriza government made a spectacular U-turn and largely went along with the Institutions' plans, in return for a partial debt write-off. The lesson was unmistakable: neither a complete revolution in the party system nor a plebiscite was enough to reverse the austerity policy, for which the NMIs were in essence responsible.[23]

In the other countries – Portugal, Ireland, Spain, and Cyprus – financial aid was similarly tied to reform requirements.[24] In addition, the European Central Bank (ECB) tied its bond purchases to conditions that affected the minutiae of economic and social policy. A notable feature of crisis management through NMIs was that they also laid down instructions for areas of policy that, according to the EU treaties, were expressly within the sphere of national responsibility; this applied to sections of social, customs, and wages policy. In these sensitive policy areas, a silent extension of powers took place.[25] All in all, the euro crisis has led to a power shift in favour of non-majoritarian EU institutions and executive organs.[26]

We are not concerned here with the economic strategy pursued by the Troika and its assessment, but with its consequences for democracy.[27] Central here is the fact that, in the countries that depended on financial aid, policy changes could not be implemented through either elections or referendums – which is why Sonia Alonso speaks of 'electing without a choice'.[28] In these countries, the ability of governments to adopt a responsive attitude towards their citizens was structurally blocked. To many, the true heads of government seemed to be not elected prime ministers but bureaucrats of the same stripe as Klaus Regling, the managing director of the European Stability Mechanism (ESM).

It was not only in the countries that received financial aid and had to comply with Troika policy recommendations that the balance of power shifted. From the outset, monetary union involved the transfer of financial and economic policies to institutions that were above majoritarian logic: they were supposed to follow the dictates of economic reason and not be subservient to the arbitrary results of political changes of power.[29] Presumably the rules of financial and economic policy before the banking crisis, the economic crisis, and the euro crisis had proven too lax and lost their normative binding force as a result of Germany's and France's unforeseen breaches of the Maastricht criteria. The crises now offered an opportunity to tighten the rules for all the euro countries. Stricter rules governing financial and economic policy were agreed to in various packages and, together, they all curtailed the competencies of national parliaments.

(1) In 2010 a stricter timeframe – the European Semester – was introduced for the reciprocal monitoring of national policies, and existing regulations were repackaged.

(2) In 2011, the Stability and Growth Pact, which covered all EU countries, was tightened through what was called 'the Sixpack' (five guidelines and one regulation). The Sixpack imposed tougher sanctions on offences against budgetary rules, put a narrower interpretation on budgetary regulations, and changed the voting procedure in a way that reversed the majority requirement for sanctions.

(3) The European Fiscal Compact or Fiscal Stability Treaty of 2012 further tightened the deficit regulations and demanded that member states legislate mandatory debt brakes at the national, preferably constitutional level.

(4) The members of the eurozone further extended the Commission's supervisory powers through the Two Pack, which was passed in 2013. National budget planning has now to be checked annually by the Commission. If it goes against the requirements of EU regulations, the Commission can ask for it to be revised.

Crises of Democracy

Thus the euro crisis led in the first instance to the institutional strengthening of the European Union,[30] alongside the fact that the power it commanded in certain areas became visible to its citizens. Many countries in the south opposed the cuts they were asked to make, while observers in the supposedly more frugal northern countries warned that the European Union was overstretching its mandate and carrying out a hidden transfer of power that would weaken both the European Parliament and national parliaments, reducing the scope for discretionary economic and fiscal policy.[31]

The liberal globalists in the EU Commission, the European Central Bank, and the European Court of Justice not only defend the achievements of European integration but drive the process further forward. They often do this without sufficiently taking into account the economic costs of Europeanization to its losers and without putting European institutions through a democratic debate. Brexit may have been fuelled by irrational arguments, but it has been clear for many years that the 'permissive consensus' of the past (i.e. the willingness to accept European compromises without questioning them) was crumbling.[32] Citizens have rejected continued European integration in several referendums – often to everyone's complete surprise.[33] In consequence, European integration and European institutions have become considerably politicized.[34] Anyone who fights for Europe should take a positive attitude to this politicization and should open European institutions to the relevant debates, so that voters may have their say. The neo-functionalist dream that, over time, more powers would automatically lead to more support for Europe was over with the financial crisis, if not before.

118   The Democratic Regression

5.3   The Refugees: Who Controls the Borders?

Starting in December 2010, a whole series of protests, uprisings, and revolutions against authoritarian regimes took place in the Arab world. This Arab Spring revived the democratic optimism of the 1990s, albeit briefly. In Syria there were demonstrations against Bashar al-Assad. Those in power reacted with rigidity. Peaceful demonstrations against the arrest of children in the southern Syrian city of Dar'a in March 2011 were violently suppressed. This incident is generally regarded as the beginning of the Syrian Civil War. It led to further protests and triggered an escalation of violence. In April 2011, the government was already sending in the military against the demonstrators. The Syrian secret services, too, demonstrated that they would not hold back in a struggle against their own population. Nevertheless, the Free Syrian Army (FSA), which was made up of army deserters and civilians, managed to drive government forces out of several areas of the country. In particular, the loss of much of the country's economic capital, Aleppo, stimulated predictions of an imminent fall of the Assad regime. But this is not what happened.

Thanks to Russian support, the Syrian military recovered and began to reconquer the territory it had lost. By autumn 2020, it looked as if the final collapse of the resistance was only a matter of time. In parallel to that, new tribal wars broke out.[35] Meanwhile the country was down and out. The war produced ruined cities and infrastructure, the destruction of valuable cultural treasures, and, above all, a humanitarian disaster. According to the Syrian Observatory for Human Rights, a body on the side of the opposition, more than 380,000 people were killed during this period; 115,000 of them were civilians and 22,000 were children. The country is almost bankrupt. According to the United Nations, 80 per cent of people live in poverty, and GDP has fallen to a quarter of its pre-war level.

The value of the currency is plummeting, prices are rising, but wages are barely rising, if at all.

Thirteen million Syrians have fled since 2013, almost half of them abroad. The number of refugees who arrived in Western Europe peaked in 2015. Asylum seekers came also from other trouble spots in the Near East, the Middle East, and North Africa. In April 2015, almost 1,000 people died in a single night when their overloaded boat capsized en route from Libya to Italy. The European Council reacted swiftly, holding a special summit on 23 April. In May the Commission presented a proposal to relocate some 40,000 refugees stranded in Greek and Italian refugee camps. The Council passed the proposal in June. At the same time the German chancellor, Angela Merkel, declared that Germany's constitution, the Grundgesetz, does not allow for a cap on the number of asylum seekers the country can accept. In July, the interior and justice ministers agreed on a further relocation of refugees and on a list of safe states of origin.[36] At the beginning of August, Merkel confirmed Germany's readiness to take in refugees.

On 19 August 2015 the interior minister informed Merkel that the number of refugees expected in Germany would be 800,000 and not 450,000, as predicted. During that period, thousands were crossing the Aegean to Greece every day, via people smugglers. Then they would take the Balkan route, through Macedonia and Serbia, to Hungary. While Greece was in the middle of the financial crisis and groaning under the burden of the refugees, the Hungarian government pursued an escalation strategy that included barely concealed human rights violations.[37] Together with the Austrian chancellor, Werner Faymann of the Social Democratic Party, Chancellor Merkel decided to suspend the Dublin Rules, which define the principle of the responsibility of the country of first entry. On 21 August the Federal Office for Migration and Refugees issued an internal directive that suspended the otherwise obligatory

120   The Democratic Regression

examination of whether asylum seekers had first set foot on European soil in another EU country and could therefore be sent back there. At the same time, all deportations to other European countries – mainly the countries along the Union's southern border, Italy and Greece – were temporarily halted. The British newspaper the *Independent* ran the headline 'Germany Opens Its Gates'.[38]

In the opening phase, Merkel's course of action received a lot of support. Large sections of civil society attempted to create a 'welcoming culture'. At the same time, however, protest swelled against the 'flood of refugees' and the burdens it brought with it. In September 2015 controls were introduced along the Austrian border and, in November, the Dublin system for dealing with Syrian refugees was restored on the instructions of the federal ministry of the interior.

For all that, the commonly used concept of a 'refugee crisis' is nevertheless misleading. The dramatic upsurge of refugees in Europe was in the first place a consequence of a deep crisis in Syria. The refuge seekers were never an existential threat to German or any other European society. In the global South, their number has been much higher for a long time. And yet the cultural, economic, and political impacts fostered a widening of social divisions in the host countries. It would therefore be more appropriate to speak of a 'crisis of integration'. In any event, the crisis hit society as a whole and was a consequence of the removal of borders around the globe. This time it originated not in the suburbs of the United States but in Dar'a, Syria. But, even from there, the spark easily jumped across state borders and escaped.

Disappointment with how little protection political borders offered played a major role in the post-crisis blame game. Opponents of open borders sought to blame the liberal cosmopolitans. With the German chancellor first in line, they were deemed responsible for opening the borders, promoting multiculturalism, and flooding the labour market with cheap

Crises of Democracy

and willing workers. The 'refugee crisis' was interpreted as yet another crisis of globalization.

There were, however, considerable differences from the financial crisis. For one thing, the crisis was not sparked off by greedy investment bankers. It was Bashar al-Assad and Vladimir Putin, his backer, who waged the brutal war against broad sections of the Syrian population. They carried out the slaughter and drove people out of their country, as refugees. The two of them can hardly be seen as liberal cosmopolitans of the first water. Moreover, it was not the strength of rigid neoliberal institutions that was responsible for the humanitarian catastrophe in Syria, but rather the weakness of the so-called liberal international security order, which could not prevent it, on account of the Russian and Chinese veto. This led to a further weakening of the cosmopolitan principle of the responsibility to protect.[39] In the end, it was not economic globalization but nationalism in Europe and power struggles in the Middle East that were the deep structural causes of the so-called refugee crisis. In fact it was the long-term effects of colonial expansion and the Nazi policy of exterminating the Jews that produced the convoluted situation in the region. To put it bluntly, the seeds of colonial globalization were sown by nationalists. Nevertheless, like the financial crisis, the refugee crisis has deepened the divide between authoritarian populists and liberal globalists, the former blaming the latter for causing the problems.

A third difference between the financial crisis and the integration crisis becomes evident if one looks at crisis management. It is true that, in the end, the influx of migrants was managed with some success. The number of asylum seekers fell without states having to resort to the most brutal means of securing their borders. Refugees have been reasonably well integrated into western societies. Unlike in the financial crisis, however, international cooperation was much less effective, even though it could have taken place largely within the framework of the European Union.[40]

122 The Democratic Regression

Through the Amsterdam Treaty of 1997, the European Union acquired the authority to develop a regional refugee policy of its own. EU legislation subsequently laid down the procedure for awarding or withdrawing refugee status. In the Lisbon Treaty of 2009, the Common European Asylum System (CEAS) was developed as a uniform procedure for dealing with asylum seekers. Article 80 of the Treaty deals with how the European Union functions and explicitly provides for the principle of solidarity and fair sharing of responsibility between member states. At the same time, the new European Border and Coast Guard Agency (EBCG) was given the task to support the member states in securing their borders and in coordinating EU operations designed to rescue refugees and combat human trafficking and people smuggling in the Mediterranean.[41]

And yet, by 2015 at the latest, the implementation of these measures had failed. Italy, Hungary, and Poland openly defied the European Union's authority on asylum and migration. Hungary erected razor-wire fences. The Italian interior minister, Matteo Salvini of the right-wing populist party The League, closed Italian harbours from 2018 on and criminalized rescue efforts by non-governmental organizations. When Italian courts called on the government to give immediate assistance to people in distress in Italian territorial waters, Salvini threatened to restrict their independence. He also rejected any legal relocation plan agreed upon between European countries, even though such relocations would have reduced Italy's burden. Only after Salvini's resignation in 2019 did the Italian government begin to support the French and German reform proposals for a relocation mechanism. Hungary, on the other hand, with Poland's support, registered a complaint against the time-limited relocation scheme, thus calling the European Union's authority into question again. These two countries and the Czech Republic continued to reject any EU interference in their control over the national borders. In the end, the

European Union was unable to deal with the crisis through a joint effort. Instead of a refugee crisis, then, one could speak of a crisis of the CEAS.[42]

No matter how one assesses these events and decisions, they functioned once again like a magnifying and burning glass, as far as alienation from democratic procedures goes. The starting point was Angela Merkel's decision not to close the borders, a decision apparently taken in isolation. In fact the decision was much less isolated than the headlines made it out to be; it was nevertheless a decision that eluded parliamentary procedure or debate. Only later, after the electoral successes of the AfD, did national politics and the majoritarian institutions come back into play. In the meantime, as with the financial crisis, an extension of EU powers took place, and at first it went unnoticed by the European public.[43] But the situation changed in the course of the crisis. Authoritarian populist parties took up the fight against the European Union's refugee policy. When they were part of the government, they obstructed and prevented the implementation of the relevant measures. Otherwise they mobilized popular opinion against the admission of migrants, which they presented as a policy imposed by cosmopolitan elites.

Under the magnifying glass, the weakening of majoritarian institutions and the cosmopolitan bias of non-majoritarian ones were clearly visible. And the longer the problem was kept under the burning glass, the more the democratic potential got burned at the stake. Double alienation progressed further. It is probably not disputed that, of all the cases discussed here, the integration crisis was the one that authoritarian populists exploited the most.[44] A significant number of people see not only the rise of the AfD but also Brexit as a direct result of Merkel's refugee policy. This view, of course, fails to account for long-term trends. In general, the integration crisis accelerated the rise of new parties but did not cause it. Unlike in the financial crisis and in the euro crisis, in the case of Brexit it was

124 The Democratic Regression

exclusively authoritarian populist parties from the right of the political spectrum that benefited.

In any case, the integration crisis revealed and accelerated social changes. The year 2016 was the first one in which the new cleavage described earlier came to dominate debate in the consolidated western democracies. For the first time, questions concerning open borders and the role of international institutions went right to the top of the political agenda.

5.4 Covid-19: The Power of Virologists

In this story, virologists play the leading role. The team around Christian Drosten at Berlin's Charité Hospital was able to lay out the complete genome of SARS-CoV-2, with all its 30,000 letters, within a few weeks of the outbreak of the pandemic. Comparison with viral structures in various animals revealed a close match to viruses in bats. But the match was not close enough yet. A mediator was needed to complete the chain. One conjecture was that the virus might have been passed to humans via raccoon dogs. These are mammals with a muzzle that resembles a raccoon's and legs like a dog's. Raccoon dogs are on sale in animal markets in China. Another thesis proposed the ancient-looking pangolin as the link. At any rate, there was plenty to indicate that the first large-scale outbreak had taken place in the city of Wuhan in central China.

A team led by the geneticist Peter Forster at Cambridge University traced the virus's path from that point. The researchers compared 160 virus genomes using phylogenetic network analysis. They were able to follow the trail from Wuhan to the automotive equipment supplier Webasto near Munich, and from there to Lombardy in Italy. Forster's conclusion was that many of the viruses in northern Italy had arrived there from China via Bavaria, then probably made their way back to

Germany later. Of course, it is not possible to assert this with absolute certainty.[45]

The virus spread like wildfire. By the middle of November 2020, more than 50 million people worldwide had been infected with Covid-19 and more than 1.3 million had died of it.[46] Without the rapid development and worldwide distribution of a vaccine, this rate of infection, if continued, would have led to a death toll comparable to that of Spanish flu in 1918–20. In spite of vaccination and remarkable efforts to prevent the uncontrolled diffusion of the virus, 6.6 million have died until 2023.

Covid is a prime example of the double dissolution of boundaries [*Entgrenzung*] that characterizes the crises of the twenty-first century. The emergence of a virus is initially a challenge to the health system. Its rapid growth makes it a problem for the whole society. To keep the death rate under control, politicians had to impose lockdowns. Despite their far-reaching effects on the economy and the limitations they imposed on basic freedoms, these comprehensive measures, which affected each and every subsystem, were largely accepted. At the same time, the virus never showed any tendency to stop at geographical borders. The crisis was a truly global one.

Against the background of this dissolution of boundaries, it may be possible in this case, too, to lay the blame at the door of neoliberalism, economic globalization, and ultimately liberal globalists. Doing so would be less easy, though, than it was in the case of the financial crisis. The virus is first and foremost an exogenous shock, not a consequence of either liberal democracy or globalization. SARS-CoV-2 emerged as a result of local practices in a region of China. The virus appeared locally and at first spread epidemically, in the region. It went global, becoming a pandemic as result of multiple connections between regional epidemics. The global map of infection depicts regional epidemics in the form of smaller or larger circles. It is not necessary to assume an intensified form of globalization for the infection to spread from region to region; normal travel links in an interdependent world would have sufficed. Only when aircrafts don't fly, ships don't sail, or trains don't run will it be possible to confine a virus to a particular region. As far back as 1831, it proved impossible to prevent Asian cholera from reaching Europe, even with a military cordon sanitaire. It is probably safe to assume that the causal contribution of the new push for globalization in the 1990s and 2000s was not decisive for the globality of the virus.[47]

By the same token, caution is required when announcing the end of globalization. Exogenous shocks usually bring about fewer changes over the medium term than the scale of the crisis might lead one to expect. Naturally, in a crisis new social practices are adopted, and later on they may become permanent if they prove to serve a useful function. So, even after the crisis is over, there may be more video conferences and fewer in-person business meetings than there were before; that would be sensible. Quite possibly, the virus would speed up the death of local retail and increase Amazon's market share still further; that would be a pity. All in all, the virus is likely to boost digitalization, which is taking place with or without it, because we will have to acquire new virtual skills. But whether this will lead to deglobalization and a revival of national economies is still an open question.

A more relevant question in our context is which governments and political ideologies will emerge from the crisis weaker and which stronger. The future of the liberal world order will depend decisively on the relative importance and strength of parties as they face each other across the new divide. And that, again, may be considerably influenced by how well or badly their protagonists perform in dealing with the pandemic. It turns out that there are no significant differences between democratic and authoritarian political systems on this front. If we look at the progress curves for infections and deaths, both autocratic countries such as Singapore and democratic

Crises of Democracy

127

countries such as South Korea have proved to be successful crisis managers. On the other hand, less successful countries included both autocratic ones, such as Iran, and democratic ones, such as Spain.

In places where authoritarian populists hold power, the virus seems to feel particularly comfortable. Populist governments have ignored the warnings of experts for too long, and replaced them with their own assessments. Brazil's president Jair Bolsonaro spoke of 'a little flu'. Taking its cue from Michael Gove's motto during the Brexit debate – 'The people in this country have had enough of experts' – the British government started out by following a strategy of herd immunity, until medical expertise was able to make itself heard again. And US President Donald Trump tried to calm the stock markets by declaring that no measures were necessary because he had everything under control. Coincidence or not, soon enough Bolsonaro, Johnson, and Trump were themselves struck down by the virus.

Hostility to experts is inherent in authoritarian populism. Since the alleged will of the majority and of the people should have an immediate effect and should be dimmed only by the pseudoneutral expertise of the governing elites (lawyers, journalists, scientists, etc.), there is no need for complex decision-making procedures to ascertain it. Rather this will is realized through the intuitions and convictions of the elected head of state and her or his entourage. For instance, Trump appointed Jared Kushner, his son-in-law, who was completely inexperienced in health matters, to be coordinator for the procurement of medical equipment. In the Covid-19 task force, Kushner seems to have consistently cut out highly regarded experts such as Deborah Birx and Anthony Fauci. According to data from Johns Hopkins University, by the end of 2020 the countries under authoritarian populist rule – the United States, Brazil, and India – were at the top of the table in numbers of people infected.[48]

128 The Democratic Regression

If we look at the number of deaths, we first notice that demographic features such as size and age of the population, as well as the proportion of previous conditions, explain most of the variation to be observed.[49] By comparison, political and social characteristics play a subordinate role. But among those, the characteristics that correlate most closely with number of deaths are absence of social trust and participation in right-wing populist forms of government. The data confirm that authoritarian populism appears to be the single relevant political variable. The statistical connection could point to a causal one: it could indicate that anti-expert political systems that bet on the populist intuitions of their heads of government do not make good crisis managers. According to surveys, support for authoritarian populist politicians actually declined somewhat at that point, at least in some countries. It is of course far too early to bet on a decline of authoritarian populism in the long run.

It is possible that the magnifying glass effect of crises will end up working against democracy again. For one thing, the importance of experts in the consolidated democracies of the twenty-first century has been demonstrated with absolute clarity. Virologists and epidemiologists set the tone in justifying many measures, and even in dictating their content. The French virologist Jean-François Delfraissy is said to have persuaded President Macron to adopt drastic measures during a crisis meeting. The epidemiologist Fernando Simón is credited with effectively steering Spain through the crisis, after politicians procrastinated for too long. Angelo Borrelli played a similar role in Italy. As for the German virologist Christian Drosten, the question 'Drosten for chancellor?' appeared in the media at once.[50] Decisions were taken in small committees in which the executive had the final word and was content to be guided by the recommendations of medical experts. Even in countries such as Sweden and Great Britain, which went their own way, the names and faces of the best-known virologists came to be inscribed in the national memory. Anders Tegnell, who set the Swedish strategy, and Chris Whitty, who persuaded the British government to change course (albeit too late), became celebrities. In Germany, comprehensive packages of measures that had a profound impact on the economy and on society as a whole were decided in conference calls between a few members of the government and the prime minister of the relevant German state alongside well-known virologists.

In addition, there were further comprehensive packages of measures at the European level. Early on, the president of the European Commission, Ursula von der Leyen, launched an initiative to finance shortfalls in workers' pay to the tune of €100 billion. A further €37 billion were made available by the Commission from the Union's structural fund to combat the pandemic. The European Investment Bank offered up to €200 billion in guarantees for loans. Member states are able to apply to the European Stability Mechanism for credit lines of up to 2 per cent of GDP in order to cover direct and indirect expenses in the health sector caused by the pandemic. Finally, the ECB launched a new loan purchase scheme designed to guarantee potentially limitless liquidity in the eurozone. The Federal Constitutional Court specifically exempted the loans purchased under this scheme from its decision against other loan purchases made by the ECB in the context of overcoming the euro crisis.

At a special meeting of the European Council at the end of July 2020, the Union's leaders agreed on a comprehensive package that totalled €1,824.3 billion and combined the multi-annual financial framework with exceptional development measures under the Union's next-generation recovery instrument. This will equip the Union with the necessary means to meet the challenges involved in overcoming the Covid-19 pandemic. Within the framework of this agreement, the Commission will be able to borrow up to €750 billion on the financial markets. Out of these, €390 billion will not be spent

130   The Democratic Regression

as credits to lending countries but will be financed by a pot that will be underwritten by the Union as a whole. This will be a step in the direction of institutionalized solidarity with the financially weaker countries – a step that the Union refused to take throughout the euro crisis.

We believe that all these measures were necessary. At the same time, it must be pointed out that the role of parliaments in making these decisions has remained marginal. For a long time, even the parties themselves followed Emperor Wilhelm II's dictum: 'Crisis knows no parties' (the emperor was talking about the war). Majoritarian institutions hardly played any role. The general trend towards the transfer of political decision-making to institutions that are beyond the control of parties or parliaments can be seen as clearly as if we looked at it through a magnifying glass.

What is more, the medium- and long-term economic effects of the crisis could bring further damage to democracy. If anything, the economic causes of the rise of authoritarian populists have been fuelled by these effects. In Germany alone, the IMF is reckoning with a fall in GDP of around €230 billion.[51] Then there are the sums made available by the German government to alleviate the situation in countries such as Italy and Spain, which have fared much worse. One consequence of the crisis will be an extremely high sovereign debt, which leaves little scope for social measures and for higher public spending on education and health care. The response to the Russian aggression against the Ukraine accentuates this development. Ultimately this will not only increase economic inequality but make it probable that politics' responsiveness to the preferences of low-income groups remains low. This bodes well for authoritarian populists. They may well end up benefiting from the Covid-19 crisis, even if they have failed at managing it.

5.5 The Paradox and the Crisis Spiral

The great crises of this century point to a paradox. In established democracies, crisis management has been successful to some extent, both historically and synchronically, by comparison to other systems. Despite this, confidence in democracies continues to erode. Alienation from democracy accelerates. Crises turn the spotlight on the relocation of power centres in democracies. The executive takes the biggest decisions in cooperation with non-majoritarian institutions. Parliaments and parties carry out a 'voluntary alignment', as it is known in Switzerland in relation to the implementation of EU law. This ultimately leads to a lack of representation, which authoritarian populist forces use for mobilization purposes. In the middle of the Covid-19 crisis, this feature allowed for abstruse conspiracy theories to flourish.[52] In the end, trust in democracy slowly melts away under the heat of the burning glass. We are faced once again with a double alienation from democracy: the real decision-making processes are distancing themselves from the democratic ideal and many citizens are disengaging from the democratic political system.

As a result, social tensions have grown within consolidated democracies. Liberal globalists in particular serve as scapegoats. Greedy bankers have cashed in, driven us into the financial crisis, and left ordinary taxpayers to pick up the bill. Multiculturalists have opened the borders so that they are able to lead a lifestyle as global as it is decadent and to have cheap labour to clean up after them. Bill Gates, Big Pharma, and the virologists have dished up a once-in-a-millennium whopper in order to gain control of society and force everyone to get vaccinated. That is one interpretation of what happened during these crises.

Another reading is that national interests prevented global financial regulation and thus created the financial crisis. The sheer power politics of the Assads and the Putins – hence the secret friends and role models of authoritarian populists – drove millions of innocent people to flee their homes and homelands. Covid-19 brought to light an ecological crisis whose root causes have yet to be addressed but whose existence cannot be denied – although authoritarian populists would like to deny it. As if that were not enough, the authoritarian populists have failed miserably in managing the Covid-19 crisis.

There is no question that the second reading is generally closer to the truth. Conversely, there is a good deal to suggest that this rapid succession of crises has something to do with the globalized state of the world. The crises have exposed the weaknesses of consolidated democracies and of the liberal world order. This, in turn, has increased the likelihood of further crises.

6

Opportunities and Dangers

Current populism is primarily authoritarian. In terms of procedure, it represents an unmediated plebiscitary implementation of the majority will. In terms of content, it represents nationalistic positions that stand against cosmopolitan elites, insofar as it plays the significance of borders and of the national will off against an open global society with strong international institutions. These convictions combine to construe an unshakeable antagonism between decent local people and a corrupt cosmopolitan elite. To that extent, authoritarian populism is against the status quo in liberal democracies.

Nevertheless, current opponents of liberal democracy still align with democracy. The paradigm here is the distinction between liberal and Christian democracy, as launched by Viktor Orbán:

> Let us confidently declare that Christian democracy is not liberal. Liberal democracy is liberal, while Christian democracy is by definition not liberal. ... Liberal democracy is in favour of multiculturalism, while Christian democracy gives priority to Christian culture; this is an illiberal concept. Liberal democracy is pro-immigration, while Christian democracy is

134   The Democratic Regression

anti-immigration; this is again a genuinely illiberal concept. And liberal democracy sides with adaptable family models, while Christian democracy rests on the foundations of the Christian family model; once more this is an illiberal concept.[1]

Authoritarian populism is successful because it is able to point out the weaknesses in democratic practice. Parties of this persuasion claim to lend a voice to the interests of ordinary people and silent majorities. They say they take it upon themselves to represent those who have been inadequately represented so far. Wolfgang Merkel speaks of a representation gap in modern democracies that will be filled by authoritarian populist parties.[2] Hanspeter Kriesi speaks even of a productive power, which allegedly will be able to advance the necessary transformation of the Western European party system.[3] Similarly, Peter Učeň sees 'the parties of the new populism' as 'non-radical challengers mobilizing a disappointed electorate against under-performing and morally failing established parties'.[4] In consequence, Christoph Möllers notes that 'the election of authoritarian figures is not undemocratic per se'.[5] All the authors cited are highly regarded scholars who cannot be accused of having a political axe to grind. As they see it, populism simply brings a long-lost confrontation back into politics.

This is how the leading intellectual lights of left-wing populism see things, too. According to Ernesto Laclau (2005) and Chantal Mouffe (2018), democracy presupposes struggles over political projects. Mouffe therefore calls for a populism of the left, which should bring democracies back to life. She regards the current political phase as a 'populist moment', in which the neoliberal hegemony is being destabilized by multiple unfulfilled demands; then she goes on to say:

> To stop the rise of right-wing populist parties, it is necessary to design a properly political answer through a left populist move-

ment that will federate all the democratic struggles against post-democracy. Instead of excluding *a priori* the voters of right-wing populist parties as necessarily moved by atavistic passions, condemning them to remain prisoners of those passions forever, it is necessary to recognize the democratic nucleus at the origin of many of their demands.[6]

Others are less optimistic about the repercussions of populism. Jan-Werner Müller (2016) points out that populism is always anti-pluralist. In his view, the juxtaposition of a morally pure, homogeneous people and an immoral, corrupt, and parasitic elite undermines democracy. Nadia Urbinati takes a very similar view. Populism is an attempt to transform representative democracy and to create a '(supposedly) direct representation between the people and the leader'.[7] What still appears as democratic when it is in opposition reveals itself to be authoritarian when it is in power. This worry is shared by many representatives of established parties. To give an example, the current president of the German Federal Republic has repeatedly expressed his concerns about the threat to democracy represented by authoritarian populists.[8]

The well-known populism researchers Cristóbal Rovira Kaltwasser and Cas Mudde take an intermediary position. They see the 'populist zeitgeist'[9] as a double-edged sword.[10] On the one hand, they share the view that populist parties take up issues that are neglected by mainstream parties. Along this line, they also credit populism with democratic potential. On the other hand, they observe how populism takes aim at the liberal pillars of modern democracy. In the end, they seem to concur with some populists' self-description as 'illiberal democrats': 'In essence, populism is not against democracy; rather it is at odds with *liberal* democracy.'[11] Of course, this assessment begs the question of whether illiberal democracy is not a contradiction in terms; for without the rule of law and basic political rights there can be no democracy.[12]

136   The Democratic Regression

The democratic potential of authoritarian populist parties is in dispute. Were authoritarian populists to reveal deficits in modern democracies, an improved form of democracy could result. Yet that seems more likely to happen in cases where authoritarian populist parties are still in opposition and the established parties react to the new challenge with a democratizing offensive. Sceptics, however, point to the content of authoritarian populism as a political ideology that calls the foundational pillars of modern democracy into question (see Chapter 3). This threat becomes particularly virulent when authoritarian populists come to power. There is something ambivalent about attacking democracy in the name of a supposedly true democracy. It is therefore wise to consider the most recent empirical developments in democracy if we are to move the debate forward.

To measure the effect of authoritarian populism on democracy, we have first to distinguish between its parties in opposition and its parties in power. After that we will take stock of the effects of authoritarian populism on international politics, then of the repercussions that these effects have on the condition of democracy.

6.1   Authoritarian Populists in Power

Once authoritarian populists come to power, they can influence the political system directly. They may take office through democratic elections, but they bring with them an authoritarian programme. When they are heading the government, they are unlikely to enhance political systems' representativeness of and responsiveness to all groups. Judging by the current practices of their leaders, authoritarian populists are more likely to challenge minority rights and attack minority lifestyles. They also strive to take control of the media, to attack constitutional courts, and to exclude anything they consider foreign. This attitude extends to rejecting international institutions as a form of foreign domination against which they invoke national sovereignty.

Whether authoritarian populist heads of government cause a deterioration of democracy can be examined on the basis of eight examples: Bolsonaro in Brazil, Erdoğan in Turkey, Kaczyński and Duda in Poland, Maduro in Venezuela, Modi in India, Putin in Russia, Orbán in Hungary, and Trump in the United States. Altogether more than 2.2 billion people live in these eight countries, making up nearly 30 per cent of world population. Our list comprises countries in Asia, Europe, and the Americas. In addition to the right-leaning examples, it includes one left-wing version of an authoritarian populist regime. In all eight countries it has been possible for authoritarian populist heads of government – thanks in part to the presidential system of government, in part to the relevant election results – to act unimpeded by complicated coalition arrangements.

Once again, we use data from the V-Dem project to find out whether authoritarian populists worsen the quality of democracy.[13] Figure 16 shows how the standing of each of the eight countries selected changed on the Liberal Democracy Index (LDI) between 2000 and 2021. The LDI has two components: the Electoral Democracy Index (EDI), which consists of measurements for the various features of free and fair elections; and the Liberal Component Index (LCI), which focuses on the rule of law, the preservation of citizens' rights, and the restrictions placed on the executive by the judiciary and the legislative. In Figure 16 the years in which governments were led by autocrats are marked in dark dots and thus distinguished from the years, marked in white dots, in which they were not.

Several trends immediately catch the eye. To start with, there are very substantial differences between the quality of democracy in these countries; and this, again, underlines, first, that tendencies towards autocratization are not restricted to

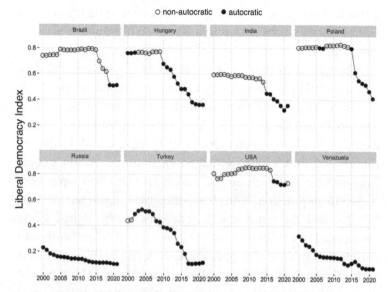

Figure 16 Democratic regression from 2000 to 2019.
Source: Data from V-Dem dataset, Version 10, 2020.

Note: The list comprises eight countries in which particularly well-known authoritarian populist governments were in office over a longer period of time. Empty circles denote non-authoritarian heads of government, filled circles authoritarian ones in the years 2000–2019. For Poland, only the years in which PiS (Law and Justice) provided both the prime minister and the president are marked as 'authoritarian', namely 2005–2007 and the period from 2015 onwards.

non-democratic countries and, second, that they do not automatically lead to the disappearance of democracy. No doubt the quality of US democracy declined under Donald Trump, but the country remained a democracy.[14] By contrast, Russia was not a democracy at any point during the past twenty years, but this did not stop its rating from falling still further.

It is also striking that, over the past two decades, the quality of democracy failed to improve in any of the countries under review. On the contrary, in six out of the eight, the LDI fell by at least 0.1 points (on a scale of 0 to 1) – that is, by at least 10 per cent. The least pronounced of all these regressions was the one in the United States, although the figure for 2020 marked a historic low. On the other hand, dramatic downtrends were registered in Poland, Hungary, and Turkey.

As Figure 16 shows, democracies decline in quality especially under autocratically minded heads of government. Naturally, it would be misleading to make specific individuals solely responsible, but in almost all instances a democratic backsliding can be seen after they came to power. With the exception of Brazil, the pattern is quite clearly marked. The condition of liberal democracy has deteriorated dramatically in the two EU countries on the list, Poland and Hungary. In the Index for 2000, liberal democracy still stood at 0.81 for Poland and 0.76 for Hungary. By 2021 it dropped to 0.41 for Poland and to 0.36 for Hungary. In no country of the world has democracy suffered a decline as steep as the one in Hungary.[15] Nowadays neither Hungary nor Poland meet the conditions that were once required for joining the European Union. In Turkey, too, any hope that the country might be on the road to becoming a liberal democracy was dashed in 2005. During the 2000s, progress was still being made and Turkey's accession to the European Union seemed a realistic possibility, but LDI figures have fallen sharply since then. The current assessment is that Turkey no longer qualifies as a democratic country.

Quite a few lessons can be drawn from the experience of autocratization in these countries. It is typical of the new wave of democratic regression that it does not limit the right to vote or do away with the principle of electoral appointments, but both the conditions for free and fair elections *and* the control of the executive by parliaments and courts are restricted. According to V-Dem data, between 2000 and 2021, in Poland, the judiciary's ability to control the executive was reduced by 30 per cent, the figure for freedom of opinion fell by 23 per cent, and parliamentary control of the government fell by 13 per cent. For freedom of association and equality before the law, the figures have also fallen by more than 10 per cent since

2000. In clear contradiction to the constitution, the Polish parliament changed the electoral law less than six months before the presidential elections. However, since the opposition can be outvoted and the constitutional court has been filled with followers of PiS (the Law and Justice party), even this clear breach of the constitution went unpunished. In Hungary, freedom of opinion and freedom of association have been severely curtailed, respectively by −28 and −23 per cent. The principle of free and fair elections has clearly been damaged as well.

The result of these observations is plain. Liberal democracy suffers when authoritarian populist parties are in power. In seven of the eight countries under review, the LDI figure for 2021 lies below or close to the critical threshold of 0.5. There are, of course, notable differences. Viktor Orbán, to take one example, has changed the political system more radically in Hungary than Donald Trump has in the United States. One reason for this may lie in the different aims of the authoritarian populist leaders in the two countries. By this logic, Orbán would simply be a more authoritarian and less democratic leader than Trump. But a much more important factor seems to be the resilience of the political system. In many countries the pre-existing institutions resist democratic backsliding more stoutly than in others. We see particularly marked and rapid declines in the quality of democracy in new or transient democracies such as those of Hungary, Brazil, Poland, and Turkey. Much smaller deviations are observed in countries with longer democratic traditions, such as the United States. But that makes no difference to the central finding of this survey: authoritarian populists in power have a negative effect on liberal democracy.

The figures show, moreover, that authoritarian populists do not confine their attacks to the liberal side of democracy but strive for an allegedly illiberal democracy, which should weaken citizens' rights but strengthen free and fair elections. The data for Hungary, of all places, point to a very extensive deterioration

Opportunities and Dangers 141

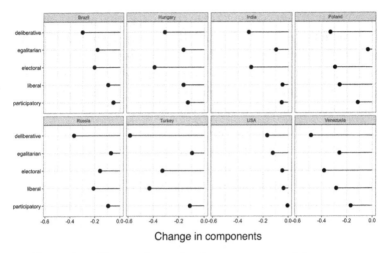

Figure 17 Change shown for the components of democracy since 2000.

Source: Data from V-Dem, Version 10, 2020.

Note: The figure shows developments in five components of democracy between 2000 and 2019. Lines that run left from 0.0 indicate deterioration; lines that run right indicate improvement.

of free and fair elections. Its euphemistic self-description as an illiberal democracy seems calculated to conceal the fact that the basic constituents of democracy are under attack. These include opposition rights, control of power, media freedom, and oversight of the executive by the judiciary. The situation is particularly obvious if we examine the individual components of the V-Dem data for the eight countries in our survey, namely the deliberative, egalitarian, electoral, liberal, and participative aspects of democracy (see Figure 17).

The rulership of authoritarian populists does not improve the quality of democracy in any way. On the contrary, it leads to no change or, more often than not, to deterioration in almost every dimension. The index of political equality (equal protection, equal access, equal distribution of resources) and the participation index (participation in civil society, direct

142   The Democratic Regression

referendums, independence of local and regional governments) have actually deteriorated, but these are all components in which, to go by authoritarian populist rhetoric, representativeness and responsiveness were expected to improve. And the electoral and liberal components have deteriorated as well. Similarly, the current deliberative component, which is made up of five subindicators (provision of reasoned justification, the common good, respect for opposing arguments, the range of elite-level advice, a politically engaged society), has deteriorated drastically in all eight countries. This breakdown points to the friend-or-foe mentality of authoritarian populists, which precludes collaborative problem solving. The capacity for deliberation seems to have declined significantly even in the United States, because the rift between Republicans and Democrats is so deep that hardly any willingness to compromise is left. These observations speak against the expectation that authoritarian populist governments might in any way improve the functioning of democracy by integrating previously disadvantaged groups or by correcting the elitist narrowing of political decision-making in favour of a broader participation of those concerned. They aim not for illiberal democracy but for electoral authoritarianism.[16] Authoritarian populists, as we have said, are careful not to destroy the appearance of democracy, because they would like to legitimize themselves through elections; but they distort democracy itself to the point of unrecognizability.

6.2 Authoritarian Populists in Opposition or as Junior Partners

If one examines how authoritarian populists behave when they govern, there is little evidence that they are willing to address the core problems of democracy. First of all, they are not interested in creating an inclusive welfare state. They may have a lot to say about the growing inequality, but their primary concern is with the preferential treatment seemingly given to individuals or groups who, from their point of view, do not belong among 'the true people'. Authoritarian populist parties aim to protect economically the native population in traditional occupations, but without seeking a more equitable distribution of resources within society as a whole. Silvio Berlusconi and Donald Trump are striking illustrations of this point. At any rate, tax cuts for the rich, the protection of national industries, and the stigmatization of specific categories of people are not measures by which social justice can be achieved.

Second, authoritarian populists show no interest in an open and self-reflective debate about lifestyles, culture, and social requirements in a diverse society. The Alternative for Germany (AfD) in Germany and the Freedom Party (FPÖ) in Austria have made that abundantly clear. They would rather work to restore the hegemony of a traditional society dominated by the (male) middle class – a middle-class society, shaped and levelled in the style of Ludwig Erhard or Helmut Schelsky, with all the cultural connotations of the model.[17]

Lastly, authoritarian populists do not fight for the democratization of complex governance arrangements in which various levels and various actors productively work together. They would much rather struggle for the uncontrolled dominance of the national executive and aim to weaken all other democratic institutions.

The democratic potential of a populist protest could be exploited only indirectly, if at all, namely via the detour of a reaction to authoritarian populism. Thus, in the final analysis, democratizing changes would depend on other actors. They might come about as a possible, though by no means certain, result of an interactive process in which the established parties react to their challengers and seek new ways to confront the double alienation from democracy. If such a dynamic should bring about a process of democratization, that would happen

144   The Democratic Regression

presumably in the face of resistance from authoritarian populists. In such a case, the relationship between populists and democratization would come closest to the pattern that Ralf Dahrendorf proposed for the correlation between National Socialism and modernization: the latter inadvertently cleared the way for the modernization of society.[18]

In order to analyse the effects that authoritarian populist parties have on democracy when they are in opposition or when they operate as junior partners in a coalition, we need to turn our attention to interactive practices. Then we shall also have to keep an eye on the dynamics that work in a different direction – that is, against democratization. Democracies can be undermined also without authoritarian populists' participation in government. Steven Levitsky and Daniel Ziblatt (2018) have studied these dynamics in the history of US democracy. It appears from their analysis that a polarization of the political process leads to the subversion of unwritten laws that are vital to the functioning of democracy. Similar developments can be detected throughout the rise of authoritarian populists in Western Europe. The general model looks something like this: the challenger party breaks taboos; the established parties respond by excluding the challenger party from the procedure, which is defined above all by informal rules; the challenger party then conquers other political positions and uses them to exclude its main rival. The situation becomes emotionally charged, which contributes to further escalation and the radicalization of aims.[19] As a result, the informal practices of democracy find themselves at risk.

Which of the two interactive dynamics has prevailed in political reality so far? Do strong populist parties in opposition or in a coalition government lead to improvement or to deterioration in the quality of democracy? We can examine this systematically in thirty countries whose political parties present various types of populism. We distinguish between cabinets in which populist parties do not participate and

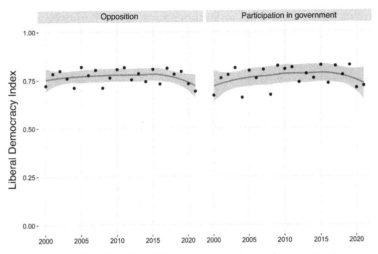

Figure 18 Quality of democracy and populist parties in government.
Source: Data from V-Dem, Version 10, 2020.

cabinets in which they participate as junior coalition partners. Once again, we use the LDI, which is based on Varieties of Democracy data. As can be seen in Figure 18, the impact on the index value is negligible when populist parties are part of a government but do not dominate it. The two lines showing developments that took place with and without populist participation are broadly parallel. In both cases, only small changes in the quality of democracy are detectable over time. When populist parties do not lead the government, they have little impact on the quality of democracy. This is illustrated by the examples of Switzerland and Austria, where authoritarian populist parties – the Swiss People's Party and the Freedom Party of Austria – have repeatedly been in government, yet this left no trace on the comparative measurements of democracy.

Together with the analyses carried out in the previous section, this finding raises serious doubts about the appraisal that authoritarian populist parties are capable of improving the quality of democracy. Much to the contrary, when populists

146   The Democratic Regression

are in power they dismantle democracy, and when they are in opposition their positive effect on democracy is nil.

6.3   Authoritarian Populism and the Liberal International Order

Along with its effects on national democracy, a further rise in authoritarian populism may change the international order. As we have seen, criticism of international institutions is part of the agenda of authoritarian populists. From their perspective, national interests and the sovereignty of the people need to be defended against European and international bodies, which are controlled by a corrupt cosmopolitan elite. Although having authoritarian populists in power has not yet led to a complete dismantling of the cooperative world order,[20] it has made international collaboration more difficult. An especially momentous example is the former US president Donald Trump, who called into question the three central, normative, and foundational pillars of the global political system established in the 1990s.[21] In the foreword to the National Security Strategy (NSS) of December 2017, he rejects the first pillar, the idea of a global common good: 'My Administration's National Security Strategy lays out a strategic vision for protecting the American people and preserving our way of life, promoting our prosperity, preserving peace through strength, and advancing American influence in the world.'[22] The global common good and the global public good have no place in his thinking. Everything is about American interests. Peace equates to American dominance – and that is that.

Second, Trump denounces international institutions as fundamentally superfluous. The United States' withdrawal from international organizations and agreements such as the Paris Agreement is presented as a 'success' of his policy. Finally, neither the president's foreword nor the NSS as a whole conveys at any point the impression that the United States and its president may be willing to explain themselves to people or governments outside their own country. There is no sign of justifying this strategy in the eyes of the world community. Once again, Trump's strategic vision differs from that of all US presidents since the Second World War. By dispensing with any justification directed at the global community, he violates the third pillar of the cooperative world order.

But the radical rejection of international institutions in the name of the sovereignty of the people endangers the stability of democratic political systems and, thus, popular sovereignty itself. The cooperative world order that took shape under American leadership between 1945 and the end of the millennium did in fact have a Wilsonian effect: it made the world safer for democracies (see Chapter 2). Already after the First World War, Woodrow Wilson tried to create a world order in which democracies could safely flourish. The Treaty of Versailles did not accomplish this goal. The world order that came into being after the Second World War was more successful in this respect.

In this respect, the anti-internationalism of authoritarian populists could prove to be the main threat to liberal democracy. Perhaps the deconstruction of a cooperative and partly liberal international order brings about the end of an environment in which democracies can flourish well. Without this context, the survival of democracies could become more difficult. But the battle for the international order is not yet over. Many see the current war in Ukraine as part of this battle. Right now, the advocates of a strong and open international order confront the proponents of a new nationalism. One could say that the new line of conflict, with liberal globalists and authoritarian populists on opposing sides, has been drawn at the global level as well. Both sides claim to be acting in the name of democracy. But neither has any good answers to the question of the future of democracy.

148   The Democratic Regression

6.4 The Democratic Dilemma in the Face of Open Borders

Elites prefer liberal globalism – the class consciousness of frequent travellers, as Craig Calhoun (2002) once pertly remarked. By contrast, authoritarian populism seems to be the political ideology of those closely attached to their homeland. If elites are using democracy and international institutions for their own ends, then it seems logical that the discontent of large sections of the locally bound population should be politicized and openly directed against the cosmopolitan selectivity of institutions. But the authoritarian populists threaten to throw the baby out with the bathwater. They are targeting the very foundations of democracy. If democratic institutions and the political rights of minorities are not made safe against the plebiscitarian will of the majority, it means that there is no democracy to speak of. Nadia Urbinati gets to the heart of the matter: without liberal individual rights, democracy cannot exist.[23] The term 'liberal democracy' is a pleonasm. This presents democracy with a dilemma.[24]

The dilemma derives from the basic principle of democratic legitimacy. The principle states that those who are affected by political decisions should play a part in making them. Both Robert Dahl (1989) and Jürgen Habermas (1996) see the right to participate of those affected as the kernel of democracy. Hence one of the historic achievements of the nation-state is to have converted the abstract principle of affectedness into membership of a territorially defined community. So long as social transactions and interactions took place within the borders of nation-states,[25] the nation-state provided a framework in which the democratic principle could plausibly be realized or institutionalized.

But this connection between the nation-state and the democratic principle was dissolved through globalization.[26] Insofar as an economic and social sphere of action extends beyond national

Opportunities and Dangers 149

borders, the situation becomes problematic. Effective problem solving that can be democratically legitimized depends on the social and the political space being congruent. If the spaces of economic and cultural transactions go increasingly beyond the political borders of nation-states, the political dominance of territorially restricted nation-states becomes normatively deficient. Then the divergence of spaces needs to be captured either through a globalization of politics or through a rena-tionalization of society. Or, to go a step further with Habermas and formulate the principle more generally, '[t]he more the complexity of society and of the problems in need of political regulation increases, the less it seems to be possible to cling to the demanding idea of democracy according to which the addressees of the law should at the same time be its authors'.[27]

The problem has both a functional and a legitimacy aspect. Functionally speaking, today's world is so tightly networked that, given the state of globalization, many transnational problems can effectively be tackled only outside the nation-state. From the point of legitimacy, we face the problem that, in a denationalized world, many decisions taken at the national level generate externalities, and thus affect people independently of whether they, *qua* members, participate in affairs of state. At least in areas like financial markets and climate change, where transactions and their effects are for the most part globalized, national decision-making infringes the affectedness principle quite spectacularly; the inhabitants of the Pacific Islands, who suffer under the climate policies of the United States, China, and the European Union, are a prime example. Against the background of this kind of problem, communitarianism and cosmopolitanism give fundamentally different answers to the question of democracy.

Just like cosmopolitanism, communitarianism is in the first place a noble political philosophy. According to communi-tarian belief, a strong democracy cannot be realized in large, heterogeneous, and territorially open spaces; rather it is bound up with the concrete social lifeworlds of the people who live in a community and requires acceptance from minorities, especially for majority decisions. An adaptation of communitarianism is currently dominant in the political sphere. It puts the nation and the nation-state at the centre of things, as bearers of popular sovereignty, and thereby severely restricts who belongs to the people. This is the programme of authoritarian populists. They can be regarded as the nationalistic descendants of the communitarian philosophy. They have achieved electoral successes as a result of their fight against European integration, globalization, multiculturalism, international institutions, and immigration, especially from Muslim countries. They claim that only a homogeneous society with sufficient interpersonal trust and national identity can exist as a community of solidarity. In such a community, then, the will of the people must be implemented.

In most cases the unconditional endorsement of majority decision-making is not only illiberal but also anti-pluralist and anti-proceduralist. It elevates majority decisions above fundamental individual and minority rights even as it denounces established procedures for determining the will of the majority. All those who are critical of the 'silent majority' are branded as members of an alienated and self-seeking elite, also accused of controlling the media and public opinion. The established procedures for deliberation and for building consensus were set up by the 'corrupt elite' as means of political patronage. The antidote should be the wisdom of the leaders of the new parties and movements. In extreme cases, those who 'know' what 'the person in the street' 'wants' are to be released from the ordinary norms of political decency, as evidenced by the long and impressively stable support for Donald Trump among certain sections of the US population, despite his failures and indecencies.

But this illiberal and anti-pluralist version is by no means the only relevant political manifestation of communitarian theories. Although these theories relate to a context of concrete communities, they are not inevitably illiberal. They may also take the form of a strong, basic democracy – as in the work of Benjamin Barber[28] or in the liberal communitarian republicanism of Charles Taylor,[29] who combines the idea of a 'right to rights' with a communitarian commitment to the common good. Craig Calhoun (2002) complements Taylor's view by criticizing cosmopolitanism on the grounds that it underestimates the contributions of national identities and borders to the promotion of solidarity and democracy. Taylor and Calhoun thus point to the possibility of reconciling liberalism and communitarianism and, in the process, of avoiding two pitfalls: reactionary traditionalism and chauvinistic nationalism on the one hand, deregulatory global capitalism on the other.

All variants of a communitarian theory of democracy have a common weakness, however. Their defence of the procedures and institutions of the democratic nation-state is built primarily on local and national communities rather than on the principle of affectedness within a globalized world. Insofar as the decisions taken by democratic nation-states in times of political and social denationalization increasingly concern people from outside the borders, and insofar as these decisions depend for their effectiveness more and more on decisions taken elsewhere, democratic mechanisms within the nation-state and democratic principles are no longer identical. This is so for two reasons: first, citizens are to a certain extent ruled by political decisions that they cannot influence; second, democracy presupposes the concept of effective decision-making, that is, the idea that political decisions are a means by which collectives are able to govern themselves.

This conjunction may well be the reason why the illiberal and anti-pluralist version of communitarian thinking is so successful. In a globalized and fundamentally pluralistic world, the nationalist defence of specific communities seems to lead

152 The Democratic Regression

necessarily to anti-liberal, anti-procedural, and anti-pluralist thinking, as is already the case in Hungary and Poland today. It is no coincidence that the rejection of supranational powers on the matter of open borders for goods, capital, and people occurs in conjunction with a preference for majority decision-making and a dispreference for minorities and individual rights. There seems to be a kind of elective affinity operating here. It is thus hardly surprising that authoritarian populist parties are the most visible manifestation of communitarianism to be witnessed today in western democracies – and also in Eastern European states and many emerging countries.

This brings cosmopolitanism into play; and cosmopolitanism confronts authoritarian populism with a global vision. To be precise, the central idea of cosmopolitan democracy is the democratization of international institutions.[30] According to Daniele Archibugi, this is about 'globaliz[ing] democracy while, at the same time, democratizing globalization'.[31] Cosmopolitans ask for the surrender of national sovereignty rights to international organizations and supranational regimes, if they do not even support the vison of a democratic world government, a world parliament, and a global civil society.[32] They advocate a transfer of powers to the United Nations and to the European Union, the multilateral regulation of business issues, world climate conferences, fiscal union in the eurozone, strong human rights regimes at a global level, and institutions that make global redistribution possible. This, of course, only makes sense if it runs in parallel with a democratization of those institutions.

Whatever the strengths of the normative content of theories of cosmopolitan democracy, the weaknesses of these theories lie in implementation. How the general principles are to take the concrete form of specific procedures and institutions is left underdetermined. Two objections are particularly relevant. First, while it is correct to say that many social, economic, and political decisions take effect across borders, setting a

Opportunities and Dangers 153

threshold on how many externalities are needed to establish the right to have a say seems arbitrary for the most part; this is the threshold value question. And, second, even if people were to agree on the requisite international institutions, it would still be extremely difficult to organize suitable democratic processes at the global level; and this is the feasibility question.

To start with the threshold value question, human actions and political decisions continually generate externalities. This means that decisions taken by individuals always influence other individuals, just as decisions taken by collectives touch other collectives. But how much affectedness do you need in order to have a say in the many grey areas of greater or lower interdependence? That the inhabitants of Pacific Island states – who are losing their homes as a result of the climate policies of the major industrialized countries – should have a say in climate policy is a comparatively clear-cut case from a normative point of view. But in other instances assessing the situation is a harder task. If, for example, the Chinese government decides to invest in computer technology, the repercussions may well affect jobs in India and in Silicon Valley; but does the government claim to be entitled to influence Chinese economic policy? The undervaluation of the euro favours German exports, but does that give other countries a say in German tariff policy?

These examples raise questions as to which institutions should be able to decide and on what basis, or who counts as part of a concerned transborder community. Should other countries have the same voting power as the country that took the decision in the first place? Which institutions should decide, and after undergoing what kind of procedure? These are unsolved normative and procedural problems, which show that the congruence or affectedness principle cannot be easily converted into concrete procedures for international politics.[33]

As for the feasibility question, one would have to conclude from a strong version of the concern principle that the rest of the world has to be granted a say in any decision taken by the United States, because its decisions always have far-reaching, in fact global repercussions. This demand may be normatively tenable, but has no hope of being realized, since the one truly global power is among the countries that fought hardest against the transfer of rights of sovereignty to supranational authorities. Other great powers such as China and Russia would equally loath to restrict their sovereignty. Other things being equal, one could even formulate a rule: that more powerful countries are less willing to cede sovereignty rights to international or supranational organizations.[34]

Liberal globalists are aware of these problems of implementation. This is why they concentrate on creating international bodies that should deal democratically with the kind of problems that can be tackled only by pooling sovereignty. Even here, however, problems are likely to arise. The bigger and more complex the political spaces, the harder it is to govern them democratically. Outside the nation-state, things like the equal participation of citizens, transparency and predictability in political decision-making, and parliamentary oversight of the executive can be implemented only in rudimentary form – at best.

The cosmopolitan answer to the feasibility problem is twofold. First, one may counter that arguments in favour of a limit to the size of democracy have no empirical support. Mathias Koenig-Archibugi (2012) notes that, apart from the existence of formal political structures, there are no necessary preconditions for democracy in the strict sense of the word. He rejects any thesis that expounds the impossibility of a global democracy and holds, on the contrary, that political communities get constructed and transformed over time. Besides, the idea of belonging to a particular nation developed only during the later eighteenth and early nineteenth centuries. Second, one may ask whether feasibility would not increase over time, if current transnational trends in economics and communications persist. If they do, then individual attitudes, political mobilization, and the distribution of political power will no longer correspond exclusively to the model of nation-state democracy.

Leaving this debate aside, liberal globalists are inclined to underestimate the tension between the arguments in favour of global political measures and the social conditions for majority decisions. They emphasize the liberal elements of democratic self-determination, especially the need to protect individual rights, the rule of law, and the power of the better argument. In so doing, they seem to forget that decisions by a majority constitute the core of democratic processes and that minority rights make no sense in the absence of majority decisions. They also partly overlook the fact that in international institutions the executive or bureaucracy takes precedence over the legislature. They thus advocate an understanding of democracy that downgrades the role of elections, parties, and parliaments while elevating the role of NMIs. This implicit understanding of democracy confirms the elitist bias of liberal globalists. It is the fear of this kind of cosmopolitanism that has facilitated the rise of authoritarian populists. Authoritarian populism, on the other hand, endangers the liberal foundations of democracy, as we have seen. Ultimately, then, both concepts are deficient in the form in which they are currently practised, and this is the dilemma of democracy under globalization: either national majoritarian decision-making excludes those affected and cancels civil rights, or lawmaking is done without democratic decision-making and participation. In any case, the Habermasian postulate that democracy and the rule of law have the same origins finds itself undermined in practice.

7

Democratic Action in the Face of Regression

In public debate, there is a tendency to exonerate oneself for the outrageous impositions of contemporary populism by explaining its rise through the shortcomings of citizens. Three different narratives can contribute, intentionally or unintentionally, to this exoneration.

The first narrative uniformly characterizes the voters of authoritarian populist parties as 'Nazis' who incorrigibly cling to racist patterns of thought, while the enlightened majority have rid themselves of them. Indeed, it cannot be denied that authoritarian populist parties are elected because some people think in racist categories or reject pluralistic lifestyles. But this does not answer the question of why so many people turn to authoritarian populist parties nowadays and why so many of them do so in the name of democracy. The second narrative characterizes authoritarian populism as a temporary phenomenon, a consequence of modernization that prompts people who live in the past to protest against the liberalization of society introduced by younger generations. In this narrative, authoritarian populist protest is not a sign of regression but a last flicker of atavism. It is enough, then, to wait patiently for the return of progress. Third and finally, in a globalized and complex world, part of the population is considered unfit for modern democracy on the grounds that it is too ill-informed or has been misled by charlatans. The main concern in this scenario is to protect the functionality of the political system from the simple-minded.

All three of these approaches relieve us of the need to ponder whether the 'system' that authoritarian populists attack is actually flawed, and why populist slogans actually work. We then don't have to explain how it is that an arrogant claim such as to be the true mouthpiece of the people does not get indignantly rejected. Nor do we have to ask why so many people believe that a billionaire like Donald Trump or a thoroughly elitist figure like Boris Johnson speaks for those who do not own skyscrapers and do not have Eton or Oxford degrees. We have tried to answer these questions in this book. We argue that authoritarian populism is listened to because there is a kernel of truth in its critique of how liberal democracy works. From this perspective, democratic action needs more than a critique of the shortcomings of authoritarian populists: it also needs a critique of the status quo in our democracies.

Politics in our democracies finds itself in a crisis of representation. It exhibits a systematic bias, which favours certain ways of thinking and social groups. On the one hand, more and more empirical studies show that not all citizens are equally well represented by parliaments. According to Mark Bovens and Anchrit Wille (2017), in a 'diploma democracy' the attitudes of the elected representatives align with the attitudes of groups whose members have higher educational levels and work in qualified professional groups, whereas the gulf that separates them from those with fewer resources is obvious. The decisions of parliaments reflect the preferences of the better-off. The concerns of the poor, and especially of the poorly educated, are taken into account only when they coincide with those of people of higher educational or professional status. Higher social classes not only are numerically

158   The Democratic Regression

over-represented in parliaments but also receive preferential treatment in the decisions that are taken there.

By the same token, more and more decision-making powers have been transferred to NMIs, which are only indirectly legitimized and cannot be sanctioned by being voted out of office. Apart from courts and central banks, NMIs also comprise the European Commission and other international institutions. These institutions are set up to take decision-making out of the political arena and hand it over to the experts. But their decisions, epistemically correct as they are supposed to be, have political repercussions and are not neutral in orientation. In particular, international NMIs aim to facilitate the free play of markets across borders and to defend individual rights against collective restrictions. This may be normatively desirable in many cases, but it advances the concerns of well-resourced liberal globalists far more than those of the less educated and the regionally confined.

The interplay between the unequal responsiveness of parliaments and their partial disempowerment exacerbates political inequality and is perceived as such. Contemporary democracy is progressively accused of a lack of openness and representativeness, and those who share this assessment vote more and more for authoritarian populism. The whole situation is socially skewed. In surveys, people with lower education or with jobs of lower social status are much more likely than their better-off counterparts to agree with statements such as 'politics is run by a closed caste and people "like me" have no way of influencing it'. Those who feel that 'the toffs' are inaccessible or deaf to their concerns often turn away from politics altogether, or else towards authoritarian populist parties. 'The toffs' can be both those who have no understanding for the socially disadvantaged *and* the liberal know-it-alls, who have no idea of the concerns of a small business owner. Anyway, when the game is rigged, or at least seems to be, you stop playing it or trying to torpedo it.[1] But it is much harder to take this

Democratic Action in the Face of Regression   159

bias seriously than to dismiss a group of citizens as hopelessly deluded or to bet on inevitable progress.

Although today's populists have put their finger on the wound of liberal democracy, their answers do not solve the problem. There is nothing to suggest that authoritarian populism does democracy any good. Where authoritarian populist parties have come to power, they damage the democracy instead of extending its reach or dismantling existing inequalities. Contrary to popular belief, there is hardly any empirical evidence that the successes of populist parties have systematically boosted voter turnout and thereby reduced one form of political inequality. The populist diagnosis of the problems does raise important questions, but, from a democratic standpoint, the answers are wrong. In Brazil, India, Poland, Hungary, and the United States the quality of democracy has deteriorated because the populists' chief concern has been to preserve their own might and to hollow out the separation of powers. Imprisoned in an 'us against them' scenario, they regard other parties as their enemies. At the same time they perceive any criticism from the media or any correction issued by courts as an attack. Anyone who believes to be the unadulterated voice of the people (understood as a kind of monad) is unwilling to make compromises and will not accept the separation of powers as a principle in exercising the law.

Unlike in the past, nowadays democratic backsliding is brought about by elected governments. No tanks are rolling through the streets, broadcasting centres are not taken by force, dissidents are not executed. But courts are manipulated or disempowered, news editors replaced, television stations turned into government press agencies, and elections rigged to rule out the possibility of defeat. Even the unwritten rules of democracy are disregarded by populists – or respected only when they can be used to the populists' own advantage.[2]

The optimism about progress that reigned after the end of the Cold War has suffered severe damage since the turn of the

160 The Democratic Regression

millennium. On the one hand, the number of democracies has dropped; on the other, the quality of democratic institutions in consolidated democracies has gone down. The past fifteen years have seen a democratic regression, which consists in a double alienation. Should this downward trend prove to be short-lived and followed by a further expansion and consolidation of democracy, this phase of autocratization could perhaps be tolerated. However, there is good reason to suspect that the enormous spread of democracy after the Second World War was tied to circumstances that do not continue to exist in the same form. A regime of 'embedded liberalism' made it possible to reconcile international integration with national autonomy, and a well-developed welfare state with high tax rates.[3] Nowadays globalization and European integration have made it more difficult to sustain national 'variants of capitalism' or 'welfare regimes', because the competition between locations has driven up the costs of protecting the disadvantaged and at the same time international organizations have made deeper interventions into national politics, thus reducing the scope for regulation in almost every area.

Globalization has created a new cleavage. Its origins are socio-structural (presence or absence of a globalization-level education) and ideological (cosmopolitanism vs communitarianism). The liberal globalists and the authoritarian populists are its organizational protagonists. There is much to suggest that this opposition has inscribed itself into political systems and is not something that will go away swiftly. The strategies that can be derived from the three justification narratives – wait and see, brush it aside, gloss it over – are therefore unlikely to succeed.

Politics faces the predicament that the tension between necessary transborder cooperation and democratic decision-making cannot be resolved unilaterally. A 'third transformation' of democracy, one that reproduced at the supranational level what had been accomplished at a national level, is not yet in sight. Meanwhile, there is a growing need to improve the fit between the political decision-making powers and economic transactions or global ecological problems that are progressively cross-border. Between half-functioning democratic participation and political problem-solving capability there is a tension that both naïve cosmopolitanism and nationally oriented communitarianism deny, each in its own way. As far as the former is concerned, it is possible to have democracy beyond states, and it would not be tied to specific preconditions that until now have been fulfilled mainly in nation-states. True, democracy cannot be inextricably linked to the nation-state from a logical or a normative perspective, but historically there has been a connection that we cannot simply ignore. Authoritarian populists dispute the necessity of cross-border cooperation. The slogan 'Make America Great Again' rests on the notion of being more successful with less international cooperation and of being able to shed one's responsibility to others. From this angle climate change must be contested, otherwise one would have to admit that this problem cannot be solved without working together. It cannot be coincidence then that the Covid-19 pandemic was played down by populist governments – by Bolsonaro, by Trump, initially by Johnson – even though this led to thousands of avoidable deaths. They would rather live with the consequences of the virus than recognize the necessity of international cooperation and the importance of scientific expertise. The predicament, then, is that we need to work together internationally, but we have not found a suitable answer to the question of how to do this successfully and democratically.

The rise of authoritarian populism has prompted some observers to conclude that the worst thing for democracy is to overstretch it. As a rule, the starting point for these considerations is an approach that transfers an economic logic to political processes. Whether people become involved in politics or simply keep themselves politically informed depends on

162   The Democratic Regression

whether, in their view, the benefits are greater than the costs. However, because keeping oneself up to date is laborious and political engagement competes with more lucrative or enjoyable activities, the estimated costs were already high overall; and in the age of globalization and regional and supranational multilevel governance they have risen still further. At the same time, the perceived benefits have sunk, because the accessibility of political systems has decreased and the number of relevant institutions has increased. As a result, it has become even harder for the individual to be heard. Many voters feel that their vote carries no weight. These assumptions about political motivation suggest that most people have good reasons not to keep themselves politically informed. Therefore, as in Schumpeter's infamous dictum, when it comes to politics the intellectual capacity of the typical citizen 'drops to a lower level'.[4] The problem with democracy, from this perspective, is that people are clueless in point of exercising reason, but are allowed to take part in decision-making.

This perspective on politics has been revived in more recent times. Bryan Caplan compares the economic attitudes of ordinary citizens with those of doctoral students in economics and comes to the conclusion that most people have no idea and one ought not to listen to them. In a popular philosophy book titled *Against Democracy* (2016), Jason Brennan divides the population into three groups: Vulcans, Hobbits, and Hooligans. Democracy, he argues, demands Vulcans, who can weigh up the advantages and disadvantages of political decisions in an unemotional and completely rational manner. They are persuaded by good arguments and always keep themselves fully informed. Unfortunately, only a few people live up to this ideal. There are instead plenty of Hobbits, says Brennan: these worry only about their immediate neighbourhood and seldom bother about politics. And, apart from this relatively harmless group of indifferents, there are also political Hooligans, who are passionate but completely deaf to rational argument.

Democratic Action in the Face of Regression   163

Hobbits and Hooligans, who seem to have sprung from Jürgen Habermas's nightmares, are unfit for democracy and therefore should be excluded from it as elegantly as possible. This is why Brennan suggests, among other things, that there should be an aptitude test that must be passed by anyone who wants to vote. If only rational people voted, the election results, too, would be more rational, and this would lead to better decisions.[5] These examples of the new elitist theory of democracy offer those who see themselves as Mr Spock a convenient explanation for the crisis of democracy: the ignorance of humankind awakens the monster of populism.

Such views are normatively untenable. Above all, they confuse the cause with the remedy. Restricting the game of democracy to Vulcans is not a good solution, if only because it would simply formalize and codify a trend that has been going on for decades: to limit access to the political decision-making system to the better educated, who possess transnational social capital and belong to a well-qualified professional group. On the contrary, it is precisely this limitation that has prompted resistance and has strengthened the authoritarian populists. The proposals of Caplan, Brennan, and others would merely accelerate the double alienation from democracy that we have noted: they would put an even greater distance between the political system and the democratic ideal, thus triggering even more authoritarian resistance to the political system.

If it is true that people are dissatisfied with how democracy works *also* because there are good reasons to be dissatisfied, then we need to think of ways to slow down the process of alienation and to make democracy more democratic. There are, from our perspective, ten points to note. We divide them into four groups: (1) general recommendations for politics and more concrete recommendations for institutional reform at both (2) the national and (3) the European and international levels; and (4) a recommendation for political education that, again, is very general in character.

7.1 General Recommendations

We start with three considerations that relate to people's political outlook and only indirectly imply reforms.

1 WITHSTAND TECHNOCRATIC TEMPTATIONS. Crises demand swift action without lengthy political debate. When a bank run or the spread of a virus must be prevented, there is little time for public deliberation. This is why crises are the province of the executive and of NMIs. When Mario Draghi, then president of the European Central Bank (ECB), famously uttered the words 'Whatever it takes' in the face of speculation about the collapse of the euro, this was effective because the ECB was ready to act immediately and did not have to go through a lengthy parliamentary process to decide on its own measures. In crises, it is the executive and expertise that are called for; parliamentary decisions, if any, are fast-tracked. This weakens parliaments as a whole and the opposition in particular. Now, this may be justified in times of imminent danger, but crisis mode must not turn into common practice. And yet, precisely because negotiation processes are so laborious, it can be tempting to bypass the public and the parliament.

This is why, for some time now, political science literature has been pointing out that a technocratic temptation lurks alongside the populist one. Technocracy and populism share a sceptical attitude towards the sluggishness of party-political and parliamentary decision-making. China in particular, but also other autocracies, Singapore for example, are viewed with thinly veiled admiration for the way their projects are pushed through, unhindered by the many opportunities for delay that constitutional democracy offers. Technocratic decision-making is justified by its supposedly superior results. Still, which outcomes are desirable or which method can best attain a given end is always controversial. Of course, all political systems legitimize themselves also through policy outcomes (output legitimacy), but this is no substitute for democratic procedure (input legitimacy).

Our recent past has already witnessed one instance of fear in the face of the superior planning capabilities of a non-democratic system. When the Soviet Union announced the launch of the first artificial earth satellite, Sputnik I, on 4 October 1957 and was able at the same time to look back on several years of impressive growth rates, it caused considerable shock among western democracies. Would Soviet communism be able to catch up with them economically and technically and leave them behind? From today's perspective, these fears seem almost absurd – which of course has a lot to do with how the western democracies developed after the so-called Sputnik shock. The successful NASA programme and the moon landing in 1969 can be mentioned here. More important, however, was the fact that the long 1960s became a decade of democratization. The civil rights movement in the United States, the student unrest in the second half of the decade, and the many and various democratic reform governments led by John F. Kennedy, Olof Palme, Willy Brandt, and others, all sent the same message: 'Dare more democracy'.

This answer rested on a belief in the superiority of democracy. Economists distinguish between static and dynamic efficiency. Static efficiency determines how, under constant framework conditions, a particular goal can be attained at the lowest possible cost. Dynamic efficiency aims at finding the best solution in the face of continuously changing framework conditions and relies on successive adjustments, second-round effects, and impacts that change over time. Even though there may be situations in which authoritarian or technocratic political systems prove superior in terms of static efficiency, democracy is better suited to attain dynamic efficiency.

We should therefore resist technocratic inclinations and look for new possibilities of democratization in order to overcome stagnation. Quite often, when the implementation of

166 The Democratic Regression

projects in western democracies is agonizingly slow, this has to do not with the democratic form of decision-making as much as with a bureaucratized and highly regulated form of implementation. This can be dealt with democratically. Technocratic political approaches, on the other hand, share with populism not only its aversion to a procedural and deliberative understanding of democracy but also its decisionism and the notion of 'this is simply a matter of doing the right thing' – and what is right is not controversial among reasonable people under given circumstances.

2 TRUST THE CITIZENS. Faced with supposedly irrational decisions such as Brexit and 'wrong' election outcomes in Brazil, Hungary, Turkey, and the United States, disenchantment with the citizenry is growing among the mainstream parties. One often hears the complaint that voters have no idea what politics is all about, especially since those who protest most loudly are conspicuously ignorant of the basics in politics. Moreover, the widespread weariness of having to argue with an ungrateful public is one of the main reasons why politicians succumb to the technocratic temptation – as already described. In Germany, disenchantment with voters also feeds on the fact that, as surveys show, with the exception of Alternative for Germany (AfD) representatives, the candidates for the Bundestag assess very positively the way in which German democracy functions, while among the population sceptical attitudes are rife. This split could invite reflection on why perceptions diverge; but it can also be read as proof of how little people understand about politics.

The second interpretation carries the risk of alienating people further; it would be better to enable a democratic politics instead. Citizens' assemblies could be used to discuss voters' perceptions of democracy and the opportunities in which they want to have a say. For their desire to participate in politics is almost as great as their mistrust of it. The

Democratic Action in the Face of Regression   167

Constitutional Convention in Ireland provides an example of how even complex topics can be negotiated with the participation of citizens.[6] But a negotiation process of this kind must have a concrete objective and should not remain without consequences. In order to embark on such a path, however, politicians would first have to accept that even a democracy that functions well by international standards can be improved. Democracy is always an ongoing process. Hence citizens and citizen participation ought to be trusted.

3 DISMANTLE CONTEXTS OF INEQUALITY. Any direct connection between income distribution and the success of authoritarian populist parties is no more than tenuous. Even so, inequality and insecurity are two drivers of political alienation, which in turn is a breeding ground for populism. The more people feel that their incomes are insecure, the less they trust politics, so that there is a close connection between economic uncertainty and political mistrust.[7] Political disenchantment is prevalent especially in regions that have experienced a relative decline – in parts of the Ruhr, in the American Rust Belt, in the north of England, and in the north-east of France.[8] In a certain way, this also applies to parts of the new federal states that were formerly part of East Germany. A striking feature of more recent times is precisely this divergent development of German regions. The resulting regional differences accumulate and progressively reinforce the three dimensions of inequality: smaller incomes, fewer assets, and a feeling of being far from the political centre and culturally detached. Contexts of inequality emerge. The socio-spatial concentration of people with poorer life chances in all three dimensions undermines the sense of being part of a society and of being recognized as an equal by those who are better off.[9]

We do not believe that there are simple economic measures that could make authoritarian populism disappear, but politics has lost sight of the need to create equal living conditions for

168 The Democratic Regression

all. This is particularly true of separate geographical areas. The thing to do is dismantle these contexts of inequality, because democracy is based on equality. Authoritarian populism, on the other hand, emphasizes difference.

7.2 Reforms to National Political Systems

The second bundle of our recommendations relates more concretely to the institutional design of democratic decision-making in national political systems. What democratic reforms could alleviate the problems described? We will start with the obvious.

4 AVOID FALSE REFORMS. In all consolidated democracies there are initiatives that have advocated political reforms for years. But the reforms they have initiated in recent times have satisfied the wishes of the middle classes rather than seriously expanding democracy. For example, the reforms to the franchise in Hamburg and Bremen have enabled electors in plural voting systems to split their votes or to give more than one vote to the same candidate, thereby enabling greater participation. But this has given rise to a franchise that is excessively complicated and disadvantages people who are less involved in politics. In districts where turnout in elections is low, the number of invalid votes, too, has risen. More democracy was created, if a wider range of choices also counts as such – but only for some.[10] The introduction of participatory budgeting in many European cities was similarly misguided. Unlike in Latin American models, here only opportunities for pseudo-participation were on offer, since the power to decide on a fixed budget was only rarely entrusted to citizens. In the end, authority over expenditure remained with the municipal administration.[11] But anyone who wants participation must let the citizens actually decide. False reforms are those that

Democratic Action in the Face of Regression 169

either increase only the surplus of academics or are primarily of a symbolic nature, and thus widen the gap between rhetoric and reality.

Two things seem particularly important in this connection. First, enhanced citizen participation should not simply repeat, let alone increase, the political selectivity of parliaments. Additional participation should therefore be decided by lot or by some similar procedure. This will encourage people to participate who otherwise would not. The logic of mini-publics can serve as a model.[12] Second, simultaneity is important in public participation. Deliberative citizen forums, as they are called, often take place in the very early stages of policy development. The results are then fed into the rest of the political process, in which not only parliamentarians but also experts and bureaucrats are involved. In the end, the original suggestions are barely recognizable. This has the potential to generate further frustration. But if experts, bureaucrats, and members of the public are all involved at the same time, the will of participants can be reconciled with practical necessities, while in an ideal scenario people should also develop an understanding of the legal and technical constraints.

5 CHANGE PARTY RECRUITMENT MODELS. Why do people not participate? Because they do not want to, because they are not able to, and because nobody asks them to – so claims a famous rule of thumb in political science.[13] They do not want to participate because the political system seems to them inaccessible or because they simply have no interest in politics; they are not able to participate because the resources are unequally distributed; and they are not asked to participate because the party recruitment models are highly selective. In a study of why blue-collar workers are so underrepresented in US politics, Nicholas Carnes showed that party selection processes that go on within parties exclude motivated and competent people. During searches for suitable candidates, the ones who

170 The Democratic Regression

get considered resemble members already active in the party – which is why white males with academic degrees are often chosen. It follows that people who do not fit this profile should be approached and encouraged.[14] The composition of parliaments not only influences the decisions that are taken there but also sends out signals to the electorate. In Britain, Oliver Heath shows that the disappearance of working-class MPs is closely linked to the decline in working-class voter turnout.[15]

The social gulf between representatives and the people they represent is harmful in another way. Representation requires, at least in principle, an ongoing dialogue between the elected and the electorate. Those who represent the population must follow their own conscience, of course; but they must also justify and explain their decisions – especially if these decisions contradict the preferences of the people they represent. Yet, although the political system in most of the consolidated democracies has numerous negotiation processes at the elite level – within coalitions, for example, or between the two houses of parliament – the dialogue with the governed is in danger of being neglected.

As far as the underrepresentation of women in politics is concerned, discussions on quota regulations have been going on for years. After an initial resistance, the equal representation of the sexes has, in various ways and to varying degrees, become a reality in many parties and committees. At this point we would like to ask – and we are deliberatively provocative here – whether the unequal gender representation that still exists in parliament is not a relatively minor problem by comparison with the unequal representation of different educational and professional groups.[16] The aim is not for one to be played off against the other. In any case, combating alienation from democracy is not solely about ensuring that women with university degrees feel that they are being heard. From the perspective of such alienation, other underrepresented groups need to be treated equally too. No one is asking for quotas for

Democratic Action in the Face of Regression 171

all groups; but, given democracy's promise of equality, it is vital that recruitment processes discriminate positively, in favour of those whose representation is, on balance, poor. Men, and especially women, from a migrant background or from the precariat in the service sector are not only underrepresented but virtually absent from parliaments.

6 MORE PUBLIC OVERSIGHT OF NON-MAJORITARIAN INSTITUTIONS. NMIs cannot be allowed to disappear from politics. This is because there are regulatory areas with high technical requirements and because both the minorities and democracy itself need mechanisms that should protect them from the passions of the population.[17] But, if it is true that the actors in these institutions have distinctly cosmopolitan inclinations (see Chapter 4), then the decisions taken there require an enhanced degree of transparency and control. The primary goal, then, should be an enhanced consultation of citizens. During every parliamentary legislative procedure, vast numbers of lawyers, economists, and expert specialists get a hearing. The majority listens to the experts before it comes to a decision. In a mirror image of this process, experts should also listen to the majority before passing judgement. Procedures are needed for consulting the groups affected by the decision of a NMI. To a certain extent, this system is already in place, but it functions on a comparatively small scale for the most part. The time allowed by central bankers for consultations with citizens is limited. This kind of consultation ought not to cast doubt on the independence, say, of judges. The principles on which NMIs make decisions should be retained but limited in scope. What matters here is transparency and a broadening of decision makers' perspective.[18]

Additionally, the courts should remain cautious in that they should not impose on politicians too detailed regulations regarding what they can and cannot do. The protection of fundamental rights should leave room for manoeuvre, but

172   The Democratic Regression

not pre-empt political decisions. Different political majorities
should be able to come to different decisions, so long as the
relevant principle is upheld. In the European Union, this also
means that there may be a multiplicity of ways in which EU
laws can be implemented in different countries (as is guaranteed for directives). From the point of view of democratic
theory, it is undesirable for courts to take the place of legislators. The separation of powers requires the judiciary to exercise
self-restraint.

7.3   Reforms beyond the Nation-State

But reforms are required in European and international
institutions too. While it is correct to say that international
institutions are very difficult to democratize, this is not an
excuse for not even trying.

7 DEMOCRATIZING THE EUROPEAN UNION. At the time of
the European elections in 2019, there were heated discussions
about whether the lead candidate principle would make the
European Union more democratic. The idea was to link the
presidency of the European Commission to the election results
in such a way that only those who had previously stood as
lead candidate for a party could become president. As is well
known, things turned out rather differently.

Viewed in isolation, a linkage of this kind would in reality
have contributed little to the democratization of the European
Union.[19] It would have had to be embedded in a batch of
reforms. On the one hand, elections are elections only if it is
possible to find out the contents of the 'package' at reasonable
expense. It must therefore be clear from the outset who is
running for what position. It cannot be just about faces. The
decisive factors are the attitudes and convictions behind the
faces and a reliable translation of the preferences associated

Democratic Action in the Face of Regression 173

with an election into European decision-making procedures. A feeling like 'Yes, I may have lost this time, but next time I can win' will arise only in the presence of these factors. Political competition in European institutions is the basic prerequisite. This calls for transnational lists of candidates and pre-polling in the European party 'families' or groups, to establish a manifesto. Then the election campaigns will no longer be primarily about national interests or about punishing the national government. Arguments will have to be made instead about the right path for Europe. So the denationalization of public debates will also be dealt with. In addition, the European Council will need to refrain from intervening retrospectively in candidate selection.

On the other hand, it should be noted that the lead candidate principle is borrowed from parliamentary systems in which the government requires the support of a majority in parliament. Then usually (though not always) it is the strongest parliamentary party that provides the head of the executive. With the help of transnational lists of candidates, the European Parliament could also form coalitions to elect a Commission president in which the strongest party is not represented. But in the parliamentary systems of nation-states all members of government come, as a rule, from the governing coalition. By contrast, European commissioners are nominated by national governments, and thus form an oversized coalition of a great variety of parties. The nomination procedure for commissioners would have to be altered as well. It is evident that the institutional democratization of the EU cannot be accomplished through isolated measures but requires a broader strategy.

A requirement of this kind is far-reaching, but not eccentric. Even in Eurosceptic Great Britain, former senior adviser Robert Cooper wrote a 'blue skies' paper on the European Commission at the prime minister's invitation, proposing that the Blair administration use genuine elections to overcome Euroscepticism in the country:

174   The Democratic Regression

> The problem with European institutions is that we have given them wide-ranging powers – probably too wide-ranging – but none of us trust[s] them. We deal with this problem by making sure that the European Union is weak. Good management consists of giving organisation[s] clear limited tasks, and giving them full authority to carry them out, and making them to bear the consequences of getting things wrong. In Europe we have done exactly the opposite.[20]

Against this background, Cooper recommends an 'elected commission'. The commission would then have to answer for its ideas and convictions to the voters. So this would not be about the lead candidates' faces; it would be about competing political programmes that have to be presented in an election campaign. Voters should be in a position to ascribe particular policies and programmes to particular actors. Only when this is achieved will an election be an election.

8 LEARNING FROM THE SWISS. Another way of democratizing the European Union can be found by looking at Switzerland. In the debate about the democratic deficit in the European Union, which has already been going on for a very long time, people often borrow from classical systems of government such as parliamentarianism or presidentialism, even though not all the conditions for these systems exist in the European Union.[21] If one looks for models, the completely untypical Swiss system could be a better bet. In this system an all-party government is in office and cannot be voted out by parliament – the Bundesversammlung (Federal Assembly). Thus the relationship between the executive and legislature corresponds to that found in a presidential system. Parliament can have shifting majorities for legislation, which is atypical of parliamentary regimes. If a party 'loses' a vote in parliament, the government does not end, and this introduces a greater degree of flexibility. The Bundesrat (Federal Council) – that is, in the Swiss system,

the government – must engage in complex negotiations and take very different (party-political) interests into account without being able to change the coalition. As result, the parliamentary and the electoral control of the government are comparatively weak.

Conversely, citizens have the possibility of exercising a direct influence on proceedings through a highly developed system of direct democracy. In Switzerland, a federal system with a high requirement for consensus is enriched through the procedures of a direct democracy. By analogy, this would call for the introduction of Europewide referendums on European issues. Such referendums would be fundamentally different from national ones. Their principal aim would be to compensate the voters for their marginal impact on the election of the government and (again as in Switzerland) to promote communal political debate in a multilingual political community.[22] The lack of a European *demos* ('people') should not give reason not to think about paths that would lead to the construction of a community. Of course, referendums are and would remain a delicate matter. Distribution issues would have to be left out, as well as small details. But voting on constitutional questions – such as new treaties – should be considered as a possibility. In any event, Europewide votes would be required, and not just a few isolated votes in individual countries.

9 COSMOPOLITAN PASSION. Advocates of the liberal world order must stop being defensive and speak out boldly for a cosmopolitan worldview. The widespread tendency to agree things on reasonable terms at international level and then sell them at home as if no alternative were available may be the simplest strategy in the short term; but in the long term it is damaging because it obstructs genuine debate in society and an open-ended public examination of world politics. Representation thrives on justification; democracy, on open competition between ideas. Ultimately there cannot be a

176 The Democratic Regression

half-cosmopolitanism that delegates decision-making to the global level and confines democratic debate to national issues. But that seems to be precisely what the strategy of many liberal globalists amounts to. And, of course, this half-cosmopolitanism simply strengthens the hand of the authoritarian populists.

The former federal chancellor, Angela Merkel, rarely campaigned passionately for her policies, often preferring to remain silent for long periods or to argue with the inevitability of decisions. If the opposition plays a role in government at least through the Bundesrat, as in Germany, it finds it difficult to dissociate itself from the government and to put forward alternative proposals. The pressure for consensus exerted by the German governmental system produces decisions that can enjoy the support of a broad coalition, but do so at the expense of preserving the difference between parties and political conflict. This invites the comment, exploited by the populists, that all other parties are pursuing the same policies. Democracy needs conflict and political competition. This conflict must be transferred to international institutions and from there reimported into national politics. The instrumentalization of international institutions for the sake of preventing political conflict domestically will prove a dead end in the long run.

This is primarily an appeal to those in government. But one should also ask whether a compulsion to debate international decisions is institutionally created. Parliamentary debates before and after journeys of the chancellery or of important ministers to international conferences could be a small, but perfectly efficient measure in this respect.

7.4 Political Education

Democracies need political education. The aims of democratic education obviously need to adapt to changed framework

Democratic Action in the Face of Regression

conditions and should train the citizenry to deal with contradictions, corrections, and conflicting aims.

10 ENCOURAGING TOLERANCE FOR AMBIGUITY. Back in 2003, none other than Sir Ralf Dahrendorf was already cautioning against authoritarian tendencies. He was aware much earlier than others of many of the developments described in this book. He said:

> Populism is simple, democracy is complex. Ultimately this may be the most important difference between these two forms of relating to the people. More specifically, populism rests on the conscious attempt to simplify problems. Therein lies its attractiveness; that is its recipe for success.[23]

Let us go back further, to 1989. A few months before the fall of the Berlin Wall, the same Sir Ralf Dahrendorf gave a one-hour video interview. The interviewer, Harry Kreisler of the University of California in Berkeley, asked him at the end what message he would like to send young people. His answer was: 'Live with complexity. . . . The world is complicated. Don't try to simplify it.'[24]

In the thirty-four years since that interview, simplification has triumphed. The Internet, the filter bubbles, and the tweets have contributed enormously. This is the cognitive soil in which populism grows and democracy withers. Political education must take countermeasures. In Germany it was introduced as a central plank of 're-education' after the Second World War. Our subject, political science, was an essential part of the strategy. Political science was established in Germany after the war as the science of democracy, although it had already taken an empirical turn in the United States. Against this background, the core of democratic education, even today, remains the doctrine of democratic ideals and of the advantages of democratic institutions. This ideal theory

178   The Democratic Regression

needs to be supplemented with knowledge of the complexity of democratic decision-making and with general competence in dealing with complexity. There are no measures that do not have problematic side effects. There are no simple fixes, and the world is full of dilemmas and paradoxes. We must recognize and take account of complexity, especially in the age of globalization. The population of a democratic state needs to be able to deal with diversity, ambiguity, and new insights that may turn out to be wrong the day after tomorrow. Fostering tolerance for ambiguity should therefore be a primary goal of political education.

None of the ten suggestions we have put forward will be uncontroversial or will, on its own, solve the problem of authoritarian populism. However, we would actually contradict the diagnosis of the crisis that we have presented if we went on to present a ready-made catalogue of reforms that claimed to revive democracy in some miraculous fashion. If there are good reasons for devolving some decisions to NMIs but doing so involves a loss of democracy, attempts to find a solution can only aim to reduce the inevitable tensions that will arise. If we take the problem seriously, there is no question of offering simple answers, as might be expected at the end of a book of this kind. Instead we need to find starting points that are consistent with our specific account of the political causes of authoritarian populism. The answer cannot be just to limit democracy, because that would ultimately lead to its abolition. The defence of democracy requires more democracy.

Notes

Notes to Chapter 1
1 Milanović 2016, p. 31.
2 Firebaugh 2003.
3 Levitsky and Way 2002.
4 Bermeo 2016.
5 Mudde 2004, p. 143.
6 Hartmann 2020.
7 Manow 2019.
8 Norris and Inglehart 2019.
9 Schattschneider 1960, p. 35.
10 Mair 2013.
11 Mounk and Kyle 2018.
12 Gosepath 2020.
13 Kriesi 2014, pp. 361–2.
14 Levitsky and Way 2002.

Notes to Chapter 2
1 Fukuyama 1989.
2 Hegel 2011, p. 18.
3 Fukuyama 1992, pp. 49–50.
4 See Koopmans 2019, ch. 2.

180 Notes to pages 17–20

5 Fukuyama was not the only one to retain an optimistic view of progress. The Harvard psychologist Steven Pinker has recently stated with force his belief in the idea of historical progress and in the concomitant spread of democracy (Pinker 2018, Part II, esp. ch. 4). In political science, this optimism is most clearly reflected in theories of modernization. With reference to democracy, the works of Ronald Inglehart and Christian Welzel are of central importance (see e.g. Inglehart and Welzel 2005). According to them, social modernization leads to a rise in the level of education, which in turn makes democratization much more probable as a next step.
6 Held 1995, p. 147.
7 See also Williams 2005.
8 Habermas 1996.
9 Keane 2009; Pettit 1999; Skinner 2002.
10 Dahl 1971, p. 1.
11 Dahl 1971, p. 3.
12 The conditions are: (1) freedom to organize (politically); (2) freedom of opinion; (3) an active and (4) a passive franchise for all adult citizens, with as few exceptions as possible; (5) the unhindered right of parties (or civil society organizations) to try to attract votes or support; (6) free and fair elections; (7) sources of information that are independent of the government; and (8) institutions that ensure that there is a connection between political decisions and the will of the majority. Dahl later cancelled the final condition, since it was implicit in the ones that preceded it.
13 Dahl used the term 'polyarchy' (rule of the many) in place of democracy as a linguistic marker of the fact that really existing forms of government are clearly distinct from the theoretical ideal. Although many later democracy indexes refer back to Dahl, they are less reticent about using the term democracy.
14 Vanhanen 2000, p. 257.
15 Schmalz-Bruns 1995.
16 Beitz 1989.
17 Bachrach and Baratz 1977.

Notes to pages 20–34

18 See Lijphart 1999.
19 Bühlmann et al. 2012.
20 For the basics, see Coppedge et al. 2011.
21 See Schmidt (2010 [1995]) for an overview.
22 This index assesses whether free and fair elections, universal suffrage, freedom of opinion, freedom of association, and separation of powers are in place and whether the legal–constitutional oversight of political decision-making is possible.
23 On different occasions Vanhanen defined different threshold values. In this instance we follow Vanhanen 2000.
24 Bermeo 2016; Diamond 2015; Foa and Mounk 2016.
25 Inglehart and Welzel 2005.
26 Jahn 2006: Zürn 2001.
27 Zürn 2018a.
28 Ambrose 1983 [1971].
29 Kolko and Kolko 1972.
30 Katzenstein 1985.
31 Ruggie 1982.
32 Esping-Andersen 1990; Hall and Soskice 2001.
33 Katzenstein 1985.
34 Esping-Andersen 1990.
35 Russett and Oneal 2001.
36 Scharpf 1987; Benedetto, Hix, and Mastrorocco 2020.
37 Leibfried and Zürn 2006.
38 Beisheim et al. 1999; Held et al. 1999.
39 Van der Pijl 1998.
40 Streeck 1995.
41 See e.g. Kelley 2004a, 2004b.
42 Schimmelfennig 2003.
43 See Brozus 2002.
44 See Kahler 1995.
45 Zangl 2006.
46 Chesterman 2004.
47 Zangl and Zürn 2003.
48 Deitelhoff 2006.

182   Notes to pages 34–52

49 Börzel and Zürn 2021.
50 Zürn, Binder, and Ecker-Ehrhardt 2012.
51 We are using the V-Dem index for liberal democracy in a desire to avoid being accused of applying an unrealistically sophisticated concept of democracy, so as to be able to issue warnings about its decline. But in essence the results would not have changed, had we chosen a more sophisticated version.
52 Lührmann et al. 2018.
53 Maerz et al. 2020, p. 1.
54 Levitsky and Ziblatt 2018.
55 One conspicuous feature of the list is that it contains five current member states of the European Union and two countries (Serbia and Turkey) that are trying to gain membership (or at least have been trying for a long time).
56 Levitsky and Ziblatt 2018; Lührmann and Lindberg 2019.
57 For this reason, the alarmist rhetoric of current reports from Freedom House has to be uncoupled from quantitative findings.
58 Maeda 2010; Tomini and Wagemann 2018.
59 See Przeworski 2019, ch. 10.

Notes to Chapter 3

1 Levitsky and Ziblatt 2018; Mounk 2018; Przeworski 2019; Runciman 2018.
2 Weyland 2017, p. 50.
3 Mudde 2004; Mudde and Kaltwasser 2017, ch. 1.
4 Mudde 2004, p. 543.
5 Freeden 2003.
6 Pitkin 1967, p. 232.
7 Urbinati 2019, ch. 2; Weyland 2017.
8 Cited in Priester 2012, p. 55.
9 Canovan 1999, p. 5.
10 Müller 2011, p. 92.
11 Rosenblatt 2018.
12 Börzel and Zürn 2020.
13 Urbinati 2019, pp. 49–50.

Notes to pages 53–62

14 See Caramani 2017; Landwehr and Steiner 2017.
15 Urbinati 2019, p. 22.
16 But see Manow 2018.
17 Rooduijn et al. 2020.
18 When Alternative für Deutschland (AfD) was founded in 2013, it set itself primarily against the euro and the policy of saving it. But after the 'right-wing populist turn' (Schmitt-Beck et al. 2017), which had been achieved by 2015 at the latest, after the arrival of hundreds of thousands of refugees in Germany, the judgement of political science research has been unequivocal. The AfD is an authoritarian populist party in our sense of the word.
19 Kriesi et al. 2012; Hooghe, Marks, and Wilson 2004; de Wilde 2019.
20 Lipset 1969; Lipset and Rokkan 1967; Rokkan 2000.
21 Habermas 2001.
22 Hooghe et al. 2004.
23 Kriesi et al. 2008.
24 Beramendi et al. 2015.
25 De Wilde et al. 2019.
26 Kriesi et al. 2008; Mair 2005; Pappi 1977, p. 493.
27 Milanović 2016.
28 In addition, the well educated and highly skilled profit as a result of linguistic and cultural borders, which remain in place. Lawyers and doctors are better protected by the particularities of national legal and medical systems than are, say, factory workers (Hartmann 2020).
29 Koopmans and Zürn 2019.
30 Pogge 1992, p. 49.
31 Held 1995.
32 Etzioni 1998; Haus 2003; see e.g. Honneth 1993.
33 Barber 1984.
34 Zürn and de Wilde 2016.
35 Rokkan 2000.
36 Kitschelt and McGann 2000, pp. 7–8.
37 Merkel and Scholl 2018, pp. 34ff.

184 Notes to pages 62–76

38 Inglehart 1977.
39 Ignazi 1992.
40 Deutsch 1969, p. 99.
41 Gygli et al. 2019.
42 Manow 2018; Flaherty and Rogowski 2021.
43 Hobolt 2016.
44 Iversen and Soskice 2019; Broz, Frieden, and Weymouth 1998.
45 Lipset 1963.
46 Gellner 1995, p. 55.
47 OECD 2015, p. 14.
48 Koopmans 2019; Kriesi et al. 2008, 2012.
49 Strijbis, Teney, and Helbling 2019.
50 Hartmann 2020.
51 Manow 2019.
52 Przeworski 2019, ch. 6.

Notes to Chapter 4
1 AfD 2017, p. 1.
2 Manow 2020.
3 AfD 2020.
4 Poushter 2019.
5 Runciman 2018, p. 72.
6 Schattschneider 1960, p. 35.
7 Gilens 2012.
8 Dahl 1989, p. 29.
9 Manin 1997, p. 232.
10 Dahl 1989, p. 95.
11 Pitkin 1967, pp. 209–210.
12 See also Schäfer 2015, ch. 8.
13 Schakel and Hakhverdian 2018.
14 Carnes 2012, 2013.
15 Carnes and Lupu 2015.
16 O'Grady 2019.
17 Giger, Rosset, and Bernauer 2012.
18 Enns 2015.

Notes to pages 76–84

19 Lessig 2011.
20 The data in question and the results summarized in the next pages are based on the combined efforts of Armin Schäfer, Lea Elsässer, and Svenja Hense. The ResPOG databank and analyses are set out in detail in Elsässer, Hense, and Schäfer 2017 and 2020.
21 Information on the incomes of the respondents was available only for some of the questions. But, since higher levels of education and more senior professional rankings generally go together with higher incomes, the findings do reflect income effects as well.
22 Elsässer, Hense, and Schäfer 2018.
23 See e.g. Schakel 2021.
24 Within the group of the resource-rich, people in technical professions incline towards the market-oriented variety of liberal cosmopolitanism and people in person-oriented professions towards the human rights variant.
25 The model is sketched in Zürn 2018b and fully worked out in Zürn 2021.
26 The surveys that collected the data to test the model were designed in the one instance in Zürn, Tokhi, and Binder (2021) and in the other in de Wilde, Koopmans, Merkel, and Zürn (2014). Supplementary data from the World Values Survey were supplied by Johannes Scherzinger.
27 WVS 2006: see Inglehart et al. 2014.
28 These are the sixteen OECD countries considered democratic by Freedom House in 2021. Data on these countries have been regularly available.
29 See Zürn 2011.
30 Dahl 1989.
31 Elster 1994; Preuß 1994.
32 Ackermann 2000.
33 See Thatcher and Sweet 2002, p. 2.
34 Krisch 2010.
35 Downs 1957.

186   Notes to pages 84–98

36 Merkel 2016b, p. 67; Przeworski 2019, p. 95.
37 Lehmbruch 1977.
38 Czada and Schmidt 1993.
39 Dahl 1965, pp. 21–22.
40 Hay 2007, p. 30.
41 Crouch 2004; Dahl 1965; Mair 2013.
42 Gerhards, Offerhaus, and Roose 2009; Moravcsik 2004.
43 Cerny 1995; Slobodian 2019.
44 Hirschl 2007, p. 1.
45 Rapaport, Levi-Faur, and Miodownik 2009; Cukierman 2008; Jácome and Vázquez 2008.
46 Jordana, Fernández-i-Marín, and Bianculli 2018.
47 Hooghe, Dassonneville, and Oser 2019; Zürn et al. 2021.
48 Zürn et al. 2021.
49 Müller 2011, pp. 143–144.
50 Zürn 2013, 2014.
51 De Wilde et al. 2014.
52 Koopmans and Statham 1999.
53 We have concentrated here only on five of the sixteen countries with data available from the WVS.
54 Strijbis, Teney, and Helbling 2019.
55 Zürn 2019.
56 Mair 2013.
57 Mounk and Kyle 2018.
58 Norris and Inglehart 2019, p. 233.
59 The area spread out between these two axes is easily distinguishable from the two-dimensional political space that we discussed in Chapter 2. It serves exclusively to identify authoritarian populist parties. The authoritarian aspect is captured by the following items: GALTAN, Nationalism, Civlib_laworder, Multiculturalism, Sociallifestyle, Immigrate_policy, and Ethnic_minorities. The populist aspect is measured by 'anti-corruption salience' and 'anti-elite salience'.
60 The countries in question are Austria, Belgium, Bulgaria, Cyprus, Czechia, Estonia, Finland, France, Germany, Great Britain,

Notes to pages 100–109

Hungary, Ireland, Italy, the Netherlands, Norway, Poland, Portugal, Slovakia, Slovenia, Spain, Sweden, and Switzerland.

61 Schäfer 2015.
62 Zürn 2011.
63 Dahrendorf 1965.
64 Bertsou and Pastorella 2017; Bickerton and Accetti 2017; Canovan 1999; Caramani 2017.
65 Urbinati 2019.
66 Slobodian 2019.
67 Crouch 2004.

Notes to Chapter 5

1 Buzan, Wæver, and de Wilde 1998; Waever 1995.
2 Kreuder-Sonnen 2020.
3 Gosepath 2020; see also Chapter 1.
4 See the discussion in Przeworski 2019, p. 9.
5 Schneckener 2020.
6 Graf 2020; Koselleck 1982. In this case, criticism was supposed to show the way out of the crisis. In 1930, Walter Benjamin and Bertolt Brecht founded a magazine called *Krise und Kritik* [Crisis and Criticism]. Appropriately enough, the first issue was entitled 'Greeting the Crisis'. Reinhart Koselleck later chose *Kritik und Krise* (2018 [1959]) [Critique and Crisis] as the title of his influential dissertation.
7 Capoccia and Kelemen 2007; Zürn 2018a, ch. 5.
8 See also Bösch, Deitelhoff, and Kroll 2020.
9 Cf. Kilper 2020.
10 Merkel 2016a, p. 6.
11 Heitmeyer 2018.
12 See Heitmeyer, Freiheit, and Sitzer 2020, p. 218.
13 Graf 2020.
14 Habermas 1976; Offe 2006; Schäfer 2008.
15 Merkel 2016a, p. 7.
16 See Offe 2003, p. 138.
17 Crouch 2004.

188   Notes to pages 109–121

18 Streeck 2013.
19 Blyth 2013.
20 Blyth 2013, p. 49.
21 Hall 2018; Hall and Franzese 1998; Höpner 2013.
22 Blyth 2013.
23 The impression that parliamentary elections are meaningless is reflected in the diminishing participation rate. Between 2007 and 2019, the traditionally high turnout in Greece went down from 74 to only 58 per cent. Relevant data are available online at https://www.idea.int/data-tools/country-view/139/40 (URL accessed November 2022).
24 Jacoby and Hopkin 2020.
25 Höpner and Rödl 2012.
26 Müller 2015.
27 Matthijs 2017; Schmidt 2015.
28 See Alonso 2015, p. 245; also Scharpf 2013 and Armingeon, Guthmann, and Weisstanner 2015 on rejections of democracy.
29 Streeck 2013; Seikel 2017.
30 Schimmelfennig 2012.
31 Admittedly, developments after the Covid-19 crisis have shown that majorities in the donor countries are not in principle against solidarity and transfer mechanisms. But they are critical of a tacit transfer of decision-making powers that removes financial policy from the arena of democratic debate.
32 Lindberg and Scheingold 1970, p. 38.
33 Hooghe and Marks 2009.
34 Rauh and Zürn 2014.
35 Reuter 2020.
36 See European Council, 'Justice and Home Affairs Council, 20 July 2015', available online at https://www.consilium.europa.eu/en/meetings/jha/2015/07/20.
37 Niemann and Zaun 2018.
38 Hall and Lichfield 2015.
39 Panebianco and Fontana 2018.

Notes to pages 121–135

40 See also Biermann et al. 2019; Börzel 2020.
41 Börzel 2020.
42 Niemann and Zaun 2018.
43 Börzel and Risse 2018.
44 Kneuer 2019.
45 Krauter 2020.
46 Dong, Du, and Gardner 2020.
47 Undoubtedly the regions of the world that were infected *first* were the ones most vigorously involved in the global society and economy. But there is little to suggest that the less integrated regions could escape the epidemic. Rather the data obtained so far show that they were systematically advancing towards it.
48 Dong et al. 2020.
49 Bosancianu et al. 2020.
50 Hornig et al. 2020.
51 On this, see the IMF's World Economic Outlook, which is available online at https://www.imf.org/-/media/Files/Publications/WEO/2020/April/English/text.ashx.
52 Of course, not all the opponents of Covid-19 policies are automatically adherents of authoritarian populist parties (on this subject, see Meier 2020).

Notes to Chapter 6
1 Viktor Orbán, opening speech at the 29th Bálványos Summer Open University and Student Camp Camp, 29 July 2018: visit https://miniszterelnok.hu/prime-minister-viktor-orbans-speech-at-the-29th-balvanyos-summer-open-university-and-student-camp.
2 Merkel 2017.
3 Kriesi 2014, pp. 361–362.
4 Učen 2007, p. 54.
5 Möllers 2017, p. 8.
6 Mouffe 2018, p. 22.
7 Urbinati 2019, p. 7.

190 Notes to pages 135–152

8 See for example Frank-Walter Steinmeier's Fritz Stern Lecture at the American Academy, titled 'Is Democracy Running Short on Reason?', Berlin, March 2019 (https://www.americanacademy.de/german-president-steinmeier-delivers-the-2019-fritz-stern-lecture), or his opening address at the 27th Congress of the German Political Science Association in Frankfurt.
9 See Mudde 2004.
10 Mudde and Kaltwasser 2017, ch. 5.
11 Mudde and Kaltwasser 2017, p. 95.
12 Habermas 1996.
13 V-Dem Institute 2019.
14 For V-Dem data, the threshold value is usually set at 0.5, in order to distinguish democratic from non-democratic countries.
15 Lührmann et al. 2020, p. 17.
16 Levitsky and Way 2002.
17 See also Reckwitz 2019.
18 Dahrendorf 1965.
19 Alter and Zürn 2020.
20 Moravcsik 2019; Stengel, MacDonald, and Nabers 2019.
21 Zürn 2018a, ch. 1.
22 The United States' National Security Strategy is available online at https://www.whitehouse.gov/wp-content/uploads/2017/12/NSS-Final-12-18-2017-0905.pdf.
23 Urbinati 2019, p. 11.
24 See Merkel and Zürn 2019.
25 Deutsch 1969.
26 Zürn 1998.
27 Habermas 2015, p. 46.
28 See e.g. Barber 1984.
29 See e.g. Taylor 1992.
30 Held 1995.
31 Archibugi 2004, p. 438.
32 Archibugi 2008; Archibugi and Held 1995; Caney 2005; Höffe 1999.

Notes to pages 153–174 191

33 For a fairly recent assessment, see Blatter 2018.
34 Zürn 2018a, ch. 3.

Notes to Chapter 7

1 Solt 2008, p. 38.
2 Levitsky and Ziblatt 2018.
3 Katzenstein 1985.
4 Schumpeter 1975 [1942], p. 262.
5 Brennan 2016.
6 Farrell et al. 2020.
7 Norris and Inglehart 2019, pp. 157–159.
8 Gest 2016; McQuarrie 2017.
9 Sandel 1998.
10 Schäfer and Schoen 2013.
11 Geißel, Neunecker, and Kolleck 2015.
12 Bächtiger, Grönlund, and Setälä 2014; Lafont 2019.
13 Brady, Verba, and Schlozman 1995, p. 271.
14 Carnes 2018; Crowder-Meyer 2020.
15 Heath 2018.
16 To dispel any misunderstanding: what we refer to as 'a relatively minor problem' is the representation of women in parties and parliaments. We regard unequal pay for men and women for the same work and the various forms of sexual violence to be a major problem.
17 Preuß 1994.
18 As with the parties, here too recruitment models have to be carefully considered. If we think of NMIs such as the Federal Constitutional Court or the European Court of Justice, then, obviously, appointment procedures can be opened only to a limited extent. In such cases advisory boards with heterogeneous appointees could be created.
19 See Grande and Vidal 2020.
20 Cooper 1998, p. 6.
21 Decker 2003; Follesdal and Hix 2006.

192 Notes to pages 175–177

22 Zürn 1996.
23 Dahrendorf 2019 [2003].
24 A video of the conversation that took place on 4 April 1989 is available online in the series Conversations with History at https://wwws.youtube.con/watch?v=Yj5pVe6hOZo or https://conversations.berkeley.edu/dahrendorf_1989.

Bibliography

Ackermann, Bruce (2000). 'The New Separation of Powers', *Harvard Law Review* 113, pp. 633–727.

Alonso, Sonia (2015). 'Wählen ohne Wahl', in *Demokratie und Krise*, edited by Wolfgang Merkel. Wiesbaden: Springer, pp. 245–274.

Alter, Karen J., and Michael Zürn (2020). 'Theorizing Backlash Politics', in *Backlash Politics in Comparison*, special issue of *British Journal of Politics and International Relations* 22.4, pp. 1–22.

Alternative für Deutschland [AfD] (2017). *Programm für Deutschland: Wahlprogramm der Alternative für Deutschland für die Wahl zum Deutschen Bundestag am 24. September 2017.* https://www.afd.de/wp-content/uploads/sites/111/2017/06/2017-06-01_AfD-Bundestagswahlprogramm_Onlinefassung.pdf.

Alternative für Deutschland [AfD] (2020). *Programm für Deutschland. Das Grundsatzprogramm der Alternative für Deutschland.* https://www.afd.de/wp-content/uploads/2018/01/Programm_AfD_Online-PDF_150616.pdf.

Ambrose, Stephen E. (1983 [1971]). *Rise to Globalism: American Foreign Policy, 1938–1976* (3rd edn). New York: Penguin.

Ansell, Ben, and Jane Gingrich (2020). 'Policy and Politics in Disjuncture in an Age of Secular Stagnation', in *The State and Future of Representative Democracy: A Comparative Perspective,*

194 Bibliography

edited by Claudia Landwehr, Thomas Saalfeld, and Armin Schäfer. Cambridge: Cambridge University Press, pp. 187–210.

Archibugi, Daniele (2004). 'Cosmopolitan Democracy and Its Critics: A Review', *European Journal of International Relations* 10.3, pp. 47–71.

Archibugi, Daniele (2008). *The Global Commonwealth of Citizens: Toward Cosmopolitan Democracy*. Princeton, NJ: Princeton University Press.

Archibugi, Daniele, and David Held (eds) (1995). *Cosmopolitan Democracy: An Agenda for a New World Order*. Cambridge: Polity.

Armingeon, Klaus, Kai Guthmann, and David Weisstanner (2015). 'Wie der Euro Europa spaltet: Die Krise der gemeinsamen Währung und die Entfremdung von der Demokratie in der Europäischen Union', *Politische Vierteljahresschrift* 56.3, pp. 506–531.

Arzheimer, Kai (2015). 'The AfD: Finally a Successful Right-Wing Populist Eurosceptic Party for Germany?', *West European Politics* 38.3, pp. 535–556.

Arzheimer, Kai, and Carl C. Berning (2019). 'How the Alternative for Germany (AfD) and Their Voters Veered to the Radical Right, 2013–2017', *Electoral Studies* 60.102040.

Bachrach, Peter, and Morton S. Baratz (1977). *Macht und Armut: Eine theoretisch–empirische Untersuchung*. Frankfurt am Main: Suhrkamp.

Bächtiger, André, Kimmo Grönlund, and Maija Setälä (eds) (2014). *Deliberative Mini-Publics: Involving Citizens in the Democratic Process*. Colchester: ECPR Press.

Bakker, Ryan, Lisbet Hooghe, Seth Jolly, Gary Marks, Jonathan Polk, Jan Rovny, Marco Steenbergen, and Milada A. Vachudova (2019). *2019 Chapel Hill Expert Survey*. University of North Carolina, Chapel Hill. www.chesdata.eu/2019-chapel-hill-expert-survey.

Barber, Benjamin (1984). *Strong Democracy: Participatory Politics for a New Age*. Berkeley: University of California Press.

Beisheim, Marianne, Sabine Dreher, Gregor Walter, Bernhard Zangl, and Michael Zürn (1999). *Im Zeitalter der Globalisierung?*

Thesen und Daten zur gesellschaftlichen und politischen Denationalisierung. Baden-Baden: Nomos.

Beitz, Charles R (1989). *Political Equality: An Essay in Democratic Theory.* Princeton, NJ: Princeton University Press.

Benedetto, Giacomo, Simon Hix, and Nicola Mastrorocco (2020). 'The Rise and Fall of Social Democracy 1918–2017', *American Political Science Review* 114.3, pp. 928–939.

Beramendi, Pablo, Silja Häusermann, Herbert Kitschelt, and Hanspeter Kriesi (2015). 'Introduction: The Politics of Advanced Capitalism', in *Politics of Advanced Capitalism*, edited by Pablo Beramendi, Silja Häusermann, Herbert Kitschelt, and Hanspeter Kriesi. Cambridge: Cambridge University Press, pp. 1–64.

Berbuir, Nicole, Marcel Lewandowsky, and Jasmin Siri (2015). 'The AfD and Its Sympathisers: Finally a Right-Wing Populist Movement in Germany? *German Politics* 24.2, pp. 154–178.

Bergmann, Torbjörn, and Kaare Strøm (2011). *The Madisonian Turn: Parties and Parliamentary Democracy in Nordic Europe.* Ann Arbor, MI: University of Michigan Press.

Bermeo, Nancy G. (2016). 'On Democratic Backsliding', *Journal of Democracy* 27.1, pp. 5–19.

Bertsou, Eri, and Giulia Pastorella (2017). 'Technocratic Attitudes: A Citizens' Perspective of Expert Decision-Making', *West European Politics* 40.2, pp. 430–458.

Bickerton, Christopher, and Carlo I. Accetti (2017). 'Populism and Technocracy: Opposites or Complements?', *Critical Review of International Social and Political Philosophy* 20.4, pp. 186–206.

Biermann, Felix, Nina Guérin, Stefan Jagdhuber, Berthold Rittberger, and Moritz Weiss (2019). 'Political (Non-)Reform in the Euro Crisis and the Refugee Crisis: A Liberal Intergovernmentalist Explanation', *Journal of European Public Policy* 26.2, pp. 226–246.

Blatter, Joachim (2018). 'Transnationalizing Democracy Properly: Principles and Rules for Granting Consociated Citizens Voting Rights and Partisan Representation in the Parliaments of Nation States', Wissenschaftszentrum Berlin für Sozialforschung

Bibliography

Discussion Paper SP IV 2018/102, June. https://bibliothek.wzb.eu /pdf/2018/iv18-102.pdf.

Blyth, Mark (2013). *Austerity: The History of a Dangerous Idea.* Oxford: Oxford University Press.

Börzel, Tanja (2020). 'That Big EU Summit: Too Little, Too Late?' SCRIPTS Blog 13/2020, 28 July. Excellence Cluster 'Contestations of the Liberal Script', Free University Berlin. https://www.scripts -berlin.eu/publications/blog/Blog-13-That-big-EU-Summit_-Too -little_-too-late_/index.html.

Börzel, Tanja, and Thomas Risse (2018). 'From the Euro to the Schengen Crises: European Integration Theories, Politicization, and Identity Politics', *Journal of European Public Policy* 25.1, pp. 83–108.

Börzel, Tanja, and Michael Zürn (2020). 'Contestations of the Liberal Script (SCRIPTS): A Research Program', SCRIPTS (Excellence Cluster 'Contestations of the Liberal Script') Working Paper No. 1/2020. www.scripts-berlin.eu/publications/Publications-PDF/SC RIPTS-WP1_final.pdf.

Börzel, Tanja, and Michael Zürn (2021). 'Contestations of the Liberal International Order from Liberal Multilateralism to Postnational Liberalism', *International Organization* 72.5, pp. 282–305.

Bösch, Frank, Nicole Deitelhoff, and Stefan Kroll (eds) (2020). *Handbuch Krisenforschung.* Wiesbaden: Springer.

Boin, Arjen (2009). 'The New World of Crises and Crisis Management: Implications for Policymaking and Research', *Review of Policy Research* 26.4, pp. 367–377.

Bosancianu, Constantin M., Hanno Hilbig, Macartan Humphreys, Sampada K. C., Nils Lieber, and Alexandra Scacco (2020). 'Political and Social Correlates of Covid-19 Mortality', SocArXiv Papers. DOI: 10.31235/osf.io/ub3zd.

Bovens, Mark A. P., and Anchrit Wille (2017). *Diploma Democracy: The Rise of Political Meritocracy.* Oxford: Oxford University Press.

Brady, Henry E., Sidney Verba, and Kay L. Schlozman (1995). 'Beyond SES: A Resource Model of Political Participation', *American Political Science Review* 89.2, pp. 271–294.

Bibliography

Brennan, Jason (2016). *Against Democracy*. Princeton, NJ: Princeton University Press.

Broz, Lawrence J., Jeffrey Frieden, and Stephen Weymouth (1998). 'Populism in Place: The Economic Geography of the Globalization Backlash', *International Organization*, 75.2, pp. 464–494.

Brozus, Lars (2002). *Globale Konflikte oder Global Governance? Kontinuität und Wandel globaler Konfliktlinien nach dem Ost-West-Konflikt*. Wiesbaden: VS Verlag für Sozialwissenschaften.

Bühlmann, Marc, Wolfgang Merkel, Lisa Müller, Heiko Giebler, and Bernhard Weßels (2012). 'Demokratiebarometer: Ein neues Instrument zur Messung von Demokratiequalität', *Zeitschrift für Vergleichende Politikwissenschaft* 6.1, pp. 115–159.

Buzan, Barry, Ole Wæver, and Jaap de Wilde (1998). *Security: A New Framework for Analysis*. Boulder, CO: Lynne Rienner.

Calhoun, Craig (2002). 'The Class Consciousness of Frequent Travelers: Toward a Critique of Actually Existing Cosmopolitanism', *South Atlantic Quarterly* 101.4, pp. 869–897.

Caney, Simon (2005). *Justice Beyond Borders: A Global Political Theory*. Oxford: Oxford University Press.

Canovan, Margaret (1999). 'Trust the People! Populism and the Two Faces of Democracy', *Political Studies* 47.1, pp. 2–16.

Caplan, Bryan (2007). *The Myth of the Rational Voter: Why Democracies Choose Bad Policies*, Princeton, NJ: Princeton University Press.

Capoccia, Giovanni, and Roger D. Kelemen (2007). 'The Study of Critical Junctures: Theory, Narrative and Counterfactuals in Historical Institutionalism', *World Politics* 59.3, pp. 341–369.

Caramani, Daniele (2017). 'Will vs Reason: The Populist and Technocratic Forms of Political Representation and Their Critique to Party Government', *American Political Science Review* 111.1, pp. 54–67.

Carnes, Nicholas (2012). 'Does the Numerical Underrepresentation of the Working Class in Congress Matter?', *Legislative Studies Quarterly* 37.1, pp. 5–34.

Carnes, Nicholas (2013). *White-Collar Government: The Hidden*

198 Bibliography

Role of Class in Economic Policy Making. Chicago, IL: Chicago University Press.

Carnes, Nicholas (2018). *Cash Ceiling: Why Only the Rich Run for Office – and What We Can Do about It*. Princeton, NJ: Princeton University Press.

Carnes, Nicholas, and Noam Lupu (2015). 'Rethinking the Comparative Perspective on Class and Representation: Evidence from Latin America?' *American Journal of Political Science* 59.1, pp. 1–18.

Cerny, Philip G. (1995). 'Globalization and the Changing Logic of Collective Action', *International Organization* 49.4, pp. 595–625.

Chesterman, Simon (2004). *You, the People: The United Nations, Transitional Administration, and State-Building*. Oxford: Oxford University Press.

Cooper, Robert (1998). Internal Government Paper on the European Commission. London. Unpublished manuscript made available to Michael Zürn by the author. Available on request.

Coppedge, Michael, John Gerring, David Altman et al. (2011). 'Conceptualizing and Measuring Democracy: A New Approach', *Perspectives on Politics* 9.2, pp. 247–267.

Crouch, Colin (2004). *Post-Democracy*. Cambridge: Polity.

Crowder-Meyer, Melody (2020). 'Baker, Bus Driver, Babysitter, Candidate? Revealing the Gendered Development of Political Ambition among Ordinary Americans', *Political Behavior* 42, pp. 359–384.

Cukierman, Alex (2008). 'Central Bank Independence and Monetary Policymaking Institutions: Past, Present and Future', *European Journal of Political Economy* 24.4, pp. 722–736.

Czada, Roland, and Manfred G. Schmidt (eds) (1993). *Verhandlungsdemokratie, Interessenvermittlung, Regierbarkeit: Festschrift für Gerhard Lehmbruch*. Opladen: Westdeutscher Verlag.

Dahl, Robert A. (1965). 'Reflections on Opposition in Western Democracies', *Government and Opposition* 1.1, pp. 7–24.

Bibliography

Dahl, Robert A. (1971). *Polyarchy: Participation and Opposition.* New Haven, CT: Yale University Press.

Dahl, Robert A. (1989). *Democracy and Its Critics.* New Haven, CT: Yale University Press.

Dahrendorf, Ralf (1965). *Gesellschaft und Demokratie in Deutschland.* Munich: Piper.

Dahrendorf, Ralf (1998). 'Anmerkungen zur Globalisierung', in *Perspektiven der Weltgesellschaft*, edited by Ulrich Beck. Frankfurt am Main: Suhrkamp, pp. 41–54.

Dahrendorf, Ralf (2019 [2003]). 'Warum es die Demokratie so schwer gegen den Populismus hat?', *Welt*, 15 July. www.welt.de/debatte /kommentare/article196864875/Ralf-Dahrendorf-Acht-immer-noch-aktuelle-Thesen-zum-Populismus.html.

Decker, Frank (2003). 'Präsidialsystem und direkte Demokratie in der Europäischen Union?', in *Reform der Parteiendemokratie: Beiträge auf der 5. Speyerer Demokratietagung vom 25. bis 26. Oktober 2001 an der Deutschen Hochschule für Verwaltungswissenschaften Speyer*, edited by Hans Herbert von Arnim. Berlin: Duncker & Humblot, pp. 79–95.

Deitelhoff, Nicole (2006). *Überzeugung in der Politik: Grundzüge einer Diskurstheorie internationalen Regierens.* Frankfurt am Main: Suhrkamp.

Deutsch, Karl W. (1969). *Nationalism and Its Alternatives.* New York: Alfred A. Knopf.

De Wilde, Pieter (2019). 'Mapping Policy and Polity Contestation about Globalization: Issue Linkage in the News', in *The Struggle over Borders: Cosmopolitanism and Communitarianism*, edited by Pieter de Wilde, Ruud Koopmans, Wolfgang Merkel, Oliver Strijbis, and Michael Zürn. Cambridge: Cambridge University Press, pp. 89–115.

De Wilde, Pieter, Ruud Koopmans, Wolfgang Merkel, Oliver Strijbis, and Michael Zürn (eds) (2019). *The Struggle over Borders: Cosmopolitanism and Communitarianism.* Cambridge: Cambridge University Press.

De Wilde, Pieter, Ruud Koopmans, and Michael Zürn (2014). 'The

Bibliography

Political Sociology of Cosmopolitanism and Communitarianism: Representative Claims Analysis'. Wissenschaftszentrum Berlin für Sozialforschung Discussion Paper SP IV 2014/102, April. https://bibliothek.wzb.eu/pdf/2014/iv14-102.pdf.

Diamond, Larry (2015). 'Facing Up to the Democratic Recession', *Journal of Democracy* 26.1, pp. 141–155.

Döring, Holger, and Philip Manow (2019). Parliaments and Governments Database (ParlGov). http://www.parlgov.org.

Dong, Ensheng, Hongru Du, and Lauren Gardner (2020). 'An Interactive Web-Based Dashboard to Track Covid-19 in Real Time', *Lancet Infectious Diseases* 20.5, pp. 533–534. https://doi.org/10.1016/S1473-3099(20)30120-1.

Downs, Anthony (1957). *An Economic Theory of Democracy.* New York: Harper & Row.

Elsässer, Lea, Svenja Hense, and Armin Schäfer (2017). '"Dem Deutschen Volke"? Die ungleiche Responsivität des Bundestags', *Zeitschrift für Politikwissenschaft* 27, pp. 161–180.

Elsässer, Lea, Svenja Hense, and Armin Schäfer (2018). 'Government of the People, by the Elite, for the Rich: Unequal Responsiveness in an Unlikely Case'. Max-Planck-Institut für Gesellschaftsforschung, MPIfG Discussion Paper 18/5, June. www.econstor.eu/bitstream/10419/180215/1/1025295536.pdf.

Elsässer, Lea, Svenja Hense, and Armin Schäfer (2020). 'Not Just Money: Unequal Responsiveness in Egalitarian Democracies', in *Journal of European Public Policy* 28.12, pp. 1890–1908.

Elster, Jon (1994). 'Die Schaffung von Verfassungen: Analyse der allgemeinen Grundlagen', in *Zum Begriff der Verfassung: Die Ordnung des Politischen*, edited by Ulrich Preuß. Frankfurt am Main: Fischer, pp. 37–57.

Enns, Peter K. (2015). 'Relative Policy Support and Coincidental Representation', *Perspectives on Politics* 13.4, pp. 1053–1064.

Esping-Andersen, Gøsta (1990). *The Three Worlds of Welfare Capitalism.* Cambridge: Polity.

Etzioni, Amitai (1998). 'Introduction: Civic Repentance', *American Behavioral Scientist* 41.6, pp. 764–767.

Farrell, David M., Jane Suiter, Clodagh Harris, and Kevin Cunningham (2020). 'The Effects of Mixed Membership in a Deliberative Forum: The Irish Constitutional Convention of 2012–2014', in *Political Studies* 68.1, pp. 54–73.

Firebaugh, Glenn (2003). 'Die neue Geografie der Einkommensverteilung der Welt', in *Mehr Risiken, mehr Ungleichheit? Abbau von Wohlfahrtsstaat, Flexibilisierung von Arbeit und die Folgen*, edited by Walter Müller and Stefanie Scherer. Frankfurt am Main: Campus, pp. 363–388.

Flaherty, Thomas, and Ronald Rogowski (2021). 'Rising Inequality as a Threat to the Liberal International Order', *International Organization*, 75, pp. 495–523.

Foa, Roberto S., and Yascha Mounk (2016). 'The Danger of Deconsolidation: The Democratic Disconnect', *Journal of Democracy* 27.3, pp. 5–17.

Follesdal, Andreas, and Simon Hix (2006). 'Why There Is a Democratic Deficit in the EU: A Response to Majone and Moravcsik', *Journal of Common Market Studies* 44.3, pp. 533–562.

Forst, Rainer (2020). 'Die Verwahrlosung der Demokratie', *Süddeutsche Zeitung*, 2 September, p. 11.

Freeden, Michael (2003). *Ideology: A Very Short Introduction*. Oxford: Oxford University Press.

Fukuyama, Francis (1989). 'The End of History?', *National Interest* 16, pp. 1–18.

Fukuyama, Francis (1992). *The End of History and the Last Man*. New York: Free Press.

Gauland, Alexander (2018). 'Warum muss es Populismus sein?', *Frankfurter Allgemeine Zeitung*, 6 October. https://www.faz.net/aktuell/politik/inland/alexander-gauland-warum-muss-es-populismus-sein-15823206.html.

Geißel, Brigitte, Martina Neunecker, and Alma Kolleck (2015). 'Dialogorientierte Beteiligungsverfahren: Wirkungsvolle oder sinnlose Innovationen? Das Beispiel Bürgerhaushalt', *Zeitschrift für Parlamentsfragen* 46.1, pp. 151–165.

Gellner, Ernest (1995). *Nationalismus und Moderne*. Berlin: Rotbuch.

202 Bibliography

Gerhards, Jürgen, Anke Offerhaus, and Jochen Roose (2009). 'Wer ist verantwortlich? Die Europäische Union, ihre Nationalstaaten und die massenmediale Attribution von Verantwortung für Erfolge und Misserfolge', in *Politik in der Mediendemokratie*, special issue of *Politische Vierteljahresschrift* 42, edited by Frank Marcinkowski and Barbara Pfetsch, pp. 529–558.

Gest, Justin (2016). *The New Minority: White Working Class Politics in an Age of Immigration and Inequality*. Oxford: Oxford University Press.

Giger, Nathalie, Jan Rosset, and Julian Bernauer (2012). 'The Poor Political Representation of the Poor in a Comparative Perspective', *Representation* 48.1, pp. 47–61.

Gilens, Martin (2005). 'Inequality and Democratic Responsiveness', *Public Opinion Quarterly* 69.5, pp. 778–796.

Gilens, Martin (2012). *Affluence and Influence: Economic Inequality and Political Power in America*. Princeton, NJ: Princeton University Press.

Gosepath, Stefan (2020). 'Zu einigen politisch–moralischen Problemen in der Pandemie' ['Practical Philosophy in the Pandemic']. Unpublished manuscript, Free University, Berlin.

Graf, Rüdiger (2020). 'Zwischen Handlungsmotivation und Ohnmachtserfahrung: Der Wandel des Krisenbegriffs im 20. Jahrhundert', in *Handbuch Krisenforschung*, edited by Frank Bösch, Nicole Deitelhoff, and Stefan Kroll. Wiesbaden: Springer, pp. 17–38.

Grande, Edgar, and Guillem Vidal (2020). *A Vote for Europe? The 2019 EP Elections from the Voters' Perspective*, Berlin: Wissenschaftszentrum Berlin für Sozialforschung.

Gygli, Savina, Florian Haelg, Niklas Potrafke, and Jan-Egbert Sturm (2019). 'The KOF Globalisation Index, Revisited', *Review of International Organizations* 14, pp. 543–574.

Habermas, Jürgen (1976). *Legitimation Crisis*. Cambridge: Polity.

Habermas, Jürgen (1996). *Faktizität und Geltung: Beiträge zur Diskurstheorie des Rechts und des demokratischen Rechtsstaats*, 5th edn. Frankfurt am Main: Suhrkamp.

Bibliography

Habermas, Jürgen (2001). *The Postnational Constellation: Political Essays*. Cambridge, MA: MIT Press.

Habermas, Jürgen (2015). *The Lure of Technocracy*. Cambridge: Polity.

Hall, Allan, and John Lichfield (2015). 'Germany Opens Its Gates: Berlin Says All Syrian Asylum-Seekers Are Welcome to Remain, as Britain Is Urged to Make a "Similar Statement"', *Independent*, 24 August. www.independent.co.uk/news/world/europe/germany-opens-its-gates-berlin-says-all-syrian-asylum-seekers-are-welcome-to-remain-as-britain-is-10470062.html.

Hall, Peter A. (2018). 'Varieties of Capitalism in Light of the Euro Crisis', *Journal of European Public Policy* 25.1, pp. 7–30.

Hall, Peter A., and Robert J. Franzese (1998). 'Mixed Signals: Central Bank Independence, Coordinated Wage Bargaining, and European Monetary Union', *International Organization* 52.3, pp. 505–535.

Hall, Peter A., and David Soskice (2001). 'An Introduction to Varieties of Capitalism', in *Varieties of Capitalism: The Institutional Foundations of Comparative Advantage*, edited by Peter A. Hall and David Soskice. Oxford: Oxford University Press, pp. 1–68.

Hartmann, Michael (2020). 'Die Kosmopoliten als Profiteure des Nationalstaats und seiner Institutionen: Zu den ökonomischen Voraussetzungen kosmopolitischer Einstellungen', *Leviathan* 48.1, pp. 90–111.

Haus, Michael (2003). *Kommunitarismus: Einführung und Analyse*. Wiesbaden: Westdeutscher Verlag.

Hay, Colin (2007). *Why We Hate Politics*. Cambridge: Polity.

Heath, Oliver (2018). 'Policy Alienation, Social Alienation and Working-Class Abstention in Britain, 1964–2010', *British Journal of Political Science* 48.4, pp. 1053–1073.

Hegel, Georg W. F. (2011). *Lectures on the Philosophy of History*. Aalten: Wordbridge.

Heitmeyer, Wilhelm (2018). *Autoritäre Bedrohungen: Signaturen der Bedrohung*, vol. 1. Berlin: Suhrkamp.

Heitmeyer, Wilhelm, Manuela Freiheit, and Peter Sitzer (2020).

Rechte Bedrohungsallianzen: Signaturen der Bedrohung, vol. 2. Berlin: Suhrkamp.

Held, David (1995). *Democracy and the Global Order: From the Modern State to Cosmopolitical Governance*. Cambridge: Polity.

Held, David, Anthony McGrew, David Goldblatt, and Jonathan Perraton (eds) (1999). *Global Transformations: Politics, Economics and Culture*. Cambridge: Polity.

Hirschl, Ran (2007). *Towards Juristocracy: The Origins and Consequences of the New Constitutionalism*. Cambridge, MA: Harvard University Press.

Hobolt, Sara (2016). 'The Brexit Vote: A Divided Nation, a Divided Continent', *Journal of European Public Policy* 23.9, pp. 1259–1277.

Höffe, Otfried (1999). *Demokratie im Zeitalter der Globalisierung*. Munich: C. H. Beck.

Höpner, Martin (2013). 'Ein Währungsraum und viele Lohnregime: Warum der Euro nicht zum heterogenen Unterbau der Eurozone passt', *Der Moderne Staat* 6.2, pp. 289–309.

Höpner, Martin, and Florian Rödl (2012). 'Illegitim und rechtswidrig: Das neue makroökonomische Regime im Euroraum', in *Wirtschaftsdienst* 92.4, pp. 219–222.

Honneth, Axel (ed.) (1993). *Kommunitarismus: Eine Debatte über die moralischen Grundlagen moderner Gesellschaften*, Frankfurt am Main: Campus.

Hooghe, Liesbet, and Gary Marks (2009). 'A Postfunctionalist Theory of European Integration: From Permissive Consensus to Constraining', *British Journal of Political Science* 39.1, pp. 1–23.

Hooghe, Liesbet, Gary Marks, and Carole J. Wilson (2004). 'Does Left/Right Structure Party Positions on European Integration?', in *European Integration and Political Conflict*, edited by Gary Marks and Marco R. Steenbergen. Cambridge: Cambridge University Press, pp. 120–140.

Hooghe, Marc, Ruth Dassonneville, and Jennifer Oser (2019). 'Public Opinion, Turnout and Social Policy: A Comparative Analysis of Policy Congruence in European Liberal Democracies', *Political Studies* 67.4, pp. 992–1009.

Bibliography

Hornig, Frank, Steffen Lüdke, Sonja Peteranderl et al. (2020). 'Die Berater der Macht', *Der Spiegel*, 13 May. www.spiegel.de/politik /ausland/corona-krise-der-einfluss-von-wissenschaftlern-auf-die -politik-a-61007227-a2fb-4755-ba96-dda3a963a7d9.

Huntington, Samuel P. (1993). *The Third Wave: Democratization in the Late Twentieth Century*. Norman, OK: University of Oklahoma Press.

Ignazi, Piero (1992). 'The Silent Counter-Revolution: Hypotheses on the Emergence of Extreme Right-Wing Parties in Europe', *European Journal of Political Research* 22.1, pp. 3–34.

Inglehart, Ronald (1977). *The Silent Revolution: Changing Values and Political Styles among Western Publics*. Princeton, NJ: Princeton University Press.

Inglehart, Ronald, C. Haerpfer, A. Moreno et al. (eds) (2014). *World Values Survey: All Rounds, Country-Pooled Datafile Version*. Madrid: JD Systems Institute. www.worldvaluessurvey.org/WVS DocumentationWVL.jsp.

Inglehart, Ronald, and Christian Welzel (2005). *Modernization, Cultural Change, and Democracy: The Human Development Sequence*. Cambridge: Cambridge University Press.

Iversen, Torben, and David W. Soskice (2019). *Democracy and Prosperity: Reinventing Capitalism through a Turbulent Century*. Princeton, NJ: Princeton University Press.

Jacoby, Wade, and Jonathan Hopkin (2020). 'From Lever to Club? Conditionality in the European Union during the Financial Crisis', *Journal of European Public Policy* 27.8, pp. 1157–1177.

Jácome, Luis I., and Francisco Vázquez (2008). 'Is There Any Link between Legal Central Bank Independence and Inflation? Evidence from Latin America and the Caribbean', *European Journal of Political Economy* 24.4, pp. 788–801.

Jahn, Detlef (2006). 'Globalization as "Galton's Problem": The Missing Link in the Analysis of Diffusion Patterns in Welfare State Development', *International Organization* 60.2, pp. 401–431.

Jordana, Jacint, Xavier Fernández-i-Marín, and Andrea C. Bianculli (2018). 'Agency Proliferation and the Globalization of the

Regulatory State: Introducing a Data Set on the Institutional Features of Regulatory Agencies: Agency Proliferation', *Regulation & Governance* 12.4, pp. 524–540.

Kahler, Miles (1995). *International Institutions and the Political Economy of Integration*. Washington, DC: Brookings Institution.

Katzenstein, Peter J. (1985). *Small States in World Markets: Industrial Policy in Europe*. Ithaca, NY: Cornell University Press.

Keane, John (2009). *The Life and Death of Democracy*. London: Simon & Schuster.

Kelley, Judith G. (2004a). *Ethnic Politics in Europe: The Power of Norms and Incentives*. Princeton, NJ: Princeton University Press.

Kelley, Judith G. (2004b). 'International Actors on the Domestic Scene: Membership Conditionality and Socialization by International Institutions', *International Organization* 58.3, pp. 425–457.

Kilper, Heiderose (2020). 'Die Interdependenz von Krisen', in *Handbuch Krisenforschung*, edited by Frank Bösch, Nicole Deitelhoff, and Stefan Kroll. Wiesbaden: Springer, pp. 59–76.

Kirchheimer, Otto (1965). 'Der Wandel des westeuropäischen Parteiensystems', *Politische Vierteljahresschrift* 6.1, pp. 20–41.

Kitschelt, Herbert, and Anthony J. McGann (2000). *The Radical Right in Western Europe: A Comparative Analysis*. Ann Arbor: University of Michigan Press.

Kneuer, Marianne (2019). 'The Tandem of Populism and Euroscepticism: A Comparative Perspective in the Light of the European Crises', *Contemporary Social Science* 14.1, pp. 26–42.

Koenig-Archibugi, Mathias (2012). 'Global Democracy and Domestic Analogies', in *Global Democracy: Normative and Empirical Perspectives*, edited by Daniele Archibugi, Mathias Koenig-Archibugi, and Raffaele Marchetti. Cambridge: Cambridge University Press, pp. 160–182.

Kolko, Gabriel, and Joyce Kolko (1972). *The Limits of Power: The World and United States Foreign Policy, 1945–1954*. New York: Harper & Row.

Koopmans, Ruud (2019). 'Who Are the Cosmopolitans and the Communitarians? Claims-Making across Issues, Polity Levels and

Bibliography

Countries', in *The Struggle over Borders: Cosmopolitanism and Communitarianism*, edited by Pieter de Wilde, Ruud Koopmans, Wolfgang Merkel, Oliver Strijbis, and Michael Zürn. Cambridge: Cambridge University Press, pp. 173–204.

Koopmans, Ruud, and Paul Statham (1999). 'Political Claims Analysis: Integrating Protest Event and Political Discourse Approaches', *Mobilization: An International Quarterly* 4.1, pp. 203–221.

Koopmans, Ruud, and Michael Zürn (2019). 'Cosmopolitanism and Communitarianism: How Globalization Is Reshaping Politics in the Twenty-First Century', in *The Struggle over Borders: Cosmopolitanism and Communitarianism*, edited by Pieter de Wilde, Ruud Koopmans, Wolfgang Merkel, Oliver Strijbis, and Michael Zürn. Cambridge: Cambridge University Press, pp. 1–34.

Koselleck, Reinhart (1982). 'Krise', in *Geschichtliche Grundbegriffe: Historisches Lexikon zur politisch–sozialen Sprache in Deutschland*, edited by Otto Brunner, Werner Conze, and Reinhart Koselleck. Stuttgart: Klett-Cotta, pp. 617–650.

Koselleck, Reinhart (2018 [1959]). *Kritik und Krise: Eine Studie zur Pathogenese der bürgerlichen Welt*, 14th edn. Berlin: Suhrkamp.

Krauter, Ralf (2020). 'Woher kam die Pandemie? Die verschlungenen Wege von SARS-CoV-2', Conversation with Michael Lange, *Deutschlandfunk*, 4 May. www.deutschlandfunk.de/woher-kam-die-corona-pandemie-die-verschlungenen-wege-von-100.html.

Kreuder-Sonnen, Christian (2020). *Emergency Powers of International Organizations. between Normalization and Containment*. Oxford: Oxford University Press.

Kriesi, Hanspeter (2014). 'The Populist Challenge', *West European Politics* 37.2, pp. 361–378.

Kriesi, Hanspeter, Edgar Grande, Martin Dolezal et al. (2012). *Political Conflict in Western Europe*. Cambridge: Cambridge University Press.

Kriesi, Hanspeter, Edgar Grande, Romain Lachat, Martin Dolezal, Simon Bornschier, and Timotheos Frey (2008). *West European Politics in the Age of Globalization*. Cambridge: Cambridge University Press.

Krisch, Nico (2010). *Beyond Constitutionalism: The Pluralist Structure of Postnational Law*. Oxford: Oxford University Press.

Laclau, Ernesto (2005). *On Populist Reason*. London: Verso.

Lafont, Cristina (2019). 'Democracy without Shortcuts', *Constellations* 26.3, pp. 355–360.

Landwehr, Claudia, and Nils Steiner (2017). 'Where Democrats Disagree: Citizens' Normative Conceptions of Democracy', *Political Studies* 65.4, pp. 786–804.

Lehmbruch, Gerhard (1977). 'Liberal Corporatism and Party Government', *Comparative Political Studies* 10.1, pp. 91–126.

Leibfried, Stephan, and Michael Zürn (eds) (2006). *Transformationen des Staates?* Frankfurt am Main: Suhrkamp.

Leininger, Arndt, and Maurits J. Meijers (2020). 'Do Populist Parties Increase Voter Turnout? Evidence from over 40 Years of Electoral History in 31 European Democracies', *Political Studies*, 17 June, pp. 1–21.

Lessig, Lawrence (2011). *Republic, Lost: How Money Corrupts Congress and a Plan to Stop It*. New York: Twelve.

Levitsky, Steven, and Lucan A. Way (2002). 'Elections without Democracy: The Rise of Competitive Authoritarianism', *Journal of Democracy* 13.2, pp. 51–65.

Levitsky, Steven, and Daniel Ziblatt (2018). *How Democracies Die: What History Reveals about Our Future*. New York: Broadway Books.

Lewandowsky, Marcel, Heiko Giebler, and Aiko Wagner (2016). 'Rechtspopulismus in Deutschland: Eine empirische Einordnung der Parteien zur Bundestagswahl 2013 unter besonderer Berücksichtigung der AfD', *Politische Vierteljahresschrift* 57.2, pp. 247–275.

Lijphart, Arend (1999). *Patterns of Democracy: Government Forms and Performance in Thirty-Six Countries*. New Haven, CT: Yale University Press.

Lindberg, Leon N., and Stuart A. Scheingold (1970). *Europe's Would-Be Polity: Patterns of Change in the European Community*. Englewood Cliffs, NJ: Prentice-Hall.

Bibliography

Lipset, Seymour M. (1963). *Political Man: The Social Bases of Politics.* Garden City, NY: Anchor Books.

Lipset, Seymour M. (1969). 'Social Conflict, Legitimacy, and Democracy', in *Comparative Government. A Reader,* edited by Jean Blondel. London: Macmillan, pp. 52–59.

Lipset, Seymour M., and Stein Rokkan (eds) (1967). *Party Systems and Voter Alignments: Cross-National Perspectives.* New York: Free Press.

Lührmann, Anna, Valeriya Mechkova, Sirianne Dahlum et al. (2018). 'State of the World 2017: Autocratization and Exclusion?', *Democratization* 25.8, pp. 1321–1340.

Lührmann, Anna, and Staffan I. Lindberg (2019). 'A Third Wave of Autocratization Is Here: What Is New about It?', *Democratization* 26.7, pp. 1095–1113.

Lührmann, Anna, Seraphine F. Maerz, Sandra Grahn et al. (2020). *Autocratization Surges, Resistance Grows: Democracy Report 2020.* Varieties of Democracy Institute, University of Gothenburg. https://v-dem.net/documents/14/dr_2020_dqumD5e.pdf.

Maeda, Ko (2010). 'Two Modes of Democratic Breakdown: A Competing Risks Analysis of Democratic Durability', *Journal of Politics* 72.4, pp. 1129–1143.

Maerz, Seraphine F., Anna Lührmann, Sebastian Hellmeier, Sandra Grahn, and Staffan I. Lindberg (2020). 'State of the World 2019: Autocratization Surges, Resistance Grows', *Democratization* 27.6, pp. 1–19.

Mair, Peter (2005). 'Cleavages', in *Handbook of Party Politics*, edited by William Crotty and Richard S. Katz. London: Sage, pp. 371–375.

Mair, Peter (2013). *Ruling the Void: The Hollowing of Western Democracy*, London: Verso.

Manin, Bernard (1997). *The Principles of Representative Government.* Cambridge: Cambridge University Press.

Manow, Philip (2018). *Die politische Ökonomie des Populismus.* Berlin: Suhrkamp.

Manow, Philip (2019). 'Politischer Populismus als Ausdruck von

210 Bibliography

Identitätspolitik? Über einen ökonomischen Ursachenkomplex', *Aus Politik und Zeitgeschichte* 69.9–11, pp. 33–40.

Manow, Philip (2020). *(Ent-)Demokratisierung der Demokratie*. Berlin: Suhrkamp.

Matthijs, Matthias (2017). 'Integration at What Price? The Erosion of National Democracy in the Euro Periphery', *Government and Opposition* 52.2, 266–294.

McQuarrie, Michael (2017). 'The Revolt of the Rust Belt: Place and Politics in the Age of Anger', *British Journal of Sociology* 68.1, 120–152.

Meier, Svenja (2020). 'Hygiene-Demos sind eine diffuse, kurzfristige Erscheinung'. Interview with Dieter Rucht, *Die Zeit*, 8 August 2020. https://www.zeit.de/gesellschaft/zeitgeschehen/2020-08/co rona-proteste-deutschland-hygienedemos-bewegung.

Merkel, Wolfgang (2016a). 'Krise der Demokratie? Anmerkungen zu einem schwierigen Begriff', *Aus Politik und Zeitgeschichte* 66.40–42, pp. 4–11.

Merkel, Wolfgang (2016b). 'The Challenge of Capitalism to Democracy: Reply to Colin Crouch and Wolfgang Streeck', *Zeitschrift für Vergleichende Politikwissenschaft* 10.1, pp. 61–80.

Merkel, Wolfgang (2017). 'Kosmopolitismus versus Kommunitarismus: Ein neuer Konflikt in der Demokratie', in *Parties, Governments and Elites: The Comparative Study of Democracy*, edited by Philipp Harfst, Ina Kubbe, and Thomas Poguntke. Wiesbaden: Springer, pp. 9–23.

Merkel, Wolfgang, and Felix Scholl (2018). 'Illiberalism, Populism and Democracy in East and West', *Czech Journal of Political Science* 25.1, pp. 28–54.

Merkel, Wolfgang, and Michael Zürn (2019). 'Conclusion: The Defects of Cosmopolitan and Communitarian Democracy', in *The Struggle over Borders: Cosmopolitanism and Communitarianism*, edited by Pieter de Wilde, Ruud Koopmans, Wolfgang Merkel, Oliver Strijbis, and Michael Zürn. Cambridge: Cambridge University Press, pp. 173–204.

Bibliography

Milanović, Branko (2016). *Die ungleiche Welt: Migration, das Eine Prozent und die Zukunft der Mittelschicht*. Berlin: Suhrkamp.

Möllers, Christoph (2017). 'Wir, die Bürger(lichen)', *Merkur* 71.818, pp. 5–16.

Moravcsik, Andrew (2004). 'Is There a "Democratic Deficit" in World Politics? A Framework for Analysis', *Government and Opposition* 39.2, pp. 336–363.

Moravcsik, Andrew (2019). '"All Bark and No Bite": Why Populist Foreign Policy Is Doomed to Disappoint'. Seminar given at Norwegian Institute of International Affairs, October. https://www.youtube.com/watch?v=KLfDyDQbomY (video).

Mouffe, Chantal (2018). *For a Left Populism*. London: Verso.

Mounk, Yascha (2018). *Der Zerfall der Demokratie: Wie der Populismus den Rechtsstaat bedroht*. Munich: Droemer.

Mounk, Yascha, and Jordan Kyle (2018). 'The Populist Harm to Democracy: An Empirical Assessment'. Tony Blair Institute for Global Change, 26 December. https://institute.global/sites/defau lt/files/articles/The-Populist-Harm-to-Democracy-An-Empirical -Assessment.pdf.

Mudde, Cas (2004). 'The Populist Zeitgeist', *Government and Opposition* 39.4, pp. 541–563.

Mudde, Cas, and Cristóbal Rovira Kaltwasser (2017). *Populism: A Very Short Introduction*. Oxford: Oxford University Press.

Müller, Jan-Werner (2011). *Contesting Democracy: Political Ideas in Twentieth-Century Europe*. New Haven, CT: Yale University Press.

Müller, Jan-Werner (2016). *Was ist Populismus?* Berlin: Suhrkamp.

Müller, Torsten (2015). 'Die Troika: Kontrolle der Kontrolleure', in *Ein soziales Europa ist möglich: Grundlagen und Handlungsoptionen*, edited by Ulrich von Alemann, Eva G. Heidbreder, Hartwig Hummel, Domenica Dreyer, and Anne Gödde. Wiesbaden: Springer, pp. 261–284.

Nguyen, Christoph (2019). 'Angry, Anxious, and Populist? The Affective Dynamics of Populist Party Support'. Center for Open

Science, SocArXiv Paper, 13 March. https://osf.io/preprints/socar xiv/e2wm6/download.

Niemann, Arne, and Natascha Zaun (2018). 'EU Refugee Policies and Politics in Times of Crisis: Theoretical and Empirical Perspectives', *Journal of Common Market Studies* 56.1, pp. 3–22.

Norris, Pippa, and Ronald Inglehart (2019). *Cultural Backlash: Trump, Brexit, and Authoritarian Populism*. Cambridge: Cambridge University Press.

OECD (Organisation for Economic Co-Operation and Development) (2015). 'OECD Income Distribution Database (IDD): Gini, Poverty, Income, Methods and Concepts'. www.oecd. org/social/income-distribution-database.htm.

Oesch, Daniel (2006). *Redrawing the Class Map: Stratification and Institutions in Britain, Germany, Sweden and Switzerland*. Basingstoke: Palgrave Macmillan.

Offe, Claus (2003). *Herausforderungen der Demokratie: Zur Integrations- und Leistungsfähigkeit politischer Institutionen*. Frankfurt am Main: Campus.

Offe, Claus (2006). *Strukturprobleme des kapitalistischen Staates: Aufsätze zur Politischen Soziologie*. Frankfurt am Main: Campus.

O'Grady, Tom (2019). 'Careerists versus Coal-Miners: Welfare Reforms and the Substantive Representation of Social Groups in the British Labour Party', *Comparative Political Studies* 52.4, pp. 544–578.

Panebianco, Stefania, and Iole Fontana (2018). 'When Responsibility to Protect "Hits Home": The Refugee Crisis and the EU Response', *Third World Quarterly* 39.1, pp. 1–17.

Pappi, Franz (1977). *Sozialstruktur und politische Konflikte in der Bundesrepublik: Individual- und Kontextanalysen der Wahlentscheidung*. Habilitation thesis, University of Cologne.

Pettit, Philip (1999). *Republicanism: A Theory of Freedom and Government*. Oxford: Oxford University Press.

Pinker, Steven (2018). *Enlightenment Now: The Case for Reason, Science, Humanism and Progress*. New York: Viking Penguin.

Bibliography

Pitkin, Hanna F. (1967). *The Concept of Representation*, Berkeley/Los Angeles/London: University of California Press.

Pogge, Thomas (1992). 'Cosmopolitanism and Sovereignty', *Ethics* 103.1, pp. 48–75.

Poushter, Jacob (2019). '10 Key Takeaways about Public Opinion in Europe 30 Years after the Fall of Communism'. Fact Tank, 15 October. Pew Research Center, Washington, DC. https://www.pewresearch.org/fact-tank/2019/10/15/key-takeaways-public-opinion-europe-30-years-after-fall-of-communism=.

Preuß, Ulrich (1994). *Revolution, Fortschritt und Verfassung: Zu einem neuen Verfassungsverständnis*. Frankfurt am Main: Fischer.

Priester, Karin (2012). *Rechter und linker Populismus: Annäherung an ein Chamäleon*. Frankfurt am Main: Campus.

Przeworski, Adam (2019). *Crises of Democracy*. Cambridge: Cambridge University Press.

Rapaport, Orit, David Levi-Faur, and Dan Miodownik (2009). 'The Puzzle of the Diffusion of Central-Bank Independence Reforms: Insights from an Agent-Based Simulation', *Policy Studies Journal* 37.4, pp. 695–716.

Rauh, Christian, and Michael Zürn (2014). 'Zur Politisierung der EU in der Krise', in *Krise der europäischen Vergesellschaftung? Soziologische Perspektiven*, edited by Martin Heidenreich. Wiesbaden: Springer, pp. 121–145.

Reckwitz, Andreas (2019). *Das Ende der Illusionen: Politik, Ökonomie und Kultur in der Spätmoderne*. Berlin: Suhrkamp.

Repucci, Sarah (2020). 'Freedom in the World 2020: A Leaderless Struggle for Democracy'. https://freedomhouse.org/sites/default/files/2020-02/FIW_2020_REPORT_BOOKLET_Final.pdf.

Reuter, Christoph (2020). 'Der Familienkrieg von Damaskus', *Der Spiegel*, 15 May. https://www.spiegel.de/ausland/syrien-assads-gegen-makhloufs-der-familienkrieg-von-damaskus-a-00000000-0002-0001-0000-000170923519.

Rogowski, Ronald (1989). *Commerce and Coalitions. How Trade Affects Domestic Political Alignments*, Princeton, NJ: Princeton University Press.

214   Bibliography

Rokkan, Stein (2000). *Staat, Nation und Demokratie in Europa: Die Theorie Stein Rokkans aus seinen gesammelten Werken rekonstruiert und eingeleitet von Peter Flora.* Berlin: Suhrkamp.

Rooduijn, Matthijs, Stijn van Kessel, Caterina Froio et al. (2020). 'The Populist: An Overview of Populist, Far Right, Far Left and Eurosceptic Parties in Europe'. https://popu-list.org.

Rosenblatt, Helena (2018). *The Lost History of Liberalism: From Ancient Rome to the Twenty-First Century.* Princeton, NJ: Princeton University Press.

Ruggie, John G. (1982). 'International Regimes, Transactions, and Change: Embedded Liberalism in the Postwar Economic Order', *International Organization* 36.2, pp. 379–415.

Runciman, David (2018). *How Democracy Ends.* London: Profile Books.

Russett, Bruce M., and John R. Oneal (2001). *Triangulating Peace: Democracy, Interdependence, and International Organizations.* New York: W. W. Norton.

Sandel, Michael J. (1998). 'What Money Can't Buy: The Moral Limits of Markets'. Tanner Lectures, Brasenose College, Oxford, 11–12 May. https://tannerlectures.utah. edu/_documents/a-to-z/ s/sandel00.pdf.

Schäfer, Armin (2008). 'Krisentheorien der Demokratie: Unregierbarkeit, Spätkapitalismus und Postdemokratie'. MPIfG (Max-Planck-Institut für Gesellschaftsforschung) Discussion Paper 08/10, November. https://pure.mpg.de/pubman/item/item _1232900_6/component/file_1232898/mpifg_dp08-10.pdf?mode =download.

Schäfer, Armin (2015). *Der Verlust politischer Gleichheit: Warum die sinkende Wahlbeteiligung der Demokratie schadet.* Frankfurt am Main: Campus.

Schäfer, Armin, and Harald Schoen (2013). 'Mehr Demokratie, aber nur für wenige? Der Zielkonflikt zwischen mehr Beteiligung und politischer Gleichheit', *Leviathan* 41.1, pp. 94–120.

Schakel, Wouter (2021). 'Unequal Policy Responsiveness in the Netherlands', *Socio-Economic Review* 19.1, pp. 37–57.

Bibliography

Schakel, Wouter, and Armen Hakhverdian (2018). 'Ideological Congruence and Socio-Economic Inequality', *European Political Science Review* 10.3, pp. 441–463.

Scharpf, Fritz W. (1987). *Sozialdemokratische Krisenpolitik in Europa: Das 'Modell Deutschland' im Vergleich*. Frankfurt am Main: Campus.

Scharpf, Fritz W. (1999). *Regieren in Europa: Effektiv und demokratisch?* Frankfurt am Main: Campus.

Scharpf, Fritz W. (2013). 'Legitimacy Intermediation in the Multilevel European Polity and Its Collapse in the Euro Crisis', in *Staatstätigkeit, Parteien und Demokratie: Festschrift für Manfred G. Schmidt*, edited by Klaus Armingeon. Wiesbaden: Springer, pp. 567–596.

Schattschneider, Elmer E. (1960). *The Semisovereign People: A Realist's View of Democracy in America*. New York: Holt, Rinehart & Winston.

Schimmelfennig, Frank (2003). *The EU, NATO and the Integration of Europe: Rules and Rhetoric*. Cambridge: Cambridge University Press.

Schimmelfennig, Frank (2012). 'Zwischen Neo- und Post-funktionalismus: Die Integrationstheorien und die Eurokrise', *Politische Vierteljahresschrift* 53.3, pp. 394–413.

Schmalz-Bruns, Rainer (1995). *Reflexive Demokratie: Die demokratische Transformation moderner Politik*. Baden-Baden: Nomos.

Schmidt, Manfred G. (2010 [1995]). *Demokratietheorien: Eine Einführung*, 5th edn. Wiesbaden: Springer.

Schmidt, Vivien A. (2015). 'The Forgotten Problem of Democratic Legitimacy', in *The Future of the Euro*, edited by Matthias Matthijs and Mark Blyth. New York: Oxford University Press, pp. 90–114.

Schmitt-Beck, Rüdiger, Jan W. van Deth, and Alexander Staudt (2017). 'Die AfD nach der rechtspopulistischen Wende', *Zeitschrift für Politikwissenschaft* 27, pp. 273–303.

Schneckener, Ulrich (2020). '"Ein Europa, das schützt": Zum Verhältnis von Versicherheitlichung und Politisierung am

Beispiel europäischer Sicherheit', *Zeitschrift für Internationale Beziehungen* 27.1, pp. 137–150.

Schumpeter, Joseph A. (1975 [1942]). *Capitalism, Socialism and Democracy*. New York: HarperPerennial.

Schwander, Hanna, Dominic Gohla, and Armin Schäfer (2020). 'Fighting Fire with Fire? Inequality, Populism and Voter Turnout', *Politische Vierteljahresschrift* 61, pp. 261–283.

Seikel, Daniel (2017). 'Verrechtlichung und Entpolitisierung marktschaffender Politik als politikfeldübergreifender Trend in der EU', *Leviathan* 45.3, pp. 335–356.

Shils, Edward (1954). 'Authoritarianism: "Right" and "Left"', *Studies in the Scope and Method of the 'Authoritarian Personality'*, edited by Richard Christie and Marie Jahoda. New York: Free Press, pp. 24–49.

Skinner, Quentin (2002). 'A Third Concept of Liberty', *Proceedings of the British Academy* 117, pp. 237–268.

Slobodian, Quinn (2019). *Globalisten: Das Ende der Imperien und die Geburt des Neoliberalismus*. Berlin: Suhrkamp.

Solt, Frederick (2008). 'Economic Inequality and Democratic Political Engagement', *American Journal of Political Science* 52.1, pp. 48–60.

Stengel, Frank, David B. MacDonald, and Dirk Nabers (2019). *Populism and World Politics*. Berlin: Springer.

Streeck, Wolfgang (1995). 'From Market Making to State Building? Reflections on the Political Economy of European Social Policy', in *European Social Policy: Between Fragmentation and Integration*, edited by Stephan Leibfried and Paul Pierson. Washington, DC: Brookings Institution, pp. 389–431.

Streeck, Wolfgang (2013). *Gekaufte Zeit: Die vertagte Krise des demokratischen Kapitalismus*. Berlin: Suhrkamp.

Strijbis, Oliver, Céline Teney, and Marc Helbling (2019). 'Why Are Elites More Cosmopolitan Than Masses?', in *The Struggle over Borders: Cosmopolitanism and Communitarianism*, edited by Pieter de Wilde, Ruud Koopmans, Wolfgang Merkel, Oliver Strijbis, and Michael Zürn. Cambridge: Cambridge University Press, pp. 37–64.

Bibliography

Taylor, Charles (1992). *The Ethics of Authenticity*. Cambridge, MA: Harvard University Press.

Thatcher, Mark, and Alec Stone Sweet (2002). 'Theory and Practice of Delegation to Non-Majoritarian Institutions', *West European Politics* 25.1, pp. 1–22.

Tomini, Luca, and Claudius Wagemann (2018). 'Varieties of Contemporary Democratic Breakdown and Regression: A Comparative Analysis', *European Journal of Political Research* 57.3, pp. 687–716.

Učen, Peter (2007). 'Parties, Populism, and Anti-Establishment Politics in East Central Europe', *SAIS Review* 27.1, pp. 49–62.

Urbinati, Nadia (2019). *Me the People: How Populism Transforms Democracy*. Cambridge, MA: Harvard University Press.

Van der Pijl, Kees (1998). *Transnational Classes and International Relations*. London: Routledge.

Vanhanen, Tatu (2000). 'A New Dataset for Measuring Democracy, 1810–1998', *Journal of Peace Research* 37.2, pp. 251–265.

V-Dem Institute (2019). *V-Dem Annual Democracy Report 2019: Democracy Facing Global Challenges*. Gothenburg: University of Gothenburg. www.v-dem.net/en/news/de mocracy-facing-global-challenges-v-dem-annual-democracy-report-2019.

Waever, Ole (1995). 'Securitization and Desecuritization', in *On Security*, edited by Ronnie D. Lipschutz. New York: Columbia University Press, pp. 46–86.

Weyland, Kurt (2017). 'Populism: A Political–Strategic Approach', in *The Oxford Handbook of Populism*, edited by Cristóbal Rovira Kaltwasser, Paul Taggart, Paulina Ochoa Espejo, and Pierre Ostiguy. Oxford: Oxford University Press, pp. 48–73.

Williams, Bernard (2005). *In the Beginning Was the Deed: Realism and Moralism in Political Argument*. Princeton, NJ: Princeton University Press.

Zangl, Bernhard (2006). *Die Internationalisierung der Rechtsstaatlichkeit: Streitbeilegung in GATT und WTO*. Frankfurt am Main: Campus.

Zangl, Bernhard, and Michael Zürn (2003). *Frieden und Krieg:*

218 Bibliography

Sicherheit in der nationalen und postnationalen Konstellation. Frankfurt am Main: Suhrkamp.

Ziblatt, Daniel, Hanno Hilbig, and Daniel Bischof (2020). 'Parochialism, Place-Based Identity and Radical-Right Voting'. Center for Open Science, SocArXiv Paper, 6 May. https://extreme entrance.github.io/pdf/ZHB_Dialect.pdf.

Zürn, Michael (1996). 'Über den Staat und die Demokratie im europäischen Mehrebenensystem', *Politische Vierteljahresschrift* 37.1, pp. 27–55.

Zürn, Michael (1998). *Regieren jenseits des Nationalstaates: Globalisierung und Denationalisierung als Chance.* Frankfurt am Main: Suhrkamp.

Zürn, Michael (2001). 'Politik in der postnationalen Konstellation: Über das Elend des methodologischen Nationalismus', in *Politik in einer entgrenzten Welt: 21. wissenschaftlicher Kongress der Deutschen Vereinigung für Politische Wissenschaft,* edited by Christine Landfried. Cologne: Verlag Wissenschaft und Politik, pp. 181–203.

Zürn, Michael (2011). 'Perspektiven des demokratischen Regierens und die Rolle der Politikwissenschaft im 21. Jahrhundert', *Politische Vierteljahresschrift* 52.4, pp. 603–625.

Zürn, Michael (2013). 'Politisierung als Konzept der Internationalen Beziehungen', in *Die Politisierung der Weltpolitik: Umkämpfte internationale Institutionen,* edited by Michael Zürn and Matthias Ecker-Ehrhardt. Berlin: Suhrkamp, pp. 7–35.

Zürn, Michael (2014). 'The Politicization of World Politics and Its Effects: Eight Propositions', *European Political Science Review* 6.1, pp. 47–71.

Zürn, Michael (2018a). *A Theory of Global Governance: Authority, Legitimacy, and Contestation.* Oxford: Oxford University Press.

Zürn, Michael (2018b). 'How the Taming of the Class Conflict Produced Authoritarian Populism', *Items,* 12 April. https://items .ssrc.org/democracy-papers/how-the-taming-of-the-class-confl ict-produced-authoritarian-populism.

Zürn, Michael (2019). 'Politicization Compared: At National,

Bibliography

European, and Global Levels', *Journal of European Public Policy* 26.7, pp. 977–995.

Zürn, Michael (2021). 'How Non-Majoritarian Institutions Make Silent Majorities Vocal: A Political Explanation of Authoritarian Populism', *Perspectives on Politics* 20.3, pp. 788–807.

Zürn, Michael, Martin Binder, and Matthias Ecker-Ehrhardt (2012). 'International Authority and Its Politicization', *International Theory* 4.1, pp. 69–106.

Zürn, Michael, and Pieter de Wilde (2016). 'Debating Globalization: Cosmopolitanism and Communitarianism as Political Ideologies', *Journal of Political Ideologies* 21.3, pp. 280–301.

Zürn, Michael, Alexandros Tokhi, and Martin Binder (2021). 'The International Authority Database', *Global Policy* 12.4, pp. 430–442.

Index

Afghanistan, 34, 40
alienation
 double alienation, 4–6, 46,
  123, 131, 163
 drivers, 167
 from political institutions,
  93–100
Alonso, Sonia, 115
Amazon, 126
ambiguity, 177–8
ancient Greece, 73–4, 104–5
anti-globalization movements,
 34–5
Arab Spring, 118–19
Archibugi, Daniele, 152
Argentina, 47
Assad, Bashar al-, 107, 118, 121,
 131–2
asylum seekers. *See* refugees
Australia, 82, 89
Austria
 coaltion government, 145
 Freedom Party (FPÖ), 51, 62,
  143

political cleavage, 57
populism, 9, 47, 145
populist support rate, 66
refugee policy, 119
autocratization, 36, 42, 137–40,
 160

Bangladesh, 38
Bank of America, 111
Barber, Benjamin, 151
Benin, 40
Benjamin, Walter, 187n6
Bergmann, Bjön, 90
Berlin Social Science Center
 (WZB), 20–1
Berlusconi, Silvio, 9, 66, 143
Big Pharma, 131
Birx, Deborah, 127
Blair, Tony, 173
blame-shifting, 87, 93
Boin, Arjen, 107
Bolivia, Morales populism, 47
Bolsonaro, Jair, 38, 127, 137,
 161

Index

Borrelli, Angelo, 128
Bosnia, 34
Botswana, 40
Bovens, Mark, 75, 157
Brandt, Willy, 165
Brazil
  Collor and Vargas populism, 47
  Covid-19, 127
  democratic regression, 5, 38, 40, 159
  population, 38
  populists in power, 137
  transient democracy, 140
  trust in citizens, 166
Brecht, Bertolt, 187n6
Brennan, Jason, 162–3
Bretton Woods conference, 28
Brexit, 65, 117, 123–4, 127, 166
Bulgaria, 32–3
Bush, George W., 104

Calhoun, Craig, 148, 151
Canada, 82, 89
Caplan, Bryan, 162, 163
Carnes, Nicholas, 169–70
cartel parties, 11, 94, 101
catch-all parties, 62, 84–5, 93
Catholic Church, 26
Center for Systemic Peace, 20
central banks, 11, 72, 80, 83, 87–8, 90, 94, 171
  See also European Central Bank
Centre for Democracy (Aarau), 20–1
Chapel Hill Expert Survey (CHES), 95–6, 98–9
chauvinism, 151

Chávez, Hugo, 47
Cheney, Dick, 104
Chile, 82
China
  autocracy, 3, 38
  challenge, 45
  climate policies, 149
  Covid 19, 107, 124, 125
  difference, 3
  escape from poverty, 2
  population, 38
  postwar order, 28
  rise, 3, 34–5
  technocracy, 164
  UNSC veto, 121
cholera, 126
Christianity, liberal vs Christian democracy, 133–4
Citigroup, 111
citizens' rights, 137, 140, 152
city states, 74
class
  populism and, 143, 148
  representation and, 75–80, 85, 102, 157–8, 170
  voter turnout and, 170
  voting behaviour, 98
cleavage theory, 43, 56–67, 90, 92, 100, 124, 160–1
climate change, 33, 92, 149, 153, 161
Clinton, Hillary, 65
Collor, Fernando, 47
colonialism, 121
communitarianism, 57, 59–60, 61, 63, 67, 102, 149–52, 160–1
Comoros, 40
complexity, 15, 127, 149, 154, 156–7, 177–8

222 Index

constitutional courts, 11, 80, 83, 87, 90, 91, 94, 129, 136, 140, 167
Cooper, Robert, 173–4
corporatism, 85
cosmopolitanism
    communitarianism and, 57, 59–60, 62, 63, 67, 102, 149, 160–1
    corruption, 11, 133, 146
    critics, 151
    direction, 90–3, 94
    globalization, 149, 160
    left-wing variant, 61
    liberal elites, 7, 35, 68, 79, 123, 133
    migration policy and, 120–1, 148
    NMIs, 13, 93, 123, 171
    populism and, 146, 152, 155
    recommendations, 175–6
    resistance to, 36
    responsibility to protect, 121
    weakness, 152–5, 161
Covid-19
    conspiracy theories, 131
    crisis, 103–4, 105, 107, 108, 124–30, 131, 132
    deaths, 125
    ecological crisis, 132
    expert power, 124–30
    genome, 124
    international responses, 127–30
    lockdowns, 125
    origins, 124, 125
    parliaments and, 130
    populism and, 127–9, 130, 161
    transboundary crisis, 125

crises
    blame, 106
    Covid-19, 103–4, 105, 107, 108, 124–30, 131, 132
    democracy and, 108–10
    ecology, 132
    etymology, 104–5
    intensification, 103–4
    Lehman Brothers, 103, 110–17
    origins, 107–8
    paradox, 131–2
    permanent state, 104–10
    populism and, 110
    refugees, 103, 108, 118–24
    remedies, 106–7
    social constructs, 105
    spiral, 132
    transboundary crises, 107, 111, 125
Croatia, 33
Cyprus, 32, 115
Czechia, 32, 40, 122–3

Dahl, Robert, 19, 20, 85, 148
Dahrendorf, Ralf, 144, 177
Delfraissy, Jean-François, 128
democracy
    after optimism, 42–3
    alternatives, 3
    basic democracy, 151
    conditions, 19–22, 26–7
    consolidated democracies, 13
    Covid-19 and, 130
    crises. See crises
    defending. See recommendations
    deliberative, 21, 142, 166, 169
    democratic action. See recommendations

Index

diploma democracy, 75, 157
direct democracy, 6, 73–4, 175
double alienation, 4–6, 46, 123, 131, 163
elections, 21
end of history, 15–17, 42–3
equality, 21
illiberal democracy, 14–15, 135, 140–1, 142, 150–2
institutions. *See* parliaments
legitimacy, 148–9, 165
liberal democracy, meaning, 21
liberal vs Christian democracy, 133–4
manipulation, 39
meaning, 2–3, 18–26
measuring, 16–43
neglect, 5
number of democracies, 22, 24, 25, 160
optimism, 15–18, 159–60
participation, 21, 148, 168–9
postwar order, 26–36, 35
representation. *See* parliaments
representative democracy, 74
reverse wave, 36–42, 43
third transformation, 160–1
thresholds, 20
trust in democratic institutions, 81–3
Democracy Barometer, 20–1
Denmark, People's Party, 62
Deutsch, Karl W., 63
diploma democracy, 75, 157
direct democracy, 6, 73–4, 175

double alienation, 4–6, 46, 123, 131, 163
Draghi, Mario, 109, 164
Drosten, Christian, 124, 128
Duda, Andrzej, 137
Dumbarton Oaks gatherings, 27–8

ecology, 132, 161
education
  diploma democracy, 75, 157
  parliamentary representatives, 75, 157–8, 163
  political education, 176–7
  trust in democratic institutions and, 98–100
El Salvador, 40
elections
  democracy, 21
  electoral autocracies, 5, 142
  free and fair, 21, 41–2
  funding, 76–7
  See also parliaments
Electoral Democracy Index (EDI), 137
elephant curve, 1–4, 31
embedded liberalism, 29–31, 35–6, 94, 160
end of history, 16–17, 42–3
equality
  dismantling inequality contexts, 167–8
  egalitarian democracy, 21
  gender, 74, 170–1
  populism and political equality, 141–2, 143
  unequal representation, 73–9, 157–8, 169
Erdoğan, Recep Tayyip, 137
Erhard, Ludwig, 143

Index

Estonia, 32
ethnic minorities. *See*
  minorities
European Border and Coast
  Guard Agency, 122
European Central Bank, 83,
  113–14, 115, 117, 129, 164
European Court of Human
  Rights, 91
European Court of Justice, 117
European Investment Bank,
  129
European Social Survey, 97–9
European Stability Mechanism
  (ESM), 115, 129
European Union
  blame-shifting to, 87
  Brexit, 65, 117, 123–4, 127,
    166
  climate policies, 149
  Common European Asylum
    System (CEAS), 122, 123
  Copenhagen criteria, 32
  Covid-19 and, 129–30
  currency union, 32
  democracy as membership
    condition, 139
  democratic deficit, 158, 160,
    172–4
  democratic regression and,
    39
  European Stability
    Mechanism (ESM), 115,
    129
  eurozone crisis, 103, 108,
    112–17
  expansion, 32–3
  Fiscal Compact (2012), 116
  Fiscal Stability Treaty (2012),
    116

global financial crisis and,
  113–15
globalization and, 91
legal implementation model,
  172
Maastricht criteria, 116
populism and, 69, 150
refugee crisis, 119–23
Stability and Growth Pact,
  116
trust in, 81
euthanasia of politics, 90–3
experts
  Brexit and, 127
  citizen pariticipation and,
    169, 171
  Covid-19 and, 124–30, 161
  crises and, 13, 164
  NMIs, 90, 91–2, 109, 158
  populism and, 45–6, 54, 100,
    127
  technocrats, 101, 114, 164–6

family values, 70, 134
fascism, 16, 101
Fauci, Anthony, 109, 127
Faymann, Werner, 119
Finland, 56, 81, 82
Forst, Rainer, 5
Forster, Peter, 124
Fortuyn, Pim, 47
France
  anti-pluralism, 49
  Covid-19, 128
  declining regions, 167
  electoral representation,
    70–1
  EU currency union, 32
  EU Maastricht criteria and,
    116

Index

Gilets Jaunes, 54
political cleavage, 57
populism, 9, 47, 54, 66
Rassemblement National, 54, 62
refugee policy, 122
trust in politicians, 85
Freedom House, 22, 23
freedom of association, 21, 41–2, 140
freedom of thought, 21, 41–2, 140
Fukimori, Alberto, 47
Fukuyama, Francis, 16–17, 26, 42

G20, 111
GAL (green–alternative–libertarian), 57, 60
Gates, Bill, 131
GATT, 28–9
Gellner, Ernest, 66
gender
parliamentarians, 74, 170–1
research, 70
roles, 71
German Democratic Republic, 7
Germany
AfD, 49, 55, 69–70, 95–6, 123, 143, 166
anti-pluralism, 49
class, 77–9
Covid-19, 124, 128, 129, 130
culture, 69–70
East–West differences, 71
election funding, 77–8
EU Maastricht criteria and, 116
euro policy, 153

Federal Constitutional Court, 91, 129
global financial crisis and, 111
globalization and, 91
modernization, 101, 144
national socialism, 101, 144
Pegida, 49, 62
political education, 177
political parties, 69, 95–6
political representation, 70–1, 77–9
political system, 176
refugees, 13, 119–21, 122
regional differences, 167
reunification, 32
right-wing violence, 108
trust in citizens, 166
trust in democratic institutions, 82
Weimar Republic crisis, 108
Ghana, 40
Gilens, Martin, 76
global financial crisis, 103, 111–17, 121, 131
globalism, 56, 61–2, 67, 68, 76, 100, 117, 121, 131, 148, 154–5, 160
globalization
anti-globalization movements, 34–5
attitudes to, 91
communitarianism and, 151
Covid-19 and, 126
democracy and, 148–9, 152, 154–5, 160
KOF Globalization Index, 63–4
losers, 66
neoliberalism, 125

Index

globalization (*cont.*)
  NMI power and, 87
  political cleavage and, 57–8,
    64–5, 100, 160–1
  populism and, 63–6, 150–2,
    156–7
  refugee crisis and, 121
  winners, 2, 3, 58
Gorbachev, Mikhail, 16, 32
Gove, Michael, 127
Great Britain. *See* United
    Kingdom
Greece
  1965–7 crisis, 108
  democratic regression, 40
  financial crisis, 13, 107, 112,
    113–15
  military dictatorship, 17
  refugees in, 119
  Syriza, 54, 115
Greens, 48, 63, 96
Greenspan, Alan, 110–11

Habermas, Jürgen, 148, 149, 163
Haider, Jörg, 47
Haiti, 34
Hakhverdian, Armen, 75
Heath, Oliver, 170
Hegel, Georg, 16
Held, David, 18
Helsinkin Declaration (1975),
    31
Hirschl, Ran, 87
Hobbits, 162–3
Hölderlin, Friedrich, 106
Hong Kong, democratic
    regression, 40
Hooligans, 162–3
human rights, 32, 35, 61, 83, 118,
    119, 137, 140, 152

Hungary
  democratic regression, 14,
    39, 40, 139, 140–1, 159
  EU membership, 32
  ideology, 152
  liberal vs Christian
    democracy, 133–4
  populism, 56, 137, 140
  refugee policy, 119, 122
  transient democracy, 140
  trust in citizens, 166
Huntington, Samuel, 17–18, 23,
    25, 26–7

Identitarians, 62
immigration. *See* migration
India
  autocracy, 37
  Covid-19, 127
  democratic regression, 14,
    38, 40, 137, 159
  globalization effect, 9
  population, 38
  populism and globalization,
    66
individualism, 59, 61
Indonesia, 38, 40
Industrial Revolution, 56
inequality. *See* equality
Ingleheart, Ronald, 95, 180n5
International Authority
    Database (IAD), 88–9,
    92
International Criminal Court,
    34
international law
  democracy and, 160–1
  populism and, 53, 146–7, 161
International Monetary Fund
    (IMF), 28, 29, 114, 130

Index

international organizations
  analysis, 88–9, 91
  cosmopolitanism, 92, 152
  democratic deficit, 158
  globalism, 62
  populism and, 146–7
  rise, 94
  Trump policy, 146–7
  welfare states and, 160
  See also non-majoritarian
    institutions; specific
    organizations
Ireland, 112, 115, 167
Islam, 34, 62, 103–4, 107, 150
Italy
  Covid-19, 124–5, 128, 130
  fascism, 17
  global financial crisis and, 112
  populism, 122
  refugee policy, 119, 122
  trust in democratic
    institutions, 82

Japan, 82, 89
Johnson, Boris, 9, 44, 66, 127,
  157, 161
Jordana, Jacint, 88
JP Morgan Chase, 111
judiciary
  constitutional courts, 90
  cosmopolitanism, 92
  democratic regression, 141
  independence, 38, 90, 137,
    171
  international courts, 91
  Poland, 139
  separation of powers, 172

Kaczyński, Jaroslaw, 137
Kennedy, John F., 73, 165

Keynes, John Maynard, 28, 90
Kirchheimer, Otto, 62, 84
Kitschelt, Herbert, 61
Koenig-Archibugi, Mathias,
  154
KOF Glaobalization Index,
  63–4
Kohl, Hermann, 32
Kosovo, 34
Kosseleck, Reinhart, 187n6
Kreisler, Harry, 177
Kriesi, Hanspeter, 134
Kushner, Jared, 127
Kyoto Protocol (1997), 33

Laclau, Ernesto, 134
Latvia, 32
Le Pen, Jean-Marie, 47
Le Pen, Marine, 44, 54, 57
Lehman Brothers, 103, 110–17
Lesotho, 37
Levitsky, Steven, 144
Leyen, Ursula von der, 129
LGBTQ+, 35, 67–8
Liberal Component Index (LCI),
  137
Liberal Democracy Index (LDI),
  22, 23, 37, 40, 137–40,
  145
Lithuania, 32
local government, 142
Long, Huey, 46
Lula da Silva, Luis Inácio, 38

McGann, Anthony, 61
Macron, Emmanuel, 57, 128
Madisonian turn, 89–90
Maduro, Nicolás, 47, 137
Mali, 40
Malta, EU membership, 32

228 Index

Marshall Plan (1948), 28
Marxism, 106
Mauritius, 40
media
 free media, 43
 German populsim, 69
 globalism, 62
 populism and, 10, 73, 136,
  141, 150, 159
Mélenchon, Jean-Luc, 54
Meloni, Giorgia, 44
Merkel, Angela, 119–20, 123,
 176
Merkel, Wolfgang, 107–8, 109,
 134
Meuthen, Jörg, 69
Mexico, 82, 91
migration
 crisis, 103
 democratic dilemma,
  148–55
 immigration policy, 62, 70,
  134
 See also refugees
minorities
 communitarianism and, 150
 globalism and, 101, 148, 155
 populism and, 136, 152
 protection, 171
 representation, 74–5
 rights, 50, 53, 83, 101, 136,
  152
modernization, 10, 23, 26, 60,
 101, 144, 156, 180n5
Modi, Narendra, 38, 137
Möllers, Christoph, 134
Morales, Evo, 47
Mouffe, Chantal, 134–5
Mudde, Cas, 7, 48
Müller, Jan-Werner, 90, 135

multiculturalism, 35, 70, 120–1,
 131, 133, 150
Mussolini, Benito, 17

Narodniks, 46
nationalism
 colonialism and, 121
 communitarianism, 61, 151
 globalization and, 151–2
 international law and, 147
 populism, 7–8, 49
 rise, 34–5
NATO, 28, 34
neoliberalism, 34, 35, 47, 61, 87,
 102, 121, 125, 134
Netherlands
 parliamentary representatives,
  75, 79
 Party for Freedom, 62
 populism, 9, 47, 56, 66
 trust in democratic
  institutions, 82
New Left, 63
Nguyen, Christoph, 67
Nicatagua, 40
Nigeria, 38
non-majoritarian institutions
 accountability, 90
 aims, 158
 attitudes to, 92
 authority, 11, 83
 bias, 95
 blame-shifting to, 87, 93
 cosmopolitanism, 13, 93, 123,
  171
 crises and, 109
 euthanasia of politics, 90–3
 global financial crisis and,
  114–15
 legitimacy, 87, 90–1

Index

229

oversight, 171–2
politicization, 93–4
populist targets, 11–12, 94, 97, 101
preferences, 13
rise, 72, 80, 81, 84–90, 94, 100, 158
technocracy, 164–6
trust in, 81–2, 87, 95, 101
See also specific institutions
Norris, Pippa, 95
North Korea, 42
Norway, 79, 82

OECD world, 30
Oesch, Daniel, 98
Orbán, Viktor, 133–4, 137, 140

Pakistan, 38
Palme, Olaf, 165
Papandreou, Andreas, 114
Paris Agreement (2015), 146
parliaments
  alienation from, 93–100
  biases, 158–9
  class and, 75–80, 85, 102, 157–8, 170
  Covid-19 and, 130
  crisis of representation, 69–102
    birth of populism, 100–2
  disempowerment, 79–93, 100
  education and, 75, 157–8, 163
  election funding, 76–8
  ethnic minorities, 74–5
  euthanasia of politics, 90–3
  gender and, 74, 170–1
  inadequate responsiveness, 73–9, 80–1, 95, 158–9

influencers, 75–9
majority principle, 80
party selection models, 169–71
representative democracy, 74
trust in, 81–4, 97
unequal representation, 73–9, 157–8, 169
wealth and, 76, 157–8
See also non-majoritarian institutions
parties. *See* political parties
Paulson, Henry, 111
Perón, Juan, 47
Perónism, 47
Peru, 47
Pew Research Center, 70–1
Philippines, 40
Pinker, Steven, 26, 180n5
Pitkin, Hanna, 75
Poland
  democratic regression, 5, 14, 39, 40, 139, 140, 159
  EU membership, 32
  globalization and, 91
  ideology, 152
  Law and Justice (PiS), 51, 62, 138, 140
  populism, 56, 66, 137, 140
  refugee policy, 122
  transient democracy, 140
  trust in democratic institutions, 82, 86
political parties
  cartel parties, 11, 94, 101
  catch-all parties, 62, 84–5, 93
  recruitment models, 169–71
  system parties, 10, 12, 69, 73
Polity IV Index, 22, 23

Index

populism
  anti-elitism, 48, 52, 53, 150
  anti-internationalism, 53, 146–7
  anti-migration, 148–55
  anti-pluralism, 8, 49, 53, 80, 135, 150–2, 156
  authoritarianism, 7–8, 52–3, 61, 133–6
  basic concept, 47–50
  breaking taboos, 144
  class and, 143, 148
  classification, 54–5
  coalition governments, 142–6
  communitarianism, 149–52
  controversial concept, 46–8
  cosmopolitanism and, 146, 152, 155
  Covid-19 and, 127–9, 130, 161
  crises and, 110
  crisis of representation and, 100–2
  cultural explanations, 66–8
  decisionism, 50
  democratic future and, 14–15
  democratic regression, 159
  deproceduralization, 51
  direct democracy, 6
  drivers, 9–13, 134
  ecology and, 132
  electoral successes, 55–6
  electoral support rate, 66
  failures, 159
  globalization and, 63–6, 150–2, 156–7
  government policies, 136–42, 159
  ideology, 48, 49–56
  inadequate explanations, 63–8
  left-wing populism, 53–4, 134–5, 137
  majoritarianism, 50, 62
  minority rights and, 53
  narratives, 156–7
  nationalism, 7–8, 49
  negativism, 53
  new cleavage, 56–63, 92, 160–1
  new populism, 6–8
  NMI targeting, 11–12, 94, 101
  number of parties, 55
  opposition politics, 142–6
  political equality and, 141–2, 143
  political strategy, 47
  PopuList dataset, 54–5
  precursors, 46–7
  racism and, 156
  remedies, 161–3
  rise, 34–5, 45–6, 94–5
  simplification, 8, 15, 127, 177–8
  socioeconomic explanations, 65–6
  targets, 11
  theory of the wrong address, 66
  use of power, 136–42
Portugal, 112, 115
Putin, Vladimir, 121, 131–2, 137

racism, 103, 156
Rappaport, Orit, 87–8
recommendations
  changing party recruitment models, 169–71
  cosmopolitan passion, 175–6

Index

dismantling inequality
contexts, 167–8
EU democratization, 172–74
facing democratic regression,
156–78
false reforms, 168–9
general recommendations,
164–8
international issues, 172–76
learning from Switzerland,
174–5
NMI oversight, 171–2
political education, 176–7
reforming political systems,
168–72
tolerance for ambiguity,
177–8
trusting citizens, 166–7
withstanding technocracy,
164–6
referendums, 13, 21, 50, 69, 114,
117, 142, 175
refugees
Arab Spring, 118–19
blame game, 120–1
crisis, 103, 108, 118–24
globalization and, 121
Regling, Klaus, 115
representation. *See* parliaments
Rogowski, Ronald, 58, 65
Rokkan, Stein, 60
Romania, 32–3
Rome Statute, 34
Roosevelt, Franklin D., 30
rule of law, 23, 35, 41, 50–1, 87,
135, 137, 155
Runciman, David, 72
Russia
2014 annexation of Crimea,
103

2022 Ukraine war, 104, 147
autocracy, 38, 138
culture, 68
Narodniks, 46
population, 38
populism, 10, 137
Serbian policy, 34
UNSC veto, 121
See also Putin, Vladimir

Salvini, Matteo, 122
Saudi Arabia, democracy and,
42
Schakel, Wouter, 75
Scharpf, Fritz, 31
Schattneider, Elmer Eric, 73,
79, 80
Schelsky, Helmut, 143
Schumpeter, Joseph, 162
separation of powers, 20, 21,
38, 39, 43, 50, 137, 159,
172
Serbia, 34, 40
Shils, Edward, 48
Simón, Fernando, 128
simplification, 8, 15, 127, 177–8
Singapore, 3, 45, 164
Slovakia, 32
Slovenia, 32, 40
social democracy, 11, 30, 57, 58,
84, 114, 119
socialism, 3, 19, 31–2, 46, 48,
58
solidarity, 49, 61, 80, 122, 130,
150, 151
Somalia, 34
South Africa, 19, 42
South Korea, Covid-19, 127
Soviet Union
collapse, 5, 32

Index

Soviet Union (*cont.*)
  Gorbachev reforms, 16, 31–2
  postwar order, 28
  sphere of influence, 17
  Sputnik shock, 165
Spain
  Covid-19, 128, 130
  global financial crisis and, 112, 115
  Podemos, 54
  trust in democratic institutions, 82
  Vox, 55
Spanish flu, 125
Sputnik shock, 165
Stalin, Joseph, 28
state of emergency, 38, 104
Steinmeier, Frank-Walter, 135, 190n8
Strache, Heinz-Christian, 51
Strøm, Kaare, 90
subsidiarity, 21
Sweden
  Covid-19, 128–9
  parliamentary representatives, 79
  populism, 56
  Syrian refugees, 107
  trust in democratic institutions, 82
  trust in politicians, 85
  welfare state, 30
Switzerland
  direct democracy, 175
  learning from, 174–5
  populist coalition government, 145
  trust in democratic institutions, 82
Syria, 107, 118–19, 121

Syrian Observatory for Human Rights, 118
system parties, 10, 12, 69, 73

TAN (traditional–authoritarian–nationalist), 57, 60
taxation, 9, 53, 66, 80, 131, 143, 160
Taylor, Charles, 151
technocrats, 45, 101, 114, 164–6
Tegnell, Anders, 129
terrorism, 103–4, 108
Thailand, 40
trade unions, 29, 30, 58
traditionalism, 151
transboundary crises, 107, 111, 153–5
Trump, Donald
  attacks on press, 51
  Covid-19 and, 127, 161
  democratic regression, 14, 38–9
  equality and, 143
  international organizations and, 146–7
  'Make America Great Again', 161
  populism, 44, 137, 138, 140
  reasons for success, 66
  socioeconomic decline and, 65
  support for, 150, 157
  tax cutting, 9
trust
  in cartel parties, 11
  in citizens, 166–7
  in democratic institutions, 81–3, 97
  deterioration, 105

Index

233

educational levels and,
  98–100
in NMIs, 81–2, 87, 93, 95,
  101
in political system, 71
in politicians, 85
Tsipras, Alexis, 114
Turkey
  culture, 68
  democratic regression, 39,
    40, 80, 139
  globalization and, 9, 66, 91
  populism, 10, 66, 137
  transient democracy, 140
  trust in citizens, 166
  trust in democratic
    institutions, 81, 82

Učeň, Peter, 134
Ukraine, 103, 104, 147
United Kingdom
  Brexit, 65, 117, 123–4, 127,
    166
  Covid-19, 127, 128–9, 161
  declining regions, 167
  Euroscepticism, 173–4
  parliamentary representation,
    57, 70–1, 76, 170
  political cleavage, 57
  postwar order, 28
  voter turnout, 170
United Nations
  globalization and, 91
  origins, 27–8
  Rome Statute and, 34
  Security Council, 33–4, 121
  Syria and, 118, 121
United Nations Framework
    Convention on Climate
    Change (UNFCC), 33

United States
  9/11, 103, 104
  2016 presidential election, 65
  anti-pluralism, 49
  Black Thursday (1929), 28,
    103, 111
  Capital Hill attack (2021),
    38–9
  climate policies, 149
  Covid-19, 127
  crises, 103, 104
  declining regions, 167
  deliberative democracy, 142
  democratic continuity, 138,
    139, 140, 165
  democratic regression, 5, 14,
    38, 40, 159
  electoral funding, 76–7
  Federal Reserve policy, 110,
    111
  foreign policy, 28
  general suffrage, 17
  globalization and, 91
  international policy, 146–7
  Lehman Brothers crisis, 103,
    110–17
  'Make America Great Again',
    161
  moon landing, 165
  New Deal, 30
  political cleavage, 65, 144
  political representatives, 75,
    76, 79, 169–70
  population, 38
  populism, 46, 48, 137, 139
  real estate crisis, 107
  Supreme Court judges, 51
  trust in citizens, 166
  trust in democratic
    institutions, 82

234 Index

trust in democratic
institutions (*cont.*)
trust in politicians, 85
See also Trump, Donald
universalism, 57, 59, 66–7
Urbinati, Nadia, 52, 135,
148

V-Dem Index, 22, 23, 24, 25,
36–8, 40–1, 137–8,
139–40, 141, 145
Vanhanen, Tatu, 19–20, 23
Vargas, Gertúlio, 47
Venezuela, 5, 47, 137
Versailles Treaty (1919), 147
Vulcans, 162, 163

Wallace, George, 46
wealth, representatives, 76,
157–8

welfare states, 29–30, 31, 61, 80,
84, 142, 160
Welzel, Christian, 180n5
White, Harry Dexter, 28
Whitty, Chris, 129
Wilders, Geert, 44, 62
Wilhelm II, Emperor, 130
Wille, Anchrit, 75, 157
Wilson, Woodrow, 147
World Bank, 1, 28, 29
World Value Survey, 81–2,
85–6, 96–7
WTO, 33

xenophobia, 103

Yemen, 40

Zambia, 40
Ziblatt, Daniel, 144